Library

Becoming a
Counsellor

Praise for the book

'This easy to read book is designed to offer support to students throughout their training. It answers many questions and guides the reader to useful additional texts for further study. The author has a remarkable capacity to recognise the needs of the trainee counsellor and to focus on a wide spectrum of subjects. This student companion is packed with a wealth of information on theory and practice and includes helpful activities. It is an ideal text for all levels of training courses. No counselling student should be without a copy.'
Irene Hill, Counselling Curriculum Head, Adam Smith College

'This is clear, concise and comprehensive. It covers all that a student of counselling should need, and it is written in a style that makes the material easily accessible to students. I particularly like the way that Kirsten has emphasised the practicalities of delivering a counselling service. To paraphrase Donald Winnicott I would say that it's more than "Good Enough". It'll be on my list of Core Texts for every counselling student from now on.'
Billy Grier, Lecturer in Counselling, Motherwell College

'The professional and personal journey encountered by the trainee counsellor can be both exciting and, at times, arduous. Amis skilfully explores in depth the issues that can arise, from the day-to-day practicalities of the training process, through to the dynamics and processes of the training group. She writes from a position of experience, and brings insight, warmth, humour and a lightness of touch that will, I believe, be a source of support and knowledge for all trainees. I strongly recommend this book for anyone in training, or contemplating it. Everything you had wanted to know about counsellor training but had feared to ask; it's all here.'
Dr Andrew Reeves, counsellor, supervisor, trainer and editor of Counselling and Psychotherapy Research

'This straightforward, easy to read companion is a tremendous support for counselling students at all level. It strikes a good balance between theory and practice and gives lots of useful examples. As a lecturer in FE I will be recommending this book as a key text for my students. Thanks Kirsten for such a useful resource.'
Alison Mcbride, Lecturer in FE Motherwell College

Becoming a
Counsellor

A Student Companion

KIRSTEN AMIS

Los Angeles | London | New Delhi
Singapore | Washington DC

SAGE Publications Ltd
1 Oliver's Yard
55 City Road
London EC1Y 1SP

SAGE Publications Inc.
2455 Teller Road
Thousand Oaks, California 91320

SAGE Publications India Pvt Ltd
B 1/I 1 Mohan Cooperative Industrial Area
Mathura Road
New Delhi 110 044

SAGE Publications Asia-Pacific Pte Ltd
33 Pekin Street #02-01
Far East Square
Singapore 048763

Library of Congress Control Number: 2010934967

British Library Cataloguing in Publication data

A catalogue record for this book is available from the British Library

ISBN 978-1-84860-881-8
ISBN 978-1-84860-882-5 (pbk)

Typeset by C&M Digitals (P) Ltd, Chennai, India
Printed and bound in Great Britain by TJ International Ltd, Padstow, Cornwall
Printed on paper from sustainable resources

MIX
Paper from
responsible sources
FSC® C013056
FSC
www.fsc.org

For Andy. Without his patience and understanding, this book wouldn't exist.

Contents

About the Author

Kirsten Amis is a full-time lecturer in counselling at Anniesland College in Glasgow where she also coordinates the student counselling service. Her research interests include counselling education, addictive behaviours and client dependency issues. She has twenty years of counselling experience within NHS, voluntary and private practice environments, and experience working with addictive behaviours. Kirsten is a Scottish Qualifications Authority Qualification Development Specialist for Counselling and is also a Director on the Board of Management for Cowal Council on Alcohol and Drugs where she provides counselling supervision.

1

An Introduction to Counselling Training

This first chapter is a basic introduction to some of the underlying principles of studying counselling, incorporating some pointers as to how to make best use of this book. The text is designed as a companion for you during your course and contains hints on how to pass your course along with some reasons why certain elements are included within your course and their use to you as a student.

WHICH LEVEL – INTRODUCTORY, UNDERGRADUATE OR POSTGRADUATE?

The content of this book has been designed to be appropriate for any level of training if you are just starting to study counselling. Many counselling students are already qualified in other professions and are seconded onto a postgraduate course so, despite being enrolled on an advanced course, it can still be a relatively new subject. Because of this, you may find that chapters apply to some courses and not others; for example, an undergraduate course may not involve primary research whereas a post-graduate course may not include a residential element. Rather than reading from start to finish, consider using the Contents and Index pages to dip in and out depending upon your current area of interest. The book has been designed to include both the process of attending classes to learn about counselling along with the theory and practice that this is based on. Throughout, the focus is on learning to work therapeutically with adults rather than with children, adolescents or specialist groups such as those living with addictive behaviours.

You will find that there are activities throughout the book. These can be completed in isolation to help you focus on particular issues, or they can be used as prompts to help if you become stuck when writing your personal journal or, alternatively, as mini self-tests so you can monitor your progress and understanding.

At the end of each chapter there are recommended reading titles listed so that if this is an area of particular interest you can expand your reading into this subject. Relevant references are also cited throughout so that, again, you are able to access the source texts that quotes originate from and read further articles, books and websites on areas covered within this book.

TERMINOLOGY

For simplicity, the term used for the practice of therapeutic talking within this book will be 'counselling' rather than 'psychotherapy' as many of the skills are shared, and at this stage we are not going to join the debate regarding any similarities and differences of the two activities. Those receiving the service will be called 'clients' rather than 'service users' or 'patients', simply as this doesn't discriminate between settings, individuals or their issues. Those currently studying counselling will be referred to as a 'student' rather than 'trainee', again to increase clarity and avoid making a distinction between levels and content of courses.

CLARIFYING PROFESSIONAL ROLES

For those who are new to psychotherapeutic services, the role of different professionals can be confusing. Here is a very simplistic definition of each to help differentiate between them:

- *Psychologist*: studied psychology (the study of the mind, mental processes and behaviour) at university, usually to doctorate level, can diagnose conditions but is not a medical doctor so not able to prescribe medication. Many specialisms such as clinical, educational, counselling and forensic. Usually qualified to deliver counselling and usually works as part of a wider team.

- *Psychiatrist*: a medical doctor who specialises in mental illness, so can prescribe medication. Often based in a psychiatric unit or outpatient department of a hospital. Not usually involved in delivering counselling. Requires referral by a general practitioner (GP) for access and works as part of a wider team.
- *Community Psychiatric Nurse*: a qualified nurse who specialises in mental illness. Rather than working within a hospital or residential setting, they are based within the community and work closely with primary care teams such as GPs and psychiatrists. Qualified to administer medication but not to prescribe it, and tend to use counselling skills rather than counselling sessions.
- *Psychotherapist* (argued by many to be interchangeable with 'counsellor'): studied psychotherapy and practises a talking therapy aimed to equip the client with the ability to cope with their personal issues. Delivers counselling. Can work alone or as part of a wider team.
- *Psychoanalyst*: a counsellor who works with Freud's psychoanalytical model of therapeutic intervention.

WHAT COUNSELLING IS AND WHAT IT IS NOT

There is often confusion surrounding the names of different psychotherapeutic interventions so some definitions may be useful here before moving on to look at counselling in more detail. This is to differentiate between the distinct roles of professional help available, which can be bewildering at first.

There are many types of help available to people in need and it is important at this point to distinguish between them. Some common strategies are:

- *Advising*: To tell someone what you think they should do, recommend a course of action or inform. Advising can involve the opinion of the advisor when they are offering options. Advising not used in the majority of mainstream methods of counselling as it devalues the client's decision-making process (this is discussed further later on).
- *Guidance*: To lead or direct (to guide). Guidance is more about showing a path or suggesting the next step. Again, this isn't used in counselling because it is up to the client to decide upon their next move.
- *Informing*: Giving information, passing on the facts or data. Informing does happen in counselling but not in the most obvious way, in that the counsellor only informs the client of the boundary issues (e.g. confidentiality, cost) during the contracting session. After that, once counselling starts, it is the client that takes over the role of informant when they inform the counsellor of their situation and difficulties.

- *Instructing*: To give direction or possibly teach an activity, and it tends to be practical. Instructing is about teaching hands-on subjects (e.g. a sailing instructor or abseiling instructor) and can often involve demonstration. This technique is sometimes used in cognitive behavioural therapy (CBT) but not in other, more non-directive therapies.
- *Negotiating*: To confer and try to reach compromise, or reach agreement. Negotiating sometimes occurs in the final stages of integrative therapy when a client is moving from setting their own goals for the future to putting them into action. Therefore it is the client that is negotiating with the counsellor, not the other way round.
- *Teaching* (doctrine, teaching fact, formal) and *Tutoring* (individual instruction): These may both be seen as helping strategies in some settings, but are not used in counselling as they are too directive and disempowering to a client.
- *Advocacy*: Speaking in support of another; representing someone or speaking on behalf of them. Advocacy is a vital skill on its own that again is not used in counselling. Advocacy is about representing a client's interests to a third party, whereas counselling is a more confidential and insular relationship. A counsellor working within the statutory sector (i.e. NHS, Social Work Department) may be required to attend case conferences but are passing on relevant information rather than speaking on behalf of the client.
- *Counselling*: A professional, objective, structured and agreed relationship involving specific skills. Counselling can be carried out in two ways, either professional counselling sessions or using counselling skills during the course of other communication. We'll look at these two separately.

DIFFERENCE BETWEEN COUNSELLING SESSIONS AND COUNSELLING SKILLS

First, counselling sessions can be either one-to-one, with couples or in group work. Before embarking on regular sessions, a contract is agreed between those involved that covers areas such as cost, timing, venue and confidentiality. The counsellor should have the appropriate qualifications and experience to be working with the client/s, and this can often be discussed openly during the contracting session.

Second, the application of counselling skills is used in many environments. It is a less formal practice as the skills are simply used as a form of communication to show that the listener is interested and cares about the client. Nurses, social workers and care staff are all likely to use skills such as empathy, active listening, summarising and not talking about themselves within their everyday jobs.

It may be that you know of a friend or family member who seems to attract people telling them their problems. This is often because they are naturally a good listener and don't jump in with opinionated comments such as 'I think …' or 'Why don't you …'. The value of counselling skills is understanding when someone wants to talk and not interrupting them.

ACTIVITY

In your opinion, what is the difference between a good and a bad listener? How can this influence your skills as a counsellor?

WHERE DID COUNSELLING START?

Counselling as we know it has evolved considerably from the first, basic talking therapies. During the mid- to late nineteenth century, central Europe was the hub of development where the first links were made between what we think, what we do and how we feel. It's hard to believe but before this, only philosophers really thought about the connections between these aspects. When talking therapies were first developed, most famously starting with Sigmund Freud, they were viewed with suspicion, which was understandable considering it was within the sphere of academia and only available to the educated or the rich. Even then, due to common scepticism, it was considered very radical.

Therapies developed from the start of the twentieth century that concentrated on the re-training of 'unacceptable' behaviours (both in animals and humans). The focus was very much on observable actions and with the interest in scientific development at the time and little in the way of ethical considerations there were some experiments carried out that would never be allowed today with our far stricter ethical guidelines.

Following the Second World War, the focus turned back to the connection between thoughts and feelings, and the locus of development shifted to USA, which was far more accepting of such interventions. Theorists like Carl Rogers, Abraham Maslow and Rollo May started to acknowledge the importance of personal autonomy and freedom of choice, which placed the client in the role of expert in their own lives. Counsellors became more facilitative and non-directive, and modern counselling really took shape.

Of course, this happened at the same time as families started moving away from their place of birth to find work so individuals and families found themselves isolated, living and working miles from their home town. This, along with the introduction of contraception and extended families no longer being the norm, meant people found there was no one close to talk to about problems. Being able to access a professional with which to unload difficulties and who wouldn't just sit and tell you what to do became a more acceptable option.

In the twenty-first century, having a wide choice of nearly 500 different methods of counselling, many of which combine the focus on behaviours, thoughts and feelings, allows the clients of today the choice to access the method of counselling they think would be most helpful for them. It should also be acknowledged that such choice can cause confusion for potential clients who might not be aware of the differences between methods. In the UK, counselling services are provided within the voluntary, private and statutory sectors, and counselling has become so mainstream that funding is available to pay for sessions through many GP practices, hospitals and schools. The USA is still ahead in the social acceptance of counselling, where individuals see it as the norm to have a therapist even if they are not facing any specific personal challenges, whereas in the UK there is still the perception that someone attending counselling does so because there is something 'wrong'.

Most think this is a fair balance as counselling is not for everyone and doesn't work for all. The thought of everyone having a counsellor all the time is uncomfortable as it suggests a culture of dependence and disempowerment, whereas knowing what counsellors do and how to access them at a time of need or crisis can be very empowering. If you would like to read more about the negative aspects of this debate, you may find the book *Against Therapy* by Jeffrey Masson interesting (see Further Reading).

AN OVERVIEW OF COUNSELLING TRAINING

There are hundreds of counselling courses available and although it might be difficult to choose which one is the most appropriate, it can also be difficult to see how they compare to each other. In this book you will find a brief overview of a selection of different levels of training and how they compare to each other. You could develop a similar map of courses in your local area to help you see the bigger picture and make an informed decision. Of course, this does not include reputation or how they are

viewed by future employers or even other courses. It would be h
there is always a robust relationship between formal training anc
with clients, so courses should always include guidance on issue
professionalism, ethics and safety.

WHAT YOU MIGHT FIND OUT ABOUT YOURSELF

The majority of clients attend counselling to help work through some
kind of issue or difficulty that they are experiencing in their life, whether
it be a situation, relationship, memory or uncomfortable feelings. However,
a small percentage of clients attend for self-development, to work through
a discovery process about themselves and the way they feel and react to
the world around them. During counselling sessions, clients attending for
any of these reasons can experience strong emotional reactions. The role
of the counsellor here is to work with the client to help establish a
meaning for these feelings and also to be comfortable being with a person
who is possibly experiencing distress, anger, frustration, bitterness, guilt,
regret or shame, although to be fair they are not always so negative! This
process of opening up and considering such personal issues can lead to the
client expressing themselves more honestly than they feel comfortable
doing elsewhere. Clients don't always like what they find out about
themselves as not everyone reacts in a way that they are expecting, so the
amount of emotional support offered by the counsellor is important.
Depending upon the type of counselling being used, counsellors tend to
be *understanding*, *honest* and *accepting* of the client. These three skills are
known as the 'core conditions' and were developed by the psychologist Carl
Rogers, and will be discussed in Chapters 3 and 10.

COUNSELLING SKILLS

In addition to qualities, specific skills are needed to encourage and support
the client. Some of the main ones are identified below:

- *Advanced empathy* is when the counsellor is listening and so in tune with the
  client that they are become aware of deeper feelings and thoughts that the
  client has not verbalised, similar to voicing a hunch.
- *Challenge* is used in a gentle and encouraging way and is in no way confrontational. An example might be 'Last session when you talked about this, you

said that it made you angry but as you are talking now, you sound more hurt.' The counsellor is challenging the client's statement but not in an aggressive or disbelieving manner.

- *Immediacy* is working in the here-and-now rather than the past or the future. It could be current feelings or a situation and may even be relating to the relationship between counsellor and client.
- *Self-disclosure* is a difficult skill to use and takes a lot of experience to get right. Some environments (e.g. addiction services or Rape Crisis) allow self-disclosure, as the counsellor making the client aware of personal experience can improve the bond or relationship. However, the danger is that the counsellor way distract from the client's situation, reducing the sense of uniqueness of experi- ence, or just introduces a tangent that allows the client to focus away from their own issues.
- *Reflection* is a skill that helps regulate the pace of the session as it allows both client and counsellor to think back over what has been said previously and to consider any impact that it has on the present issue. It allows the client to hear what they have said anew. Consideration can be of feelings, situations, relationships or attitudes – almost anything really that is relevant.
- *Summary* can be used throughout a session but is particularly useful at the end to bring together the main issues that have been raised or remind the client of what has been covered. This allows them to leave with a sense of completion and progress.
- *Active listening* is vitally important as we don't often engage so totally with a speaker in general conversation. Passive listening is simply allowing a voice to continue without much concentration on what is being said, whereas to be active involves clarification to ensure that you heard correctly, or open questions to check the context in which speech is used. Reflection may be used as a method of active listening. It can be exhausting to concentrate so hard for 50 minutes!
- *Focus* is essential. It is difficult to imagine how chaotic a session may be without the counsellor helping the client to focus on their issue and helping them to examine around it! In conversations we go off on tangents and talk about ourselves, but this wouldn't be therapeutic for the client so can't be done. There has to be total concentration to work through the client's choice of issue so that some therapeutic development can take place.
- *Evaluation* tends to come nearer the end of the counselling relationship when the counsellor encourages the client to reflect back over a change or develop- ment that has occurred and assess its value in the context of their life. This helps coping mechanisms emerge as the client is able to identify what works and what doesn't for them. It may well be that after the evaluation, the session reverts back to a previous stage where planning takes place and the cycle begins again. Alternatively, if successful, this can be the end of the counselling sessions.

As you can imagine, all of these take quite a lot of practice, particularly when using some them at the same time. Counselling really is very different to a ordinary conversation!

WHAT YOU MIGHT FIND OUT ABOUT OTHERS

During and following a programme of counselling, there is a risk that changes in attitudes and behaviours can alienate family and friends. One of the core aims of talking therapies is *empowerment*, which can result in the client reassessing the quality of their lives and relationships and can lead to subtle or drastic changes in circumstances. For example, if a client is living in an abusive relationship, counselling may equip them with the confidence and assertiveness to alter the situation to ensure their happiness or at least their safety. The strength of familial and friendship bonds can be put under strain during any process of development and change. Even studying on a counselling course can lead to shifts with others, although they are usually very positive!

LEARNING CURVE

A central part of the counselling relationship is the ability for the client to make changes, either in thought patterns, feelings or behaviour, to accommodate their new outlook. Part of this process is the ability for the client to accept change and learn from the practice. Unfortunately, it can be painful to let go of previous habits and automatic responses.

Figure 1.1 depicts a fairly typical learning 'curve' and shows how learning and change does not proceed smoothly: the peaks, plateaux and troughs are normal features of the process. Of course, as a counselling student, you too will experience a similar process whereby you may have to unlearn old methods before learning new ones, and progressing from being not very good at some aspects through to them becoming second nature and part of who you are.

Figure 1.2 shows a different way of looking at the process of change and learning, which was developed by Reynolds (1985).

Both figures are taken from the excellent website focusing on methods of learning by J. S. Atherton (2005) *Learning and Teaching: Learning curves*, which can be found at www.learningandteaching.info/learning/learning_curve.htm.

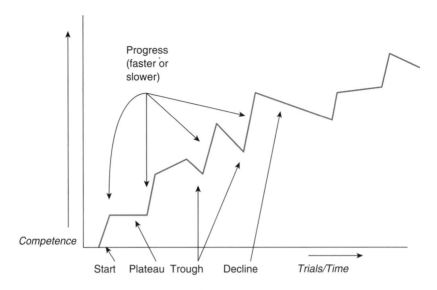

Figure 1.1   A learning 'curve' is far from a straight progression (Atherton, 2005). Reproduced with kind permission from Atherton (2005).

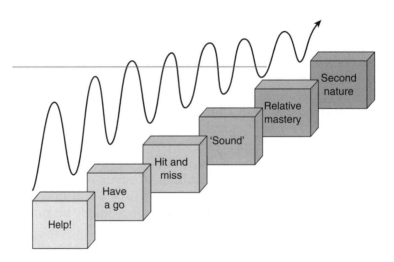

Figure 1.2   The process of change and learning. Reproduced with kind permission from Atherton after Reynolds (1985).

BECOMING COMFORTABLE WITH EMOTIONS

When a counsellor first meets a client, they are essentially strangers who are meeting with a shared purpose. The counsellor is expected to be professional enough to work with whatever the client decides they would like to share at that time. If it is the first time that the client has felt comfortable talking about an issue or if there has been a build-up of tension in their lives, the first session can often be a very emotional time where trust is hopefully established. The counsellor must be able to reflect on their acceptance of how others communicate intense feelings so that the client does not feel embarrassed or ashamed of any honest expression of emotion. This is an important element of counselling training and personal development.

ACTIVITY

If you are keeping a personal journal as part of your course, this would be a good time to reflect upon what you have just read. Consider how the contents of this chapter makes sense to you and identify if you are able to establish any links with your previous experiences or understanding.

FURTHER READING

BACP (2007) *Towards Regulation: The Standards, Benchmarks and Training requirements for Counselling and Psychotherapy*. Lutterworth: BACP.

Buchanan, L. and Hughes, R. (2000) *Experiences of Person-centred Counselling Training*. Ross-on-Wye: PCCS Books.

Claringbull, N. (2010) *What is Counselling & Psychotherapy?* Exeter: Learning Matters.

Cross, M. (2001) *Becoming a Therapist*. Hove: Brunner-Routledge.

Masson, J. (1992) *Against Therapy*. London: Fontana.

Sanders, P. (2003) *Step in to Study Counselling*. Ross-on-Wye: PCCS Books.

2

Starting Out

Starting out in counselling training can be a nerve-wracking experience as the learning and teaching tend to be so different in approach and style from other courses. Here we will look at the main areas that can cause concern for new students.

WHICH LEVEL DO I START AT, COLLEGE OR UNIVERSITY?

Deciding between college or university isn't as straightforward as it sounds. For example, the following questions are just a few that can influence this crucial choice:

1 What are the entry requirements, and can you meet them?
2 Is this progression the next level on from your previous qualifications?
3 Does the application process acknowledge accredited prior learning?
4 What value is placed on your past life experience (e.g. addiction and successful rehabilitation)?
5 What is your focus on the future (i.e. how do you wish to use the award or qualification)?
6 Are you ready and able to meet the academic requirements for your chosen level of course?
7 Do you hope to link levels with employment and further study?
8 How much will it cost, and can you afford it?
9 Is this the right time in your life to study?

10 Did you feel a sense of support, encouragement and warmth from the interview process?
11 How confident do you feel?

You may have already made that decision and be waiting to start, or already studying on your course, or you may still be at the stage of trying to decide, so the following sections may help clarify any concerns or questions you may have about how to study rather than what to study. At this point, you may also find the map of qualifications in Chapter 18 useful as a guide.

There are many differences and similarities between courses which are hard to quantify as they differ between establishments, areas and countries too. The focus should not be so much on college or university as on further or higher education. A *very* rough approximation would be that:

- Colleges usually offer introductory or certificate-level courses, although other higher levels are offered if it is a higher education college. Progression can often be provided by the one establishment.
- Colleges have a different funding structure so can offer fee waivers that cover costs for students in receipt of certain benefits.
- Colleges deliver mainly vocational qualifications and are appropriate for students who may lack confidence in their academic abilities.
- Colleges tend to be local as they are built within communities.
- University courses tend to offer courses at a higher academic level so the entry requirements are higher.
- University courses have a different funding structure so courses are more likely to need to be paid for.
- Universities offer post-graduate courses as well as undergraduate courses.

These are by no means applicable to all institutions but rather aspects for consideration.

WHAT ARE ATTENDANCE REQUIREMENTS?

Due to the complex nature of counselling training, students are not expected to simply attend lectures and tutorials but rather more focus is placed on the student's own engagement with the overall course content. A minimum of 80 per cent attendance is usually expected but your values, attitudes, communication skills and commitment along with academic ability are all very important. Essentially, treating your fellow students with the care and respect you would bestow on a client is expected. This range of requirements is often incorporated into a learning contract,

In acceptance of an offer to study the **Certificate in Counselling**, I hereby agree to the following clauses:

- I agree that I will treat colleagues with the care and respect I would wish to receive myself.
- I agree that issues discussed within class remain within class and will not be discussed outside the group.
- I agree that attendance to the Community Group is compulsory.
- I agree to be honest and genuine as I recognise that these qualities underpin the ethos of the course.
- I agree that attendance of a minimum of 80 per cent for each unit.
- I agree that I will be punctual and accept that I will not interrupt the community group by being late.
- I agree that assignments have a formal cut-off date for submission. If I am unable to honour this, I will formally negotiate an extension with the subject tutor a minimum of 14 days prior to the original submission date.
- I agree that my relationship with my co-counsellor will be professional and respectful, and I will treat it as I would any other session with a client or with a counsellor.
- I agree that I will adhere to the recognised ethical guidelines within the course.
- I agree that I will ensure my mobile phone is switched off during class. I can be contacted in an emergency via the number below.
- I agree that if I am unable to attend, I will contact _____ on _____ or e-mail _____.

In return:

- I will be offered academic support and professional advice throughout the course.
- I will be kept up to date with current developments within counselling, including via e-mail.
- I will be able to ask questions and request guidance at any point.
- I will be provided with opportunities for personal, academic and professional development.

Name _____   Signed _____

Tutor _____   Date _____

Figure 2.1   An example of a basic counselling course contract

especially if the orientation of your course values working within contracts such as 'transactional analysis' or CBT. An example of a basic learning contract is given in Figure 2.1.

SECONDMENT, PART-TIME OR FULL-TIME?

The pattern of attendance may be determined already by employers, family, time or finance, but commitment is necessary for each. There are benefits and drawbacks to each, but the availability and choice allows personal flexibility in attendance. In addition to this, you should be aware of how each are viewed by the accrediting bodies if you are hoping to become registered:

- *Secondment* is ideal if you are working and your employer requests that you attend. If this is the case, they usually cover your fees as it is a vocational stipulation. Attendance can be either full- or part-time and you may also be offered study leave to complete assignments, etc. If you are already working within a counselling environment, you may be able to use your place of work as your placement for the course.
- *Part-time* may be more appropriate if you have family commitments or you are doing this in your own time for your own interest and your employer is not supporting your application. Usually one or two days a week for one or two years, this can also include weekend commitments. Higher-level courses such as PhD or other doctorate may take up to six or even eight years for completion.
- *Full-time* differs in definition from institution to institution and can be influenced by funding requirements. It may cover the method of attendance or it may simply mean that you are not engaged in any other formal activity whilst studying on the course (i.e. you are a full-time student).

STUDENT EXPERIENCE 2.1   HEATHER

I found that being part-time has a slight disadvantage concerning travelling costs as it affected my application to qualify for funding. However, I most certainly could only have begun my studies because it was part-time due to work commitments and although I am not sure where I am headed career-wise, I am confident that the course has only enhanced my learning within the line of work I wish to pursue.

Juggling work, home life and college work was a big challenge to begin with but did get easier over the course as I began to prioritise how important completing my assessments was to me personally. The practical work reinforced my learning as I identified the need to use this as an opportunity to put the theories into practice.

HOW MUCH DO COUNSELLING COURSES COST?

This is difficult to answer as every course will have its own cost and options how to pay, but they can vary between £100 for a short introduction course up to £10,000 at post-graduate level once supervision and personal therapy are included. If you are being seconded by your workplace, you are lucky enough not to have to worry about this as the invoice will be sent to your employer to pay. If you are in receipt of certain benefits, it may be that there is the availability of a fee waiver, especially in further education. The rules regarding help with course funding change often so it is always worth sourcing up-to-date information before making a decision. Details of funding options can be found at these websites:

England: www.direct.gov.uk/en/EducationAndLearning/index.htm
Scotland: www.student-support-saas.gov.uk/
Northern Ireland: www.studentfinanceni.co.uk
Wales: www.studentfinancewales.co.uk/

Costs can rise steeply for degree and post-graduate courses although as with most things, depending upon the level of course and institution, it is likely to be based on your individual circumstances. It is better to contact the finance department or student services department of your chosen course for specific advice regarding their payment procedures. If your course is being provided by a private organisation, it is less likely that a government payment scheme will be accepted but it is not unheard of, so again speak to the company directly – it may well be that the fee can be paid in smaller instalments. Counselling courses within voluntary agencies are different again. Most of these are provided free on the under-standing that you commit a set amount of time to volunteering for the organisation, usually two years. This is ideal if you are just wanting to help out within a specific setting rather than work towards accreditation.

CONTINUING EDUCATION, ADULT RETURNER OR CPD?

Where you are in your academic career path can also have an impact upon your experience within the course. If you are already in the habit of studying and have developed a learning structure that works for you, you are doing well. However, if you lack confidence – maybe you are an adult returner – then considering the questions on how you work best in Chapter 11 might be a good place to start so that you feel that you are establishing control over your own progress and development. Alternatively, studying as part of your continuing professional develop-ment (CPD) can impact upon your motivation, interest and level of commitment. For this reason, it is not ideal if you are being seconded onto a course that has been chosen for you by your employer but, rather, it should be your decision that is supported by your employer. A subtle but crucial difference! It is a good idea to measure the level of support you feel you might need as soon as you can so they are in place for the duration of the course. You will be acquiring personal learning skills and application skills as well as the content of the course, so there are many aspects that meet the needs of CPD.

STUDENT EXPERIENCE 2.2   JANE

This was to be my first academic qualification since leaving school (I was 37 when I started the course). I was apprehensive about whether or not I would be successful in completing assessments. Now that I am half-way through I appreciate that my commitment to the course is paying off and I am now looking forward to my second year with more confidence and optimism. I was initially nervous about being in a large group setting but over the year I have got to know my fellow students and have found that we all gel in a way that is beneficial, especially at times when we need support and encouragement because of other commitments outside college. Overall I welcomed the opportunity to meet with new people.

LEARNING STYLES AND HELPFUL HINTS

The overall aims of most counselling courses are to provide the opportunity to further develop the knowledge, skills and attributes relevant to the theory and practice of working with people and counselling through:

- examining the many concepts of psychology which may be applied in a counselling setting
- investigating support networks and supervision within the counselling field
- exploring interpersonal and group skills
- developing personal effectiveness
- turning theories into practice to increase confidence and understanding
- increasing individual study skills through personal guidance
- including personal and professional development which is central to all units
- improving personal communication skills.

This is a wide and varied remit and as such demands many different methods of learning. One of the most destabilising aspects of this process that can result in losing motivation is that in order to gain new skills, it is necessary to lose old ones that are not correct or helpful. Being told or shown that what you previously thought to be correct is not can be soul-destroying, and the period of time between losing your old ways and being comfortable with the new can leave you feeling devalued and vulnerable. The way round this is to expect it, recognise it and plan how you hope to deal with it in advance. This reduces the feelings of loss, potential resistance and resentment of new ways of being.

ACTIVITY

Think about how you learn at present. Write this down in your personal development or learning journal if you keep one. Identify any areas that you consider weaknesses or barriers to you learning. Then consider any methods you could use to counteract this – your own personal solutions.

OTHER STUDENTS

As mentioned earlier, treating your fellow students with the care and respect you would bestow on a client is expected. You can never guess in advance who else might be studying on the course and their experience, backgrounds and personalities. This is a parallel experience to meeting new clients and provides instant situations to allow you to bring your feelings about fellow students into your awareness so that you can be honest about how you deal with the relationships you develop on the course. Some of the areas for consideration may include issues such as:

- own participation
- taking responsibility
- openness to learn
- openness to feedback
- resistance
- relationship with group members
- relationship with facilitator
- reaction to conflict
- reaction to emotion
- collusion
- fear of rejection
- scapegoating
- dependence
- trust
- disclosure
- friendships
- discomfort.

The role and importance of these relational issues are further developed in Chapter 13.

STUDENT EXPERIENCE 2.3   JOHN

On first starting the course I had a bit of a rough time and lots of self-doubt as to whether I could actually do the course, but by sticking to my guns and some amazing help/support from support services and my tutors I am starting to believe in myself and my abilities. Also the type of course that counselling is, you really are looking deeply at yourself and others so there really is growth from the outset/onset. It also made me realise that no one is perfect.

EXPECTATIONS

On first starting attending a course, it is important to separate the educational experience of learning about counselling from the therapeutic environment of counselling. A counselling course is not a series of counselling sessions and the other students are not counsellors to provide personal therapy! If you are struggling with personal issues that go beyond any co-counselling opportunities available, then attending personal therapy is a more professional and safe route than opening up to colleagues in informal and unsafe situations.

The first day of the course can be daunting, so remember that it's the first day for everyone else there too. This is the time when it is difficult to concentrate as so much is happening. Often, the first day is just about completing paperwork, meeting fellow students, finding out where to go and meeting tutors and lecturers. This is a list of topics that might be addressed on the first day:

- Welcome
- Health and safety/toilets
- Fire evacuation procedure
- First aid
- Enrolment form, photo for student card, confirmation of payment
- Student guide
- Learner induction pack
- Student welfare form
- Provision of student services
- Library – induction details

- Support for learning/extended learning support
- School booklet/course booklet
- Timetable
- Placement requirements
- Course review teams/class representatives
- Guidance/individual learning plans
- How work is collected/stored
- Class contract to sign
- Recommended reading list and course texts
- Support groups/study groups
- On-line resources
- Co-counselling partners
- E-mail addresses for all
- Community group
- Journal
- Ice-breakers
- Retention requirements
- How do you learn?

WILL IT TAKE OVER MY LIFE?

The simple answer is yes, if you let it. There are potential challenges that may surface but these can be managed, pre-empted and planned for in advance. First, there are practical issues such as time management – balancing studying with the rest of your life, friends and family. However, it is not so easy to plan for changes in attitudes, values and behaviours which are almost certain to accompany a counselling course, and how these impact on those close to us. Despite this being a widely acknowledged phenomenon, there appear to be no studies and little formal evidence to support it, but it would be very interesting to find any research conducted into the relationship between counselling training and personal relationships.

STUDENT EXPERIENCE 2.4   YVONNE

Being on summer break from college has allowed me to reflect and appreciate just how much I have learned and how this benefits me on a day-to-day basis – so much so that I have recognised just how focused and positive attending college keeps me. The holidays have reinforced just how much effort it takes to keep my own identity and the importance of keeping a healthy attitude.

It is highly likely that you will be issued with a recommended reading list which will guide you towards texts that you should be reading to reinforce your classroom learning. This is to inform your work, place your understanding and essays in a wider context and increase your comprehension. Think of each chapter or article you read as the subject being explained to you in a different way by a different voice. Reading one text may give you some information but reading two or more is going to reinforce your learning and understanding more than simply listening to your tutor. Background reading is a way of demonstrating that you are able to grasp the relevance and surroundings of a concept and is necessary in academic writing. Chapter 11 includes guidance on citing references and avoiding plagiarism.

STARTING TO STUDY

There is no such thing as a step-by-step guide for preparing to begin a counselling course as they are all so different, as are students. However, listed below are some main areas that require consideration and planning before embarking on a counselling course:

- What courses are available in your area?
- What level is most appropriate for you to study at?
- Is the chosen course appropriate for you final goal or aim?
- What is the application procedure?
- How much does the course cost?
- How often are you expected to attend?
- How much support is available to you both through the course and at home?
- What barriers may prevent you from completing the course?
- How will you overcome these barriers?

If you are an 'adult returner', meaning it is some time since you attended formal education, it may be helpful to ask about additional support that is available. Additional classes are often available in essay writing, spelling, grammar, time management, study skills, etc., which can be very helpful and in some cases make the difference between success and failure. Here are some examples of methods of learning and teaching that are used in counselling courses:

- *Formal and informal lectures*: Classroom-based, requiring personal attendance and handouts are often provided. Note-taking may be expected and PowerPoint presentations are often included.
- *Experiential workshops*: Allowing the linking of theory and practice.

- *Role play*: For student safety and depending upon the level of the course, practice is often using role-play scenarios, although many courses prefer you to use examples from your own life.
- *Self-directed study*: There is an expectation that students feel confident to work alone, particularly as background reading is necessary.
- *Multi-media resources*: The institution will normally provide free use of on-line computers for all students as well as books and current and back copies of counselling and psychology journals. There may also be relevant study packs available to use at home.
- *Co-counselling*: Included in many courses for skills practice (see Chapter 9).
- *Case studies*: Examples of client situations allows practice to be viewed in context. These may be provided or based on clients you are working with.
- *Individual guidance*: Time is allotted within each course term for time to be spent with the course tutor on a one-to-one basis to investigate areas of challenge and progression.
- *Group discussion*: An integral part of all counselling courses lies in the benefit of honest discussion.
- *Reflective journal*: A log or diary of personal and professional development maintained throughout the majority of courses.
- *Demonstration and practice*: Lecturers usually demonstrate relevant techniques.
- *Regular community groups*: A non-directive community group involving everyone on the course. This provides an opportunity for honest discussion within a non-threatening environment.
- *Personal development groups*: A facilitated and directed group designed for members to focus on particular aspects of self-development.
- *Book reviews*: Students are encouraged to read, evaluate and actively engage with relevant texts. Reviews might be fed back to the group or added to an on-line learning environment.
- *Video*: Films and programmes are occasionally used to illustrate certain theories, practice or service provision. Audio or live recordings may also be made of your practical sessions, which will allow you to monitor your practice more objectively.

WHAT TYPE OF LEARNER ARE YOU?

Such a wide variety of methods tend to be used as it has long been recognised that individuals learn in different ways. It is a good idea to identify which type of learner you are so that you can use it to help you make sense of methods which you are less comfortable with. A good course will incorporate many different ways of learning so that all different types of learners can connect with elements of the course. It is also interesting to be taken out of your comfort zone so that you can reflect on exactly what it is that makes you uncomfortable or resistant to certain styles of learning. Consider which description relates to you:

- *Alone or with others?* If you prefer working in groups and with other students, you are a social learner.
- *By hands-on activities?* If you prefer learning by doing (i.e. practice, experimentation or rehearsal), you are a tactile learner.
- *By looking and watching?* If pictures, colours and graphics make more sense to you, you are a visual learner.
- *Creative or structured?* If you respond more positively to free-flowing and autonomous sessions, you are a creative learner, whereas a structured learner prefers consistent, sequential steps to their learning.
- *Formal or informal?* If you would rather sit at a desk with a chair as in a traditional classroom, you are a formal learner. Informal learners prefer alternative environments that allow for freedom, such as sitting in circles or groups.
- *Movement or stillness?* If movement is important to you when you are concentrating, then you may be a kinesthetic learner.
- *Through listening?* If you prefer lectures, discussion and activities involving sound, you are an auditory learner.
- *Quiet or noisy?* Not so much a learning style but rather an aid to supporting positive learning. Background noise may be either stimulating or a distraction. Decide which and choose your private learning environment accordingly.

FURTHER READING

Karter, J. (2002) *On Training to be a Therapist*. Buckingham: Open University Press.

3

Theoretical Orientation

There are estimated to be more than 500 different talking therapies. This chapter introduces the background, theory, techniques and benefits of the major models that have been most influential in counselling.

WHAT DOES ORIENTATION MEAN?

Differences in the underpinning models or approaches of courses and how this can influence the content and ethos of the course.

With more than 500 different 'talking cures' available, the method of counselling that you are trained in will depend very much upon the psychological theory underpinning the course. It would take an enormous and very heavy book to cover all of these in detail so this chapter will provide a brief, and in some cases very brief, synopsis of the approaches listed in Figure 3.1. To compensate, there is a more comprehensive Further Reading list included at the end of the chapter in the hope that any interest stimulated can be further developed by additional reading.

PSYCHODYNAMIC THEORY

Mapping the mind

The expression 'psychodynamic' is an umbrella term that covers many different methods of therapeutic intervention, all based (some more

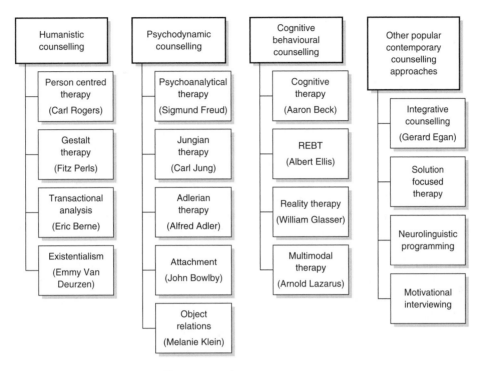

Figure 3.1   The main counselling approaches

loosely than others) on Sigmund Freud's psychoanalytical theory which is a good place to start. Freud (1856–1939) is recognised as the first psychologist to develop investigation into the mind and the influence that our past experiences, particularly in childhood, have on our personality as an adult. He argued that the mind is divided into the conscious, which we are aware of; preconscious, which consists of memories and feelings that we have 'put in storage' but can be retrieved when we need them; and the unconscious. The unconscious part of the mind consists of elements of our past that would cause us such anxiety and upset that we are unable to recall them without professional analysis. These distressing factors can influence our reactions, emotional responses and actions without us being aware of them. There were several methods that Freud employed, such as dream analysis and free association in psychoanalysis (or talking therapy) which were ground-breaking at the time. You'll notice that they involve *analysis* which requires a trained expert to interpret and untangle potentially damaging responses. Freud believed that dreams were a coded representation of our anxieties stored within the unconscious and that the process of dream analysis could move these into the conscious where the process of psychoanalysis would deactivate them.

Id, ego and superego

In addition to this, Freud continued to develop his theory of the workings of the mind when he identified the three aspects of the personality: *id*, *ego* and *superego*. He argued that we are born with an id which remains in our unconscious and controls our most basic drives, such as aggression, and biological drives, for instance sexual urges, and demand immediate gratification. Sometimes the demands of the id are illustrated by what are referred to as 'Freudian slips': when we say the wrong word without thinking, but as this is directly from the unconscious it indicates what we really feel. The id can also become apparent through coded representations within our dreams. Because this is such a fundamental force, it satisfies the pleasure principle when we meet our more immediate needs. Second, the ego develops at approximately six months of age, sits both in our conscious and unconscious, and is controlled by the reality principle so keeps our feet on the ground. It is the peacekeeper between the demands of the id and the control of the superego, ensuring that we meet our needs in a socially acceptable manner. Third, the superego is regulated by the morality principle and is divided into two parts, the ego-ideal and the conscience, which also sit in both our conscious and unconscious. The role of the superego is rather like that of a parent as it is concerned with controlling the urges of the id and enforcing our values and morals that we learned through childhood. The ego-ideal is similar to Carl Rogers' actual and ideal self in that it consists of the image of how we would like to be compared with how we actually are. The wider the gap, the less happy and more distressed we are. The conscience, however, controls how we feel about ourselves if we fail to live up to our ideal and meters out feelings of guilt or punishments. For example, clients with eating disorders such as anorexia nervosa are often thought by psychoanalysts to have a particularly powerful superego.

Psychosexual stages of development

In addition to theories of the mind, Freud also focused on the importance of our developmental progress during childhood and the impact this has upon our personality as an adult (see Table 3.1). His theory was not popular at the time of origin but has since been expanded and elaborated on by many psychologists. Basically, Freud maintained that child development is

Table 3.1   The developmental progress through childhood (after Freud)

Stage of development	Age	During the developmental stage	Impact of fixation on adult
Oral	0–6 months	The baby's mouth is the principle erogenous zone. Gratification is gained by sucking and chewing.	Still gain pleasure from putting things in mouth, e.g. smoking, chewing pens, overindulgence or, more obliquely, might have 'biting' wit.
Anal	1–3 years	The principle erogenous zone is the anus. Gratification is gained by the voluntary withholding or expulsion of faeces.	Obsessive-compulsive type behaviours with belongings, money, etc. Could also result in the opposite, e.g. untidiness or extravagance.
Phallic	3–6 years	Gratification comes from the manipulation of the child's genitals. It is during this stage that the *Oedipus* or *Electra Complex* takes place.	Sexuality – heterosexual or homosexual relationships.
Latency	6–puberty	During this period, the libido hibernates and previous developments are repressed but still present. Friendships take priority.	Ability to make friendships, abandonment issues.
Genital	After puberty	The libido re-emerges. Gratification is gained from sexual curiosity and the development of intimate relationships.	Control and independence issues.

motivated by the effect of our libido (i.e. sexual energy) and produced a developmental 'map' of childhood. If a child grows up in a loving and supportive environment, they should move through each stage without difficulty. If, however, they experience conflict during any stage, they can fixate or remain at that stage until psychoanalysis allows them to bring it into their conscious, resolve it and move on.

Defence mechanisms

How we protect ourself emotionally was also under scrutiny from Freud. He believed that we use both conscious and unconscious methods to avoid anxiety and emotional pain, the investigation and analysis of which is a fundamental element of psychoanalytical therapy. Freud's daughter, Anna, developed this theory further (see Table 3.2).

Table 3.2   Defence mechanisms (after Anna Freud)

Emotion	Reaction
Compensation	Where we try to make up for our unconscious urges or apprehension; we counterbalance what we see as our inadequacies with the opposite behaviour.
	Example: an insecure manager might appear aggressive as they are counteracting their lack of confidence.
Denial	When we reject an impulse ever having taken place.
	Example: a boxer continuing to fight despite being diagnosed with brain damage.
Displacement	Here we might substitute a safe recipient to our negative response rather than the actual quarry.
	Example: we kick the chair instead of our colleague.
Projection	If we unconsciously attach our own unacceptable thoughts onto someone else to make it feel more acceptable.
	Example: we are cross with a friend but uncomfortable with that so accuse them of being angry with us.
Rationalisation	When we explain our behaviour in a way that makes it seem more acceptable to others.
	Example: we might say 'I leave everything to the last minute because I work better under pressure' when we actually rush our work so the result isn't an accurate reflection of our ability and, if we fail, we can then say that it was because we rushed it.
Reaction formation	Here we may behave the opposite to how we really feel.
	Example: You may be attracted to a fellow student on your course but behave as though you dislike them.
Repression	If we have experienced a traumatic or unpleasant incident, we might unconsciously block it out as a form of protection.
	Example: You may have no memory of being in a car accident.
Sublimation	When we change unacceptable impulses into more socially acceptable ones.
	Example: You go cycling when angry so your energy is channelled into a healthy activity.

Impact of mind on health

All of these developmental and unconscious and conscious pressures affect who we become as adults. If the process has not progressed smoothly and we have experienced conflict as a child, there are two potential consequences: neurotic or psychotic behaviour.

- *Neurosis*: Unhealthy behaviour which is in the conscious – the client is aware of it (e.g. depression and phobias). Interestingly, obsessive compulsive disorder (OCD), although mainly neurotic, can also present with psychotic features. The ego remains unharmed.

- *Psychosis*: Unhealthy behaviour which is unconscious – the client is unaware of it (e.g. hallucinations and delusions). There is a loss of awareness of reality.

Putting theory into practice

In addition to Freud's original theory, there are many other psychodynamic theorists who have built upon his original ideas. Carl Jung, Alfred Adler, John Bowlby, Melanie Klein, Erik Erikson, Donald Winnicott, Karen Horney and Erich Fromm are just some of the influential intellectuals influenced by the underlying philosophy of the psychodynamic tradition. As with many models, some overlap more than one school of psychology, such as Eric Berne's transactional analysis, which can be viewed as both psychodynamic (ego states) or humanistic (positive self-regard, organismic valuing). Fitz Perls' Gestalt therapy is similar in that it bridges psychodynamic (recognition of unconscious forces) and humanistic schools (present rather than past). All of these approaches have their own blend of values, skills and methods that best serves their needs and often require a more long-term approach to the therapeutic alliance.

Despite being criticised and discredited over the years, it is now recognised that Freud's psychoanalytical theory has influenced the majority of contemporary counselling, and much of Freud's language and terminology is still in use today. His multi-dimensional ideas have evolved into successful working models of therapeutic practice.

COGNITIVE BEHAVIOURAL THERAPY

Behavioural psychology – J. B. Watson (1878–1958), B. F. Skinner (1904–1990), Ivan Pavlov (1849–1936)

Often referred to as the 'second force', behaviourism removed the focus from the inner workings of the mind where Freud had placed such importance, and relocated it to actions and observable behaviours. This more empirical, scientific approach dismissed the significance of thoughts and feelings and replaced them with objective, measurable outcomes. To do this, experimentation became the principal technique, and because no discussion was necessary (monitoring sufficed) animals could be utilised as well as humans, although many behaviourists then applied the results to human behaviours. Examples of behaviourist theories are 'classical' and 'operant conditioning'. During this period, ethical guidelines did not exist in the same way that they do today, so some experiments are considered inhumane and unethical in retrospect. There are basic assumptions purported, such as that we are born as a blank slate. If behaviour can be learned, it can be unlearned; there is a relationship between trigger (stimulus) and our response which can be manipulated.

Social learning theory (SLT) – Albert Bandura (1925–2007)

Bandura is believed to be the first psychologist who determined links between behaviour, thoughts and feelings. At the heart of SLT is the study of *why* we do what we do and where we learn it from. According to Bandura, there are several answers to this. We watch others (role models), although it is important to recognise that modelling is not just copying others but determining the rules that lie behind the behaviours so we can recreate the behaviour ourselves if we so wish. How likely we are to re-enact the behaviour is influenced by intrinsic reinforcements (such as our conscience) and our underlying personal characteristics (such as how extroverted and introverted we are). In addition to this, self-efficacy or how successful we believe we are going to be, which we base on previous experiences, has an impact too.

Cognitive therapy (CT) – Aaron Beck (b. 1921)

Compared to other models, CT is a fairly recently developed approach. As the name suggests, cognitive therapy concerns itself with the workings of the thinking mind and the impact that this has on our overall sense of wellbeing. Beck indicated that our behaviour, feelings and thoughts are all interrelated (see Figure 3.2) and any change in one will automatically alter the other two. Schemas and negative automatic thoughts are challenged. The counselling that results from this involves some methods from other models as 'in practice, the actual distinction between cognitive therapy and CBT is more historical and semantic than practical' (Sanders and Wills, 2005: 121–122). Behavioural experiments are devised that will support cognitive change.

Cognitive behavioural therapy (CBT)

CBT is an amalgamation of several aspects of both behavioural and cognitive counselling. Similar to other cognitive approaches, it is recognised

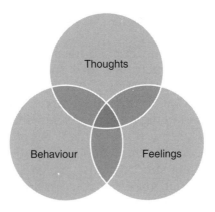

Figure 3.2   Our behaviour, feelings and thoughts are all interrelated

that our thoughts influence the way we feel, how happy or sad we are. The focus is on the present rather than the past and involves action, doing and challenging rather than solely thinking and talking. As the ultimate goal is to replace negative behaviours with positive ones, CBT is often used for the treatment of phobias, OCD, addictions, etc. Distinct change in behaviour is observable, therefore measurable, and so presents a currently popular approach enthusiastically adopted by the National Health Service (NHS). Not all CBT practice involves a therapeutic relationship as CDs, DVDs and self-help books are often used as an alternative.

Rational emotional behaviour therapy (REBT) – Albert Ellis (1913–2007)

REBT (sometimes referred to as REBC if the 'therapy' is replaced with 'counselling') was originally developed during the mid-1950s and established a relationship between thoughts, feelings and behaviours. It centres on the sense of achievement and success people experience when they achieve or are working towards set goals or aims. Ellis believed that irrational and illogical thoughts and behaviours led to unhappiness and a failure to succeed, so the therapy is designed to challenge negative falsehoods and teach the client how to replace these with factual, logical and more positive ways of thinking. His ABC model (action–belief–consequences) was developed to distinguish between actual events and appropriate or inappropriate emotional responses.

Reality therapy – William Glasser (b. 1925)

Reality therapy is a treatment designed for people experiencing difficulty in meeting their needs which can lead to irresponsible or damaging behaviour and differs from therapies used before 1965. The approach is based on the client's morality with judgements made on worthwhile or 'satisfactory standards of behaviour'. Glasser claimed that our values and behaviours parallel our sense of self-worth. According to Glasser (1975: p. 24), 'therapy is a special kind of teaching or training which attempts to accomplish in a relatively short, intense period what should have been established during normal growing up'. An interesting aspect of this approach is that mental illness is cited as an avoidance tactic or excuse for negative behaviour, as are unconscious concepts such as transference. The client's past is of absolutely no interest as it cannot be changed. The counselling practice involves teaching clients how to fulfil their needs in a positive and moral way. Although fairly radical by today's thinking, reality therapy is often used when working with addictive behaviours and can be integrated with the Minnesota model (12-step programme).

Multimodal therapy – Arnold Lazarus (b. 1932)

This is a psychoeducational framework which encourages improvisation and incorporates some elements of SLT. The therapy assesses seven separate but connecting modalities: Behaviour, Affect, Sensation, Imagery, Cognition, Interpersonal factors and biological considerations/Drugs, abbreviated by the acronym BASIC ID. When working with clients, bridging and tracking are techniques often used. Bridging is when the counsellor moves from one modality to another, such as from the client's mood (affect) to how the how their body feels (sensation) or how others view the situation (interpersonal factors). This is successful in adapting to the client's current frame of mind and providing a uniqueness to each session. Tracking is being aware of a client's train of events or firing order when they create a destructive frame of mind. Other methods used are the Multimodal Life History Inventory and Structural Profile Inventory.

Revision checklist for cognitive behavioral therapy

- If behaviour can be learned, it can be unlearned.
- Identify triggers (stimulus) to manipulate response.
- Objective rather than subjective.

- Training and practice can re-establish healthier behaviours.
- How we think influence how we feel and behave.

HUMANISTIC THERAPY

This is a wide-ranging school of psychology and therapy which is often referred to as the third force (with psychoanalysis being the first and behaviourism being the second). Originally believed to have been named by Abraham Maslow, humanistic theory focuses far more on the individual's experiences and perceptions of their life rather than the more scientific explanations that went before. Such a phenomenological and existential standpoint took the focal point away from the external framework of the client and placed it firmly at the internal framework. It is a hugely popular approach to counselling and there are currently many different humanistic counselling courses available.

Person-centred therapy (PCT) – Carl Rogers (1902–1987)

PCT is often the first counselling model that jumps to mind when thinking of humanistic approaches. However, there are many, some developed as a practical framework to working with clients in a therapeutic setting, through to others that are more a philosophy or framework for viewing the world around us. Carl Rogers carried out much work in this field with his formulation of non-directive therapy, later renamed client-centred therapy which then became known as person-centred therapy during the 1970s. There are several elements to this method of therapeutic working that make up the 'pure' model, although PCT is well used as one of the major component theories for integrative counselling too.

- *Counselling or psychotherapy*: Rogers and many person-centred counsellors make absolutely no distinction between these two activities. These two labels for similar activities, methods and approaches have become interchangeable.
- *Non-directive*: Unlike the previous therapies available, Rogers acknowledged that the client was the expert in their own life and as such it would be inappropriate to offer advice. The counsellor does not know the situation, history, people involved or indeed exactly how the client truly feels, so is in no position to direct them. Rather, the counsellor is there to provide the conditions (see below) to value and recognise that the client is a unique individual who is capable of making their own decisions.

- *Core condition*: There are six core conditions or qualities that Rogers argued were necessary in the therapeutic relationship. Purists claim that these are all that is necessary for a positive outcome, whereas many counsellors from differing theoretical backgrounds utilise them to build a warm and trusting relationship. Rogers' core conditions are:

  1 *Psychological contact*: Members of the therapeutic relationship feel a deep level of supportive connection.
  2 *Client incongruence*: The client is aware that there is something they are unhappy about, that they require counselling and that they choose to be present.
  3 *Congruence*: There is true honesty and genuineness demonstrated by the counsellor; Rogers referred to this in levels of 'transparency'.
  4 *Unconditional positive regard*: A warm, accepting and non-judgemental attitude toward the client, which is a major constituent for a positive relationship.
  5 *Empathy*: A deep understanding of the client's inner world from the client's perspective.
  6 *Client perception*: The client not only needs to feel supported and listened to by the counsellor but, more importantly, needs to be aware that the other conditions are present. The client must be aware of the fact that they are not being judged, that the counsellor is making every effort to truly see the world from the client's viewpoint and that they are being honest and genuine.

- *Actualising tendency*: The base motivation that all humans have for improvement and development. There are similarities with Maslow's self-actualisation in the hierarchy of needs, although the process is different. Being such an optimistic and valuing therapeutic model, Rogers believed that everyone has an innate ability to work towards their potential as long as they are living in a supportive and encouraging environment. Prevention of this can lead to unhappiness and frustration.
- *Organismic valuing*: Doing more of the things we like or being attracted to what we think is good for us. This can be as obvious as choice of food but can also be behavioural, such as taking part in activities that give us pleasure rather than those that don't. Sometimes our environment and those around us have a negative impact rather than a positive one in the process of personal decision making.
- *Conditions of worth*: The framework of guiding principles and expected behaviours that we grow up with influenced by our parents, peers, teachers, media, etc. Being told what is acceptable and unacceptable makes it clear what those around us value, and in turn we also adopt that value base. This can be reinforced through reward and punishment; if you steal you could go to prison gives the message that, if you don't steal, you are 'worthy' or a good person. If you work hard and gain qualifications, you are rewarded with a wider choice of better-paid jobs.

- *Fully functioning person*: can be read as a 'healthy' person, someone who is in touch with their real self and comfortable, has a positive self-concept and is interested in new experiences and development. According to Rogers, a fully functioning person would hopefully show:

1 A loosening of feelings.
2 A change in their manner of experiencing.
3 A shift from incongruence to congruence.
4 A change in the manner in which, and the extent to which, they are willing to communicate self.
5 A loosening of their cognitive maps of experience.
6 A change in their relationship to their problems.
7 A change in their manner of relating.

(Tudor et al., 2004, with permission)

Hierarchy of needs - Abraham Maslow (1908–1970)

This is not so much a therapy as a basis or framework for considering motivation and development throughout life. It has become an underpinning element in many areas of care, such as social work and nursing. Luckily, it is most usually represented graphically through the use of the now well-recognised triangle which highlights the sense of progression and growth (see Figure 3.3). Maslow felt that an individual could only move up the hierarchy once they had already met the needs of the previous stage. For example, it would be highly likely that a client who was currently homeless would be worried more about food and shelter than considering which degree course to apply for.

Gestalt therapy - Fitz Perls (1893–1970)

Gestalt therapy is based on viewing our lives in a holistic way with a wider focus that allows us to see both the immediate or obvious situation (foreground) as well as the contextualisation and underlying influences (background). This is in association with ensuring that we finish what we start to avoid frustration and encourage satisfaction. This is done by placing the moment-by-moment present under the microscope: 'Now is the chasm we constantly bridge between the entirety of the past, which has been refined into this moment of existence, and the not-yet-existent future. From second to second it is the place of exquisite decision, which will in turn help form the next gestalt and the next' (Houston, 1995: 11). We can only view our life as a whole as opposed to

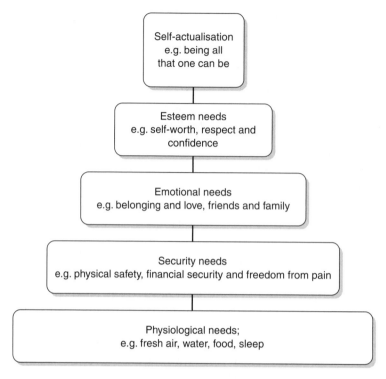

Figure 3.3   Maslow's hierarchy of needs (Maslow, 1943). Reproduced from *Psychology Review* (1943), 50(4): 370–396 (now in public domain).

the individual constituents due to the impact each aspect has over other parts. The therapy often utilises an empty chair and the client is invited to imagine placing people or the difficulties they are experiencing on the chair so that a channel of communication can be opened up with what might previously have been an isolated, esoteric, intellectual or indistinct problem. Perls' most famous demonstration was as part of the Gloria sessions (*Three Approaches to Psychotherapy*: Shostrom, 1965), although there is much more to the therapy than was evident in that 30-minute session.

Transactional analysis (TA) – Eric Berne (1910–1970)

TA also has a very optimistic viewpoint of people in common with other humanistic models. In TA, this derives from the premise that all people have the ability to take control of how they feel and react; they have the

Table 3.3 Ego states and effect

Ego state	Effect
Parent	Controlling, protective, influencing others.
Adult	Very much in the present, balance between parent and child.
Child	Dependent, influenced by the past.

ability to control the direction that their life takes them in (life script). As a therapy, TA focuses on the interpersonal and relational aspects of the client and the role of communication within these (ego states – see Table 3.3). There is recognition that how others communicate with us on a physical and emotional level feeds how we feel (positive or negative strokes). The task of contracting with the client takes on a more significant role than in other therapeutic approaches to reinforce the 'people are OK' assertion, introduce negotiation and establish commitment.

Existential therapy (ET) – Rollo May (1909–1994), Victor Frankl (1905–1997)

Being a counselling model and a philosophical way of thinking, existentialism is a common basis for approaching constructive and healing work in counselling. Placing the client within the context of their personal experiences and then understanding the sense they make from what has happened to them can help to create a sense of independence, free choice and positive decision making. Traditionally, existentialism was a reaction to control by a society that only really valued objective, scientific evidence which challenged this by rehumanising people and recognising individuals as unique. This standpoint impacts on counselling practice in that clients often distance themselves from positive aspects of their lives and have grown to reduce their awareness to only the negative aspects. Existential therapy, therefore, is about encouraging a client to develop an awareness of the whole picture, reduce the negative feelings and recognise and acknowledge the positive ones.

Revision checklist for humanistic therapy

- The client is the expert in their own life.
- Actualising tendency/self-actualisation.
- Assumption that people are essentially good.

- Methodology is client led and non-directive.
- Unhappiness is caused by disparity between ideal and actual self.
- Core conditions.
- Establishing a positive rapport is essential.
- Client must choose to be present.

INTEGRATIVE THEORY

During the 1980s, a growing number of practitioners began the integration of some of the major therapeutic models (which is sometimes mistakenly referred to as 'eclecticism'). By the 1990s, a substantial number of counsellors used some form of integration within their practice and, by the 2000s, the majority of counsellors used some form of amalgamation of models. There are arguably many different methods for using this approach, but currently many are based on Egan's 'Three-stage Model of Helping'.

Each of Egan's three stages is divided into three separate areas of focus beginning with encouraging the client to tell their story which tends to involve a level of clarification. The helper or counsellor might help to identify aspects of themselves or the situation the client is unaware of (known as blind spots). There might be an element of challenge surrounding this, especially during the process of searching for leverage when beginning to confront the issue.

Stage two moves the client on to consider preferred scenarios and consider possibilities. These would then be transformed into practical aims and goals while the client is then directed towards the reality of change and what might help motivate them when working toward their goal.

The final stage is more strategic and pragmatic in approach. The client is encouraged to brainstorm for ideas that will help them initiate change and then pick the most suitable strategies before integrating them into a plan for progress.

As each stage has a slightly different focus, each is underpinned by a different psychological approach.

Stage 1 is humanistic in perspective as the focus is on exploration and encouraging the client to tell their story. This requires building a warm and trusting relationship, and the use of qualities such as the core conditions are successful within this process. Stage 2 involves the client setting goals and is therefore a more cognitive process. Finally Stage 3, the action stage, is based on changing behaviour and as such has a more behavioural bias.

Other methods of integration are not always so structured and so can be approached in several ways. Counsellors may start by combining compatible theoretical basis that underpin different approaches when working with a client, which can result in the creation of a blend of method-ology. Alternatively, counsellors may use a range of diverse techniques and skills from a range of models without necessarily considering or believing in an underpinning theory. Then again, the process can be far less planned, with the counsellor cherry-picking elements of differing approaches without considering a wider picture. This is known as 'syncretism'. Although this can be successful, it takes a very experienced counsellor to have the ability and the confidence to discriminate in this way. All three of these methods can only succeed if the theories and methodology chosen are compatible, but when used correctly can result in a unique and tailor-made style of therapy that is moulded to the client's individual needs. Clearly there are dangers to this, with the major one being focusing so much on the process that you lose sight of the reason that the client is attending counselling in the first place. Of course, there is also the need for the counsellor to be highly skilled and adept in a number of orienta-tions to allow for a professional and therapeutic practice that ultimately helps the client.

The single element that all these approaches have in common is the desire to support the client whilst they develop coping mechanisms and new skills to deal with a situation that they can then put into practice themselves at a later date without the need to return to counselling; building new frameworks for dealing with issues.

Messina (2005) identified eight specific motives for the trend in integration:

1 Proliferation of therapies.
2 Inadequacy of a single therapy relevant to all clients and problems.
3 External socioeconomic realities: insurance reimbursement.
4 Popularity of short-term, prescriptive, problem-focused therapies.
5 Opportunities to observe and experiment with various therapies.
6 Paucity of differential effectiveness among therapies.
7 Recognition of therapeutic commonalities' major role in therapy outcomes.
8 Development of professional societies aimed at integrating psychotherapies.
(Reproduced with kind permission. To read more of Jim Messina's work please visit www.jamesjmessina.com)

Revision checklist for integrative therapy

- Several different methods of integration.
- Currently very prevalent.
- Every session totally unique to each client.
- Designed to provide client with coping skills for future.
- Counsellor needs to be highly skilled in more than one orientation.

SOLUTION-FOCUSED THERAPY

Unlike other approaches that we have covered, there is no one definition, history or founder of solution-focused therapy. Instead it has evolved from the amalgamation of methodologies from other modalities, in particular CBT, motivational interviewing and the work of Adler and Erikson. There is no set number of sessions but the underlying philosophy is to encourage the client to focus more on the future and the solution than on the past and the problem and to encourage positive thinking. The techniques are designed to help the client concentrate on their strengths and skills, so replacing a defeatist outlook with a reminder of past achievements that would boost the empowerment and autonomy of the client. The 'miracle question' is often used (if a miracle occurs and your problem is resolved, what is the first sign that you know it's happened?) within the structure as a tool to help this. Some simple guidelines are identified by O'Connell and Palmer (2003: 10):

- If it isn't broken don't fix it.
- Small change can lead to bigger changes.
- If it's working keep doing it.
- If it's not working stop doing it.
- Keep therapy as simple as possible.

Confusingly, the term 'brief therapy' has nothing to do with solution-focused therapy but is often applied to counselling sessions that are restricted within a reduced timescale, such as 6–10 sessions within a GP's surgery, although this definition remains open for debate.

AS A STUDENT, WHAT DO THESE DIFFERENCES MEAN?

Differing teaching methods

You will find that a variety of teaching methods are used according to the orientation of the course you have chosen. For example, person-centred courses tend to allow students to make sense of the learning in their own way so there is an emphasis on the feelings experienced and less direction, whereas cognitive behavioural courses place more importance on matter-of-fact structure and specific skills. Psychodynamic courses insist on students attending personal therapy as well to explore elements such as their drives and transference. There is further information on this subject in Chapter 2.

How will it affect my practice?

Now that we have looked at a range of orientations, the question remains as to how the application of theory may affect the use of skills and the therapeutic alliance. There are some logical and fairly basic impacts on practice; for example, a directive model where the counsellor is the expert, such as in psychoanalysis and CBT, introduces a potential power imbalance between client and counsellor (patient and therapist/analyst). Other non-directive approaches make a conscious effort to restore a balance of power, which can be a challenge considering the counsellor is usually perceived by the client to be a trained professional and sessions take place in an unfamiliar environment, immediately giving the counsellor the upper hand.

Why does it matter?

As far back as 1980, Smith et al. published a detailed survey that claimed that no one therapeutic approach was preferable to any other as they were all fairly effective. There is also much current evidence to show that it is not so much the orientation or method of counselling that is used with a client but rather the therapeutic relationship that is achieved. A client who feels supported, encouraged and valued will have a more successful outcome than one who feels disconnected from their counsellor. Whether you are training to be a psychoanalyst, psychotherapist, counsellor or studying for CPD within a helping occupation, your success during therapy comes down to your warmth, understanding and acceptance of others. That is the true indicator of how successful you will be, hence the value of personal development activities in courses.

Will it be easy to find a job?

If we, for a moment, reflect upon the current trends within employment of counsellors, it is apparent that there has been rapid growth of CBT within the NHS. This is a consequence of both the importance of robust outcome evaluation, which secures funding along, together with the convenience that methods which take fewer sessions are cheaper to fund, more clients can be seen and waiting lists are more manageable. Additionally, this directive, pragmatic and measurable method slots easily within the medical model of care.

There is such a wide range of counselling settings and services that it is difficult to pair up organisations with preferred orientations, so it is always better to contact any service you would like to work for directly, and check their preferred approach if you wish to tailor your training to meet their requirements. An aspect for consideration here is the paucity of paid posts compared to the availability of voluntary opportunities, which differs from area to area. A great number of counsellors within the UK are working on a voluntary basis, which makes it essential to ensure that you are studying the right orientation at the right level to meet your future career needs.

FURTHER READING

Psychodynamic therapy

Elliott, A. (2002) *Psychoanalytic Theory: An Introduction*. Durham, NC: Duke University Press.
Higdon, J. (2004) *From Counselling Skills to Counsellor: A Psychodynamic Approach*. Basingstoke: Palgrave Macmillan.
Howard, S. (2006) *Psychodynamic Counselling in a Nutshell*. London: Sage.
Jacobs, M. (2004) *Psychodynamic Counselling in Action*. London: Sage.
Klein, M. (2006) *The Psychodynamic Primer*. Ross-on-Wye: PCCS Books.
Mander, G. (2000) *A Psychodynamic Approach to Brief Therapy*. London: Sage.

Cognitive behavioural therapy

Sanders, D. and Wills, F. (2005) *Cognitive Therapy: An Introduction*. London: Sage.
Westbrook, D., Kennerle, H. and Kirk, J. (2007) *An Introduction to Cognitive Behaviour Therapy: Skills and Applications*. London: Sage.

Humanistic therapy

Lister-Ford, C. (2002) *Skills In Transactional Analysis Counselling & Psychotherapy*. London: Sage.

McMillan, M. (2004) *The Person-centred Approach to Therapeutic Change*. London: Sage.

Merry, T. (2002) *Learning and Being in Person-Centred Counselling*. Ross-on-Wye: PCCS Books.

Perls, F., Hefferline, R.F. and Goodman, P. (1951) *Gestalt Therapy*. New York: Julian.

Rogers, C. (2004) *On Becoming a Person*. London: Constable & Robinson.

Thorne, B. (2003) *Carl Rogers*. London: Sage.

Tudor, L.E., Kemar, K., Tudor, K., Valentine, J. and Worrall, M. (2004) *The Person-centred Approach: A Contemporary Introduction*. Basingstoke: Palgrave Macmillan.

van Deurzen, E. and Arnold-Baker, C. (2005) *Existential Perspectives on Human Issues: A Handbook for Therapeutic Practice*. Basingstoke: Palgrave Macmillan.

Integrative therapy

Culley, S. and Bond, T. (2011) *Integrative Counselling Skills in Action*, 3rd edn. London: Sage.

Egan, G. (2001) *The Skilled Helper: A Problem-Management and Opportunity-Development Approach to Helping*, 7th edn. Belmont, CA: Wadsworth.

Lapworth, P., Sills, C. and Fish, S. (2001) *Integration in Counselling & Psychotherapy: Developing a Personal Approach*. London: Sage.

Palmer, S. and Woolfe, R. (eds) (1999) *Integrative and Eclectic Counselling & Psychotherapy*. London: Sage.

Solution-focused therapy

Bor, R., Gill, S., Miller, R. and Parrot, C. (2004) *Doing Therapy Briefly*. Basingstoke: Palgrave Macmillan.

Coren, A. (2010) *Short-term Psychotherapy: A Psychodynamic Approach*. Basingstoke: Palgrave Macmillan.

Macdonald, A. (2007) *Solution-focused Therapy: Theory, Research and Practice*. London: Sage.

Milner, J. and O'Byrne, P. (2002) *Brief Counselling: Narrative and Solutions*. Basingstoke: Palgrave Macmillan.

O'Connell, B. and Palmer, S. (eds) (2003) *Handbook of Solution-focused Therapy*. London: Sage.

Tudor, K. (ed.) (2008) *Brief Person-centred Therapies*. London: Sage.

4

Who Needs Counselling?

Starting a counselling course may be daunting but there are commonalities with starting a counselling relationship. Before moving on to other areas of counselling training, we will consider the role of counselling from the perspective of a client to contextualise their perception and process. This will be from an individual therapy perspective rather than group work.

WHO IS THE CLIENT?

Anyone can be a client. We never know what may happen in our lives and how we may perceive it or respond to it. For this reason, counselling can cover a vast range of circumstances and situations. Issues can involve both the external and internal framework. The external framework is the situation that the client is in, the world and people around them, whereas the internal framework refers to the client's inner world, their thoughts, feelings, perceptions and fears. During counselling sessions it is hoped that the counsellor can encourage the client to forge links between the external and internal to develop a greater understanding prior to instigating any necessary change. This may also involve taking into account the past, present and future so that difficulties can be viewed in a more objective manner or simply from alternative perspectives. Because of this complex process clients can experience many different responses, such as distress, resistance, frustration and anger. In general, it isn't until later in the process when changes are imminent or already happening that more positive feelings may surface, although these can be accompanied by fear or trepidation.

There are so many issues that clients might present with that there isn't room to cover them all here, but some more common ones are:

- loss
- addiction
- relationship difficulties
- dissatisfaction
- managing feelings
- fear
- medical conditions
- change
- coping with memories
- financial difficulties
- self-development.

This should give some indication of the wide range of issues with which clients can present. Counselling training is purposely involved and intensive so that on completion we are ready and able to work in a dynamic way with such a diverse array of client difficulties. Despite referral being an option, particularly with some practitioners specialising in a particular issue, it is not always the most advisable route. Ideally, clients should have the freedom to make that decision because where you may hear 'referral' as a positive and supportive option, your client may hear 'your problem is too complex for me to deal with', which can result in the negative consequence of 'my problem is so bad that even a counsellor can't help me'. Developing the skills and confidence to work with a range of issues comes with experience, hence the use of placements and personal challenges during training to prepare you. Even after the course there is a requirement for counsellors to continue learning, developing and expanding knowledge through continuing professional development (CPD). No counsellor ever reaches the point of knowing it all – there is far too much to know and clients are far too unique for this to ever happen.

This individuality extends to other areas, such as how a client finds a counsellor in the first place. Very often, this is by GP referral if the counselling practice is approved by the NHS; however, self-referral is also common, which can result from a search on the Internet, telephone directory, reading an advert in a local newspaper or libraries, etc. Occasionally a well-informed client my seek information from a professional body such as BACP, but frequently it is as a result of word of mouth and reputation.

Here are some common assumptions made *about* clients:

- The client wants to talk.
- The client wants to be present.
- The client knows how they feel.
- The client is able to explain how they feel.
- The client is comfortable with opening up to a stranger.
- The client understands the process of counselling.
- The client is motivated for change.

Clearly, these are not all going to be true and it is the counsellor's responsibility to consider how they might work with this. Unfortunately, there is no easy list of solutions that can be provided but honest reflection and self-evaluation by the counsellor, client or both can result in the formation of ideas and options for facilitating the therapeutic process.

A CLIENT'S VIEW

Take a moment to consider attending counselling from a client's perspective. Here they are making a commitment to turn up regularly to speak about personal, private and sometimes embarrassing feelings with a stranger who they have only just met. The environment is not usually somewhere they have been before so they are not in their comfort zone. This may be accompanied with discomfort or embarrassment at attending counselling. It is only after attending several sessions that the process becomes more natural and secure. Naturally, there are going to be concerns.

COMMON CONCERNS AND ISSUES CLIENTS CAN EXPERIENCE

Concerns regarding boundary issues

One of the most common concerns that clients express is regarding confidentiality. Understandably, clients who are new to counselling can be anxious about where information goes once it has been divulged, but reassurance can be given during the initial contracting session. Concerns can be about the storage of and access to notes as well as the sharing of verbal content. Agencies and organisations have policies and procedures to follow regarding this but private practitioners are required by accrediting bodies to develop their own ethical system. This is a considerable concern to clients who attend counselling in rural rather than urban settings due to the dual roles the counsellor may have, such as also being a colleague on a committee or a fellow parent in a school. Although not solely a rural issue, this is, understandably, more prevalent within smaller communities where privacy can be more challenging. Other concerns regarding boundary issues can be cost and affordability, regularity of attendance and private access to the location, all of which should be considered by the service provider.

Client's uncertainty as to their role

Mention was made earlier to specific concerns first-time clients may experience regarding the organisation of the sessions, and here we will consider uncertainty regarding the content of the sessions. Worrying thoughts such as those below can result in the possible development of barriers and resistance that can impede the therapeutic process:

- How will this be different to talking to my friends?
- Will I like my counsellor?
- What happens during the session?
- What happens if I become upset?
- What if I find out things about myself that I don't like?
- What if I find out what I'm really like?
- What if I'm asked to do something I don't want to do?
- What will happen if I really open up about my feelings?
- Will I be say something stupid?
- Will I feel under pressure?
- Will I have to take risks?
- Will I talk too much about myself?

It is part of the counsellor's role to anticipate such concerns and to discuss calmly and professionally any fears regarding the process during the first meeting. This will help allay fears, encourage a trusting relationship and stimulate notions of autonomy, negotiation and empowerment.

Dependency issues

Involvement and over-involvement may be clear to an experienced counsellor following ethical guidelines, but a client doesn't have that security: 'For a number of clients, this independent interest and focus can be perceived as a personal caring by the counsellor over and beyond professional responsibilities. The resulting compulsion or reliance upon this process and experience is referred to as dependency' (Amis, 2008: 172). This perception of the counsellor as a friend rather than a professional can blur boundaries and impede the process of autonomy within the client. You, as the counsellor, are required to remain alert and aware in case this becomes apparent. However, there are arguments that a level of dependency is necessary for the therapeutic process to succeed: 'I believe ... that dependency is, for the course of the treatment, essential, even if it takes the form of an underlying commitment to the process' (Young, 2002). Only training, experience and regular supervision can inform as to where that boundary lies.

Expectations

Clients new to counselling may enter the relationship with some interesting perceptions, such as 'this is an instant solution', or 'an expert will sort everything out for me' or 'a counsellor will tell me what to do, give me advice and guidance'. This is one of the main reasons for the contracting session – it is for introducing the method practised which in turn allows the client to make an informed decision as to whether they wish to proceed with that particular method of intervention.

IMPORTANCE OF CONTRACT SESSION

A contract session (sometimes integrated with an assessment) takes place before counselling begins. This is an opportunity for swapping information – the counsellor provides information on the counselling process they provide, and the client shares information about why they feel they need counselling. Then both make a decision as to whether there is a good match and they feel comfortable enough to build a trusting, warm and professional relationship. Within this time, the counsellor may establish clarity by sharing appropriate information about their boundary issues. Boundary issues are the guidelines, rules or boundaries that a counsellor adheres to, to remain professional – essentially everything that moulds the counselling sessions, apart from what takes place during them. These can include:

- *Ethics*: informed by a professional body, e.g. BACP, the values, principles and moral qualities that you adhere to for the safety of yourself and your client.

- *Contracts*: agreements to establish commitment, especially within approaches such as transactional analysis.
- *Confidentiality*: clarifying your policy on sharing and storage of information.
- *Beginnings and endings*: the decisions and methods used to start and stop counselling.
- *Referral*: where clients may be referred from and where they may be referred to.
- *Supervision*: counselling support and monitoring that is used to support the service.
- *Education and training*: qualifications and experience.
- *Number of sessions*: whether this is decided by client, counsellor, agency policy or funding limitations.
- *Cost of sessions*: hourly rate or funding provider, e.g. NHS.
- *Timing of sessions*: how long each lasts (usually a 50-minute therapeutic hour), also the number of sessions and how regularly they take place.
- *Orientation*: the psychological school, model or approach that underpins your practice.
- *Settings*: voluntary, statutory or voluntary service provision plus counselling environment.

The client and the counsellor both need to be very clear about the process before agreeing to begin, in much the same way as they might with a surgeon, chiropractor or piano teacher. The aims may be to encourage the client to consider the situation from various viewpoints, to help the client make breakthroughs and to facilitate changes in direction, but importantly, this also includes allowing the client to feel empowered to decline continuing if they so wish. Clearly this is not the case in compulsory counselling, when a client is obligated to attend by a court or school, etc.

ACTIVITY

- Consider why confidentiality, referral, supervision and ethics are necessary boundary issues within counselling environments.
- Why, in your opinion, is training so important before working with clients?
- How can a) the setting and b) the counselling orientation influence the client's needs?

Information regarding boundary issues ensures transparency and gives the client the opportunity to question the process prior to formally entering into a therapeutic relationship. This is predominantly highlighted within humanistic approaches where equality and openness are particularly valued.

STUDENT AS CLIENT

Socrates said, 'When I must first know myself, to be curious about that which is not my concern, but to do this while I am still ignorant of myself is ridiculous' (Plato, 360). Gibson and Mitchell (1999) suggest that being an effective client, in turn, augments our effectiveness as a counsellor. The self-awareness, personal insight and therapeutic process provide a valuable outlook into the world of the client, helping identification of issues such as transference, dependency and vulnerability. Until fairly recently, many courses (including all BACP accredited courses) stipulated that students as well as practitioners must be engaged in regular personal therapy. This is no longer the case; it recently became optional, so there is now a situation where some courses insist on personal therapy and others don't feel it to be necessary. The orientation of the course has a bearing here as psychodynamic courses, due to their nature, consider personal therapy to be a compulsory element, whereas CBT courses are far less likely to recognise any benefit at all. If your course expects you to engage in therapy or if you feel that it would be of personal benefit, there are several ways that you can find a suitable counsellor to meet your needs. First, local counsellors may be recommended by your tutor, although if this is not the case, then it is very simple to set about finding one yourself by accessing lists of appropriate and accredited counsellors directly through the websites of the accrediting association that you hope to form allegiance with yourself. (A list of websites has been provided at the end of this chapter.)

Personal therapy allows you to genuinely experience and hopefully understand what you may consider to be potentially problematic or awkward aspects, for instance, ethical guidelines from an alternative perspective that would both inform and benefit your own practice. How immersed you become in this process is a very personal decision. Andrews et al. (1992: 571) felt that 'the unique needs of the individual student or client would be violated by insisting on a single modality of uniform length'. This argument suggests that a school of thought that purports autonomy, freedom of choice and empowerment (such as PCT) would be denying these fundamental components for students by insisting on a prescriptive and formulaic counselling process during training. On some introductory or basic-level courses, a possible alternative to external personal counselling is the process of co-counselling, which is described in detail in Chapter 9. Some courses suggest co-counselling in addition to external personal therapy, whilst others don't consider it an option. This, of course, is in addition to counselling supervision, which is a very different process (see Chapters 6 and 12 for information on counselling supervision). Essentially, your course tutor, course curriculum, counselling supervisor and accrediting body will guide you as to your requirements.

WHO DOESN'T NEED COUNSELLING?

The use of the word 'need' here can be questioned, as surely entering such an invasive and involved relationship is a personal decision and, if we are to value the autonomy of the individual, this decision cannot be made on another's behalf, so perhaps 'want' would be more appropriate. It might be counter-productive to work with a client who did not want to discuss their issues or even to be present in the sessions. This is a recurrent issue when working in settings with clients who have been referred against their will, for example through the courts as in many statutory and voluntary addiction or anger management services. Here a diverse range of skills are required in addition to counselling skills to encourage the client to trust, open up, but also see merit in the process. This is a very different context to simply recognising that not everyone feels the need to talk about their difficulties; many people would rather work through them privately in their own way or ignore them without coming to any harm at all. Counselling is not some great panacea, otherwise it would be compulsory for all!

So far we have made the assumption that the counselling process has a positive effect on the client but it would be irresponsible to ignore considerable arguments that counselling sometimes has no effect, or indeed a negative effect, on the client. There have been many advocates over the years who argue that counselling intervention makes no difference or may even be harmful (Masson, 1992; Smail, 1987). Much of this is rooted in the more historical interventions used traditionally within the medical model and, to some extent, psychiatry. Many past and present interventions can be questioned from an ethical and moral standpoint, particularly in the areas of power imbalance (psychoanalytical approaches) and advice-giving (CBT). Masson writes extensively and articulately on this subject (see Further Reading). However, even when working with what are percieved as more gentle and personalised approaches, such as PCT, Masson asserts that:

> The therapist is *not* a real person with the client, for if he were, he would have the same reactions he would have with people in his real life, which certainly do not include 'unconditional acceptance, lack of judging, or real empathic understanding'. (1992: 232)

This is an interesting viewpoint as Masson is arguing that it is deceitful to claim to be yourself when demonstrating the core conditions, as they are additional attitudes we are trained to adopt rather than natural, innate ways of being. Humans need to have a level of judgement and condemnation to maintain their own safety. Are we then required to dismiss our own values and adopt those of the client at will?

There is also a substantial accumulation of evidence that supports the assertion that the depth and impact of the complex therapeutic relationship, with the combination of dedicated, concentrated time, benefits the client more than any specific methodology (Mearns and Cooper, 2005). This is discussed in more detail in Chapter 13.

ACTIVITY

- Who do you choose to talk to if you are upset?
- Why do you choose to talk to them in particular?
- How does it make you feel when you have talked about your problem?
- What are you good at when you are listening to people?
- List any communication skills that might help people talk to you.

RELEVANT WEBSITES

British Association for Counselling and Psychotherapy: www.bacp.co.uk
UK Council for Psychotherapy: www.ukcp.org.uk
The British Psychological Society: www.bps.org.uk
Counselling and Psychotherapy Central Awarding Body: www.cpcab.co.uk
UK Association of Humanistic Psychology Practitioner: www.ahpp.org/about/statpurpose.htm
Counselling and Psychotherapy in Scotland: www.cosca.org.uk

FURTHER READING

Masson, J. (1992) *Against Therapy*. London: Fontana.

5

Counselling Contexts

An understanding of where counselling takes place can influence your choice of course and future career plans. In this chapter we will examine the various settings and the differences between them, both for the counsellor and for potential clients.

WHERE COUNSELLING TAKES PLACE

Counselling within the statutory sector includes agencies, organisations and services that are centrally funded such as:

- GP surgeries
- schools
- prisons
- hospitals
- social work departments
- community addiction teams.

Essentially, there is no cost to the client at the point of delivery and staff are trusted as being thoroughly vetted for competency and trustworthiness.

Funding for voluntary sector settings is raised independently through public donation, applications to funds such as the National Lottery or fundraising activities, etc., so does not have the same level of certainty afforded to statutory sector services. However, it is also common that voluntary services can be partially funded by local councils, NHS or social work departments (SWD) if they are alone in providing a vital service to a community and meet the necessary requirements (such as approved policies and procedures). If registered as a charity, they are a non-profit making organisation where any surplus income must be reinvested into the service. Sometimes, clients are asked to make a donation for their counselling, if they can afford it, to help cover costs. They can be small, local services or national concerns. Well-known examples are:

- Childline
- Women's Aid
- Samaritans
- Relate
- Cruse
- Place2be.

Private counselling settings are different yet again (see Figure 5.1). Based on profit making, the intention is to generate an income. Counsellors may

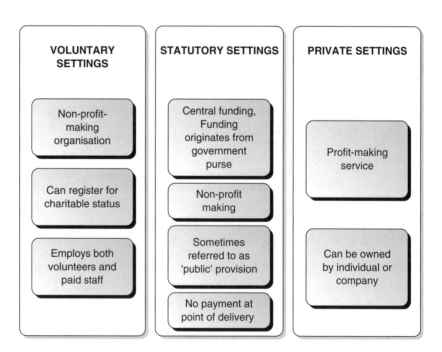

Figure 5.1   Comparison of counselling settings

work alone or with colleagues in private practice or be employed within a privately owned service. Counselling provision within private hospitals such as the Nuffield and BUPA hospitals would also fall within this category. The underpinning commonality is that a profit is generated.

The differences are more complex than simply sources of funding. There are also organisational differences, e.g. statutory and private sector services are more likely to deliver counselling by a structured appointment system, whereas charitable organisations encourage flexibility to meet the needs of potential clients so drop-in sessions, self-referral and word-of-mouth play a greater role in access to the service and methodology of counselling. Statutory sector services may use a variety of approaches but, following the Increasing Access to Psychological Therapies (IAPT) agreement, CBT is more prevalent. Some counselling services, particularly in health settings, include a greater level of information giving (such as detailing what may happen during surgery) to allay fears. Very generally speaking, voluntary sectors opt for a more person-centred approach although here, too, some information may be included, such as in debt counselling or working with addictions. Counselling services available within the private sector are different again as there are a vast array of approaches available. These can be found through the websites of professional bodies (see list at end of Chapter 4) or counselling service websites or through local advertising.

At present, there is a considerable discrepancy between paid and voluntary posts. The vast majority of counselling posts are unpaid within the voluntary sector which, on the one hand, can be helpful for accruing practice hours for accreditation but, on the other hand, cannot generate an income. Because of this, many volunteer counsellors cannot afford to seek accreditation or work as full-time unpaid counsellors but continue volunteering their time to a local agency to gain personal satisfaction. In addition, voluntary agencies usually insist upon new volunteers attending specific internal training courses designed and certificated by the agency, but it is becoming more common that there is a charge for these courses, possibly due to a high turnover of volunteers. This can be an unexpected additional cost and frustrating if courses are only delivered infrequently. Vacancies for volunteer counsellors are often advertised locally, such as in libraries, local papers, leaflets or on the agency website if they have one.

The route to employment as a salaried counsellor is slightly different because, by comparison, there is a paucity of posts. Advertising tends to be more widespread (e.g. newspapers, professional journals or websites) and require the applicants to be already qualified to a particular level, so additional training in-post would be classed as continuing professional development (CPD) and funded by the agency, not the counsellor. Standards required tend to be higher than those asked for in the voluntary sector and are determined by recommendations by professional bodies such as the BACP. Salaries are comparable with other care professionals such as nurses and social workers but dependent upon qualifications, experience and the role fulfilled. Table 5.1 illustrates some major differences between the three settings.

Table 5.1   Differences between counselling settings

Setting	Confidentiality	Access	Funding implications
Statutory	Shared confidentiality between those in primary care team. Notes are stored on premises, although may move between departments.	Referral from GP, social worker, teacher, prison doctor, etc.	Not paid for by client but indirectly from National Insurance contributions.
Voluntary	Session content remains with counsellor, although will be discussed with counselling supervisor. Agency aware of name of client. Only discussed with line manager if client considered to be a danger to self or others. Notes are stored according to organisational policy.	Usually self-referral, although may require appointment to be made by telephone first.	Usually free, although may request donation or means-tested charge.
Private	Session content remains with counsellor, although will be discussed with counselling supervisor. Notes are stored according to individual policy or following recommendations by accrediting body.	Self-referral by telephone or e-mail.	Varying individually set fee, which is sometimes based on client's income.

THE COUNSELLING ENVIRONMENT

Any environment that is alien to us can make us feel uncomfortable but with a client it can immediately distort the power balance in favour of counsellor who is on 'home ground'. To compensate for this, this is another reason why counsellors need to be welcoming and open, encouraging the client to relax when they first meet. Before we go any further, imagine that you are a client and take a few minutes to list anything that you would like to be in a room where counselling takes place. This could be large items like different types of furniture, or less obvious aspects like lighting. Even having music playing in the area outside the door to prevent overhearing session content can have an impact on the comfort of the client and their perception of a safe and non-threatening environment.

Although this may be purely academic depending upon the setting that the sessions are taking place in, the following items may be in some counselling rooms, although available funding is also an issue here. It is worth considering the impact that each might have on the counselling process.

- *Sofa*: On the one hand, a sofa may appear homely, informal and inviting, encouraging the client to feel relaxed and at home. It might also be interesting to see how individuals choose their seating in family or group therapy. On the other hand, it might take up a lot of room, be disconcerting for a new client that doesn't want to sit next to someone else, or be difficult for a less-able client to get in or out of.
- *Chairs*: Should chairs be armchairs or more formal and upright? This would often depend upon the setting as counselling rooms within the statutory sector, such as social work departments and the NHS, usually have a more formal seating arrangement whereas the voluntary sector uses what falls within their budget, although this might also be very informal. The private sector varies but often has a larger budget to access for furniture.
- *Telephone*: A telephone might, at first thought, appear to be necessary in a working environment and would certainly be an advantage in a violent or crisis situation. It would also aid communication with a receptionist or colleagues. Alternatively, a client might view it with suspicion, worried that it might ring during the session, disturbing thoughts or flow. Because of this, it is better not to have a phone on view in the room.
- *Window*: Natural light is important for counsellors who spend many hours a week in their room, and a good view might be thought of as relaxing. A window that reduces privacy (especially when people passing can look in) would be inappropriate as this would compromise confidentiality. Also, for a client to be sitting looking out of the window could be argued to be offering a distraction that they can use to avoid focusing upon difficult or painful issues. For similar reasons, glass doors would also be unsuitable.
- *Carpet*: We might take a carpet for granted but counselling rooms in the statutory sector often have hard floors for ease of cleaning. Carpets can make a room feel less clinical, especially in a hospital setting, and can also deaden sound, making the room slightly more private.
- *Tea and coffee machine*: Hot drinks are considered to be soothing in Western cultures, which might aid a difficult process but the time it takes to make a drink

can be used by procrastinating clients to put off starting a session or to distract from sensitive issues. Therefore, it is better not to have hot drinks available but rather to have a jug of water and clean glasses within reach. Alternatively, offer a drink before the session begins that the client can take in with them.

- *Comfortable lighting*: Lighting can be dictated by the setting too. For example, overhead strip lighting can be very harsh and formal, as it is in a hospital. To have smaller lights or uplighters can provide a more diffused light, making the room more inviting and comfortable.

- *Table or desk*: A desk or table between counsellor and client is providing a physical barrier which gives the perception of the counsellor keeping a distance or removing themselves from the immediate situation. It is also reinforcing a position of powerful and disempowered, can make the counsellor appear disdainful and prevent any sense of connection within the relationship.

- *Computer*: A computer in the room is handy for storing typed records and files but must be turned off during sessions and kept locked with passwords to prevent unauthorised access. However, it would change a dedicated counselling room into more of an office and would mean that the counsellor would potentially be spending far more time in the room.

- *Filing cabinet*: As with a computer, a filing cabinet should be securely locked to prevent clients accessing confidential records and it would be quite dominating in a small room, turning what would otherwise be an informal room into an office or storage facility.

- *Clock*: A clock on the wall can be distracting for the client, as if they are aware of the passage of time it can influence their thought process, causing them to withhold or rush the sessions. If only the counsellor can see the clock, it could be interpreted as an element of power or control, but logically, the counsellor does need to be in control of the time to maintain boundaries.

- *Tissues*: Having tissues within reach does not suggest that all clients will become upset or need them, but it is surprising how often they are used. To have a client who is upset sitting sniffing for any length of time can result in them feeling very uncomfortable because they start to think less about the subject being discussed and more on how much they need to blow their nose!

- *Fish tank*: Some people find fish tanks very soothing, which is why they are often found in dentists' waiting rooms. If the counselling room is quite small, a fish tank would dominate and be noisy. Also, like a window with a view, it could provide a distraction that a client may use to avoid concentrating on a disturbing or upsetting issue.

- *Certificates on view*: The decision to hang certificates on the office or therapy room walls is not as straightforward as you might think. Consider the impact it can have on the therapeutic relationship; are you wanting to put your clients' minds at rest that you have successfully completed courses in counselling and want to establish a professional basis for your practice, or is it because you want to be seen as the 'expert'? This choice will be influenced by the orientation of the counselling, whether directive or non-directive.

> ## ACTIVITY
>
> Consider your placement (or a counselling environment you have visited). What was your initial feeling on entering the counselling room? Why do you think this was? How might this affect the client?

COUNSELLING AS A PSYCHIATRIC INTERVENTION

Here we will consider how counselling and psychotherapy are used within the medical treatment model which is found mainly within the NHS, most commonly hospitals and GP surgeries. The medical model makes some basic assumptions regarding clients and their presenting conditions, such as the locus tending to lie within the individual and that any help offered needs to take control of the situation. In the past, there was little if any recognition of the role of socio-cultural or psychological factors in a person's condition, although this is now acknowledged, particularly within the field of psychiatry. The focus was more on establishing whether a physical or hereditary cause might be underlying, such as a chemical imbalance or organic disease. Because of this, the medical model is sometimes referred to as the 'disease model' despite it being accepted that disease is not always present. Medication might be the first treatment option, although CBT resources such as DVDs and books are becoming more commonly prescribed by GPs. Websites such as Living Life to the Full (www.livinglifetothefull.com) are also recommended, which demonstrates a growing interest by the medical profession in cognitive behavioural alternatives to protracted drug therapy.

Many counsellors contest this approach due to its lack of awareness of the client in the context of their own life and often distrust the heavy reliance upon chemical intervention (i.e. antidepressants and other commonly prescribed medication). Additionally, 'Opponents of the model also point out that the disease model can lead to people avoiding self-responsibility, believing that the disease must be attended to by experts, rather than the changes coming from within (albeit with help from others)' (Clark, 2006). Despite still being the dominant view of those responsible for treatment, this reduction in autonomy and responsibility couldn't be more different from the underpinning goal of increasing autonomy, dependence and successful coping mechanisms which is core to the majority of counselling practices.

A few medical settings provide access to psychoanalytical therapies, which are different again. Here the patient (not client) is analysed in the context of their childhood and development to establish their neurosis and then pinpoint how they are expressing unconscious conflict. Then the psycho-analyst encourages them to address and free-up any conflicts that have resulted in fixation (see Chapter 3 for more details). As this is a highly intensive and extended process, and funding is certainly an issue here.

SOCIAL CONTEXT

Attitudes towards counselling and psychological interventions have changed over time, gradually moving from a lack of awareness of any benefit, to general suspicion, to measured acceptance. Although there is a height-ened awareness of psychotherapeutic interventions, the USA still leads the way in the normalisation of talking therapies; counselling is not viewed as a negative remedial treatment but as an acceptable method for sharing issues or concerns. In the UK, however, there is still a sense that counselling and psychotherapy are for working through psychological crisis and the general assumption is that if you attend sessions there must be something wrong with you. Hopefully, this will continue to change over time to gain acceptance as a personal choice rather than as a prescribed treatment. This shift in societal perspective is reflected in the funding available for potential clients. A wider recognition and approval of methodology results in a wider availability of resources.

CULTURAL CONTEXT

We have touched on the recognition and value placed on counselling in the UK and USA and, hopefully, this demonstrates an inconsistency between just two countries. If you were to consider the awareness and acceptance of counselling around the world, there is very little uniformity between cultures. This could be explained in several ways:

- by the very active role of religion and reliance on religious leaders in some cultures where lives are to be lived within the guidelines of religious doctrine
- the deterministic view of life being in the hands of a greater being and there-fore beyond an individual's control
- communities where practical assistance to solve problematic issues such as access to clean water is far more pressing than talking about these problems
- cultures where care professionals are respected as experts to the extent that they are expected to give advice and solve problems.

As evidence is gathered in support of the positive benefits of counselling, it may well become more available over time. Then again, counselling skills can be easily integrated into many other roles to improve general communication.

COURSE CONTENT AND THE COUNSELLING SETTING

Table 5.2 outlines how course content relates to particular counselling settings.

Table 5.2 Course content and its relation to counselling settings

Course content	How this is relevant to particular settings
Theory	Statutory settings tend to favour CBT, medical model and psychoanalysis. Voluntary settings work predominantly with PCT and CBT amongst others. Private settings offer an extensive range of approaches. Having a sound basis in theory ensures practice is based on recognised and tested methods.
Placement	Your previous experience informs your practice. It provides you with the confidence to make informed future career choices.
Practice/triads/ co-counselling	The practice of counselling skills and sessions in a structured, supported and safe environment develops confidence and the skills necessary to work with vulnerable clients in a successful and professional manner.
Group work	As groups are cheaper to run than one-to-one sessions, they are popular in a wide range of settings, e.g. addiction services. Facilitation is a complex skill and experience is crucial.
Personal development/ journal	The more comfortable you are with yourself, the more comfortable you will be with your clients. Reflective practice is an integral part of all counselling settings. Your journal can be requested at interview as it is a personal barometer of your learning and development.
Supervision	A mandatory requirement of practice. Your time spent in supervision is crucial in the monitoring of your work, and working with this mentor-like relationship ensures that you are an independent practitioner but do not feel alone.
Research	How do we know what works if we don't check? Research is crucial in that it informs our work and allows us the confidence to continuing developing. It is also used as part of reflective practice.
Accreditation	Vital for monitoring professional standards and necessary for working within the statutory sector. Working within stated ethical guidelines protects ourselves and our clients.

ACTIVITY

Using available resources (library, *Yellow Pages*, telephone directory, friends and family, Internet, etc.) find out as much information as you can about counselling settings within your local area. You would be able to gain an overview for comparison if you collate the following information:

- name of organisation/setting/agency
- location and method of access
- funding details
- usual client group
- required or provided staff training
- details of counselling service provided.

FURTHER READING

Bor, R., Miller, R., Gill, S. and Evans, A. (2009) *Counselling in Health Care Settings: A Handbook for Practitioners*. Basingstoke: Palgrave Macmillan.

6

Who's Who on the Course

Counselling is fundamentally about communicating positively with others, so this chapter will consider counselling relationships within two distinct contexts: first, with our colleagues on a counselling course; and second, within the therapeutic relationship. Examples of responsibilities are provided as a guideline.

WHAT DOES THE LECTURER DO?

Studying on a counselling course will bring you into contact with many different professionals whose role it is to support and guide you through your training. For the sake of clarity, the main roles are identified below.

Course tutor

This title may vary according to the setting in which your learning takes place, but essentially your course tutor is the individual who monitors your progress and provides individual support and guidance throughout the duration of your study. In some institutions you may be allocated a new course tutor each year, although for continuity and the development of a deeper, more understanding relationship it is preferable to remain with the same person throughout a counselling course. They do not necessarily teach you and you may only meet with them during regular appointments, but they are your first line of contact if you are experiencing any difficulties. Examples of tutor responsibilities are:

- supporting students
- providing individual guidance
- monitoring progress, attendance, etc.
- liaising with lecturers
- maintaining relevant course documentation.

Course lecturer

A lecturer is one of many professionals who deliver teaching on the course. This may appear like stating the obvious, but Loewenthal and Snell highlighted the multi-faceted role the role of the lecturer in counselling training as 'tutor, lecture/seminar leader, workshop facilitator, academic supervisor, co-assessor, large and small experiential group facilitator, clinical supervisor or leader of case discussion group and administrator' (2006: 61). This indicates that although on paper a lecturer is simply there to pass on information, knowledge and stimulate learning, in reality they fulfil other roles. Loewenthal and Snell argue that so many roles, rather than having a confusing or harmful impact, 'can allow for playful and very fruitful forms of interaction, interpretation and learning'. This ensures that the relationship counselling students have with their lecturers is rather different to that which other students have on other courses. There is a responsibility for care, of encouraging personal development along with academic and professional learning. Connor (1994) identifies 'staff will need to offer a sensitive mix of support and challenge', which is more significant than when studying less individualistic subjects. Examples of lecturer responsibilities include:

- delivering course content
- support and encouragement
- setting submission dates
- delivering lectures and other teaching methods
- encouraging participation
- maintaining safe boundaries.

Counselling supervisor

Some courses recommend particular supervisors for students, some provide supervision and others just state that it is compulsory to attend supervision. This is dependent upon the level of course you are studying and the setting in which it takes place. Courses within voluntary agencies are more likely to provide supervision for students, whereas university courses (undergraduate and post-graduate) are more likely to recommend individual supervisors by providing a list. More basic or foundation courses that do not include an assessed placement may well recommend engaging in supervision but do not oversee attendance as it is the students' responsibility rather than a requirement of the course. When you are the client of a counselling supervisor, you have the opportunity to discuss your counselling practice, skills, values, challenges and client work with an experienced professional. This is a mixture of support and monitoring to help your therapeutic work remain professional and ethical. It is usually recommended to choose a supervisor who practises the same model of counselling that you are learning, although once qualified it is often more developmentally challenging to work with a supervisor from a different orientation; personal choice dictates. This section is fairly brief as counselling supervision is discussed in considerably more detail in Chapter 14. Examples of counselling supervisor responsibilities include:

- meeting with you regularly
- discussing your counselling practice
- monitoring your relationship with clients
- challenging and supporting
- catalyst for self-reflection.

Group facilitator

Throughout your course you will be expected to attend and contribute to some form of group, whether it is a directed or non-directed personal development, self-awareness or community group. In many courses, the group facilitator is a member of staff who does not have direct teaching responsibilities on your course. This allows for group members to be open and honest without worrying about any contributions they make affecting their marks. Examples of group facilitator responsibilities include:

- arranging and facilitating regular groups
- monitoring your relationship with group members
- providing opportunities for challenge and support.

Placement mentor

A placement mentor is your adviser and guide when you are in practice with clients during your course. They are a named individual who often has responsibility for monitoring your practice, log book or developmental journal and sometimes even practical assignments. It is also their responsibility to ensure that you are provided with clients and working situations to meet the requirements of the course. More information on the role of the placement is provided in Chapter 17. Examples of placement mentor responsibilities include:

- monitoring your relationship with clients
- completing necessary course paperwork
- facilitating appropriate learning opportunities
- providing opportunities for practical experience
- liaising with the course staff.

Personal counsellor/therapist

It may be a condition of the course that you have a certain number of hours of personal counselling yourself. This allows you to experience personally the role of client, maintain self-care, work on your own issues and develop an awareness of possible transference and counter-transference. The apparent inconsistency between courses in this area is clearly explained by Daw and Joseph in their study of how qualified therapists experience personal therapy:

> Although many would consider the reasons for undertaking personal therapy to be self-evident, there remains much debate about the role of personal therapy and whether it should be part of therapists' training curriculum, with different branches of the profession taking different stances. Neither the British Association for Counselling and Psychotherapy nor the UK Council for Psychotherapy stipulate a number of hours for which therapists are required to engage in personal therapy in order to be accredited. The amount of personal therapy deemed necessary is left to the discretion of the training course upon which the person is enrolled. This varies considerably across courses. (2007: 227)

Unsurprisingly, such disparity is a keen source of debate in the world of counselling training. Most importantly, even if your course does not insist on students attending therapy for a set number of hours, you can still arrange it yourself in your own time if you feel it would be useful – it certainly helps provide discussion within your personal development journal. Examples of personal counsellor responsibilities include:

- providing an environment for discussion of personal issues
- use of counselling skills to facilitate personal development
- reflection on past, present or future

- use of specific orientation
- maintaining agreed boundaries
- professional, agreed and structured therapeutic relationship.

Other students

As we have previously established, studying on a counselling course is unlike any other. Individuals often divulge personal information that wouldn't arise if on an English literature or computing course. This can lead to far deeper and more complex interpersonal relationships developing. There are three different ways that students can view their colleagues: as friends, as clients or as co-learners. Clearly, the first two can lead to occasional difficulties. It can't be denied that working with people at such an intimate level for an extended period of time is bound to lead to significant friendships developing, some of which can be very long-lasting indeed. A danger here would be to assume that every supportive and encouraging comment received in class automatically meant that it stemmed from a friendship. Remember that other students have their own agenda and are learning to communicate positively in the same way that you are, and view your relationships in this light. However, for the sake of honesty and realism, it is unlikely that you will like everyone on the course, but it is how you choose to manage that which can impact considerably upon your enjoyment of classes. If you struggle with individuals who talk too much, try to establish informal leadership, detract or distract or behave in a manner that you are uncomfortable with, view it as an excellent opportunity to examine the reasons behind your feelings and responses. Why do you feel frustration, anger or intolerance? Does that mean that you would feel the same with a client who demonstrated such behaviours? Such insight can be invaluable if, later in your career, you are working professionally with a colleague or client who exhibits similar traits. By then you will already have developed a positive way of coping in your relationship with them.

The second, viewing co-learners as clients, is also beset with pitfalls and is slightly more inappropriate. Apart from the hint of condescension and superciliousness that accompanies this approach, there would be a lack of congruence and honesty on your part. It might be a useful coping mechanism at times, but essentially you are all in the same role and as such can learn from your reactions, but not to the extent of confusing relationships. It is hoped that the values and attitudes that underpin a counselling course are intrinsic, though an important element of learning to be counsellor is developing comfortable personal boundaries. This new way of being can inform the way you are, but it is unreasonable to believe that you can be a counsellor 24 hours a day. Not only would it be exhausting, but your friends and family would probably find it a struggle too.

Personal boundary issues like this aren't just the remit of the students; one of the difficulties for tutors during the application and interview stage is ensuring that applicants who are offered a place want to study counselling and are not mistaking it for needing to be counselled. If an individual is fragile or vulnerable, the thought of spending one or more years surrounded by people who are interested in others can be a seductive attraction. The interview plays a considerable role in filtering the student intake to ensure that those applying are at a time in their life when they are strong enough to engage in what can be a very tough and draining course. One of the main risks of finding yourself in this situation when you are not psychologically ready is that of developing dependency on others in the class. From a psychodynamic perspective, Chu (1988) argues that such dependency results from either the individual re-enacting some negative past experience that has involved rejection or desertion, or more fundamentally of poor ego functioning. Clearly, this can alter the learning dynamic and lead to frustration and a hindrance to the process.

Who has power?

Power is an interesting concept in relation to counselling training. Carl Rogers (1967; Rogers and Freiberg, 1969) wrote extensively on learning and teaching, much of which is relevant to the area of power and power imbalance. He argued that nothing that is worth learning can be taught; that it is the experiencing and individual processing that makes sense, not that of someone else (i.e. a teacher). Understandably, this led to some very controversial presentations at conferences. It is relevant here, though, as it illustrates the balance between knowledge, experience and a way of being. Course tutors and lecturers are traditionally viewed as having the power to pass or fail a student, depending on their successful adherence to set learning outcomes and performance criteria. However, with counselling training, the focus is also on the student's internal world (e.g. values, attitudes and principles) so strangely you are far more in control of your vocation than you may think you are. Don't be afraid to request detailed feedback or enter into a discussion if you receive a result you feel is inaccurate. It maybe that there are remedial steps that you can take to rectify the situation. The way our work is understood by others is not always representative of how we intended, but this usually improves over the duration of the course as we learn not just content but also how to jump through the assessment hoops necessary to pass.

AS A STUDENT, WHAT IS MY ROLE?

Table 6.1 outlines the responsibilities of the student and some suggestions on how to maintain them.

Table 6.1 Student responsibilities

Example of responsibilities	Suggestions
Meeting deadlines	Make sure that you know exactly when deadlines are and devise a structured but realistic plan to complete work on time. This will help considerably with your relationship with lecturers.
Engaging with the content	Finding the time to immerse yourself in your learning will help enormously. Establishing links between theory and practice or experience will help you understand rather than just remember what you have been learning.
Working with trust	No one is expected to be comfortable with trust immediately, but being honest and open about reservations or difficulties will make them a lot easier to deal with.
Taking an active role in your own learning	Seeing yourself as in control, empowered and directing your learning allows you to become far more involved. The lecturers are not in control of your learning – you are.
Remembering background reading	The reading list on the course is compiled to provide a relevant and balanced background to the content of lecturers and class exercises. Keep up to date with your reading and you will have a wide range of references to cite in your written assessments.
Maintaining an interest	Not easy when the course becomes more challenging and intensive. Remind yourself of your aims and goals, read through your original statement of application and note down your difficulties in your personal journal. Bring any issues up in individual guidance with your course tutor too.
Expecting difficulties	No course worth doing is ever problem-free. If you pre-empt potential difficulties (e.g. time management, waning interest, financial concerns) you can plan how to work through them if they occur.
Developing coping strategies	Linked to the previous point, if you discover your best way of dealing with barriers or situations that impede your enjoyment or progress, it will make you a stronger and more committed student.
Access help if you need it	By admitting that you are struggling sooner rather than later, specific support can be put in place to help you continue on the course. This might be practical, like financial information, or pragmatic, like time management guidance, or academic, such as additional support for writing essays or presenting assignments if you have been out of education for some time.

HOW CAN I PASS THE COURSE?

Periods of self-doubt are natural within such an intensive course format. Some common fears can be worked through very simply as long as you remain honest and upfront about your reservations. You might like to consider the following questions:

1 How can I arrange my life around the course?
2 What if my family are unsure of the changes in me?
3 What if I discover elements about myself that I don't like?
4 If I struggle with the course content, what should I do?
5 What will the other students on the course be like?
6 How might I make sure that I meet submission deadlines?
7 I have been out of education for years, what if I can't keep up?
8 How can I afford the time and money to undertake the course?
9 What impact might this have on my future?
10 How can I overcome barriers that might prevent me from succeeding?

WILL THIS HAVE AN EFFECT ON FAMILY AND FRIENDS?

During your course, you will change and develop as a person. The way you communicate will also change and this can come as a shock to friends and family who know and love the 'old' you. Common experiences tend to follow patterns, a common one being that initial support dissolves into boredom and frustration. Boredom with listening to you using new terminology and talking about the course and your new experiences that they aren't able to be a part of, and frustration may arise if you find that you have changed a lot and aren't the same as you were. Clearly this can lead to relationship difficulties if you are not prepared for change and have not discussed it with those close to you. Importantly, change is usually for the better; you become more understanding, patient and encouraging. You may value the time you spend together more, and develop a greater sense of the separate worlds within your family. For most, this makes you a better partner, parent, etc; however, negative responses such as resistance to change and even open hostility can be reactions from those around you if they feel they are being left behind as you move on in your personal development. Luckily, the impact of increased self-awareness will provide you with greater coping mechanisms and methods of working with any feelings of alienation in an understanding and patient manner. Even for those who feel supported and encouraged by their family, specific areas such as confidentiality can cause upset. For some, this may be the first time they are not able to discuss everything with a partner or friend because of boundary issues, which can result in concern about secrets or hidden areas within an individual. Although by itemising such negative scenarios gives the impression that there is a huge risk in beginning a course, this is not the case; other professionals manage to separate their professional and personal lives successfully, and with time and practice, so can you.

FURTHER READING

Chu, J. (1988). 'Ten traps for therapists in the treatment of trauma survivors', *Dissociation*, 1(4) 34–32.

Clark, D. (2006). *The Disease Model of Addiction*. Retrieved 14 August 2007 from: www.drinkanddrugs.net.

Connor, M. (1994) *Training the Counsellor: An Integratve Model*. London: Routledge.

Houston, G. (1995) *The Now Red Book of Gestalt*. London: Rochester Foundation.

Loewenthal, D. and Snell, R. (2006) 'The learning community, the trainee and the leader', *European Journal of Psychotherapy and Counselling*, 8(1): 61–77.

Rogers, C. (1967) *On Becoming a Person*. London: Constable & Robinson.

Roger, C. and Freiberg, H.J. (1969) *Freedom to Learn*. New York: Merrill.

Tudor, L. E., Keemar, K., Tudor, K., Valentine, J. and Worrall, M. (2004). *The Person-Centred Approach: A Contemporary Introduction*. Basingstoke: Palgrave Macmillan.

7

Personal Development

Self-awareness, personal insight and self-perception are recognised within most approaches as being vital for the effectiveness of a counsellor, therefore it is a necessary requirement for the counselling student. Here we will examine what personal development is, the methods by how it is encouraged on counselling courses and the complexity of assessment.

WHY DO YOU NEED TO KNOW ABOUT ME?

Many studies show that the practice of self-reflection and personal insight are linked to positive growth, change and development, which is why they are referred to as personal development in the context of counselling training. Such application is not unique to counselling as reflective practice is also a condition within other interpersonal professions, such as nursing, teaching and social work. To be successful at this ongoing process, time and effort need to be spent on the distinct activity of examining the self and being able to see the self in relation to others. Our values, attitudes and interpersonal connects are often influenced by others and therefore changeable. Awareness of this allows us to harness and mould such changes so that we are constantly aware of ourselves and the impact that we are having on others, particularly our clients.

This awareness of self within the therapeutic relationship has er
impact upon the counsellor and our practice. If we hope to work
cally and professionally, then shouldn't that include our own rol
the therapeutic alliance? Our use of skills, awareness of the cli
interpersonal (between ourselves and others) connections all in
how successful we are as a counsellor. An awareness of our intra,
or internal processes is of equal importance. There is considerable
evidence to show that it is not so much our theoretical orientation or
use of skills that result in success or failure as a counsellor, but rather the
depth and warmth of the relationship that we have with the client. This
is considered in more detail in Chapter 13.

For this to sit comfortably within our course, Connor (1994) placed the
core elements of personal development (from an integrative perspective)
into the following lists which are included here in their entirety due to
their clarity:

The core of the model: Intrapersonal development

Learning objectives

1 To develop understanding and appreciation of self.
2 To become aware of and utilise personal strengths and assets.
3 To become aware of blind-spots, blocks and vulnerabilities.
4 To identify areas to work on in personal counselling.
5 To appreciate experientially the significance of developmental stages in
   personal development.

The core of the model: Interpersonal development

Learning objectives

1 To understand areas of strength and areas for development in a range of
   interactions: with peers, staff, clients and in personal and professional
   relationships.
2 To gain confidence in appropriate self-sharing.
3 To develop skills of giving and receiving feedback.
4 To facilitate growth in self and others through active participation in personal
   development groups.
5 To develop helping relationships with clients.
6 To continuously reflect upon successes and setbacks and to use such reflection as the basis for setting realistic objectives for development.
7 To develop the internal supervisor, active not only during sessions with clients
   but also in other interactions whether group of individual.

(Connor, 1994: 31–2)

STUDENT EXPERIENCE 7.1 WILLIAM

William felt totally at ease within the student community group and established trust and openness almost immediately. He often felt uncomfortable with silence so saw stepping in at these points as 'rescuing' the group. William felt totally safe in the group as he claimed that he didn't worry about what happened to the information he disclosed. As a direct result of his previous involvement with groups, he felt strong enough to say that it was the responsibility of the other members to work within the agreed confidentiality boundaries and that he couldn't worry about something that might not happen. He was aware that other students in the group may not feel so safe, which is why they felt less inclined to contribute.

An important aspect of personal development which is often forgotten is that of self-care. If we are to manage our practice safely and develop coping strategies for dealing with difficulties, it is crucial that we develop an awareness of our own feelings and reactions. Hopefully, much of this would be identified and examined within regular supervision, allowing for honest reflection on both the interpersonal and intrapersonal aspects of the counselling relationship. This process can unearth links that we might have otherwise been oblivious to, such as over-familiarity with a client who happens to resemble a close friend, disassociation issues with a client we don't agree with, or the lack of achieving distance, for example, between a client's recent bereavement and our own previous bereavement (see also Figure 7.1) By raising awareness of this, changes can be made that allow us to work with ourselves concurrently to working with the client, ensuring both client and counsellor are working safely.

For this process of constant evaluation to be embedded within our practice right from the start, it has to be included in our counselling course. As a result, counselling training recognises the fundamental role that self-development plays in our professional life, and a range of differing reflective and evaluative activities will be introduced. Activities such as personal development groups, journals, personal therapy, supervision and exercises that promote mindfulness are introduced to encourage students to look inwards as well as around them.

It is very difficult to identify all of the benefits that personal awareness can have on counselling practice as it is so wide ranging, but the ability to be mindful of the ongoing interaction and the part we play in that is fundamental to our success as a professional therapist. However, it is completely untrue that all practising counsellors are mature and wise. The

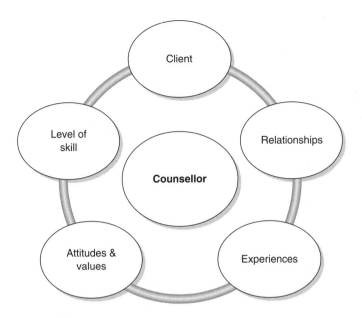

Figure 7.1   There are many influences affecting the counsellor

ability to be honest with one's self and be prepared for change is certainly an indicator of maturity but is in no way connected to actual chronological age. It is, however, a major factor that is considered during the selection process when applying for training. This is a contentious issue as maturity is more a way of being, and as such is very difficult to quantify. Evidence of self-awareness is usually a requirement to be accepted onto a counselling course. This ensures that tutors know there is a basis on which to develop, as opposed to introducing the concept from the beginning. To return momentarily to the subject of wisdom, understanding, insight and perception may be considered to be attributes but real wisdom comes from being aware of faults and inadequacies whilst still being able to manage these in a positive manner that benefits our self and others.

STUDENT EXPERIENCE 7.2   STEPH

At the beginning of the course, Steph didn't know the purpose of the community group and remembered that some members dominated the sessions, but she felt uncomfortable challenging others. Sometimes sessions were interesting as it provided a good space for discussion. Steph found that she preferred the smaller groups run on the Higher National Certificate (HNC) courses to the larger groups on the post-graduate diploma course. The size of the group had an impact on her perceived safety within the group as she felt considerably less safe in a larger group when she did not know all the members. There were personal benefits of attending the community groups. Steph developed more confidence on hearing her own voice and eventually become more comfortable with the differences between group members. In her opinion, this led to her becoming less judgemental and more open to others.

STRUCTURED PERSONAL DEVELOPMENT GROUPS

The active engagement in learning and the humanistic bias of personal development groups in counselling training has emerged from the process of several elements that feature in this type of group: shared goal setting; active learning opportunities; valuing of existing experience; recognition of the practical implications of learning; recognition of the need to know; and acceptance of maturity and developmental growth (Johns, 1996). This increased emphasis on experiential learning (Rogers, 1967) engages group members in a very personal and unique way, aiding the transition of theoretical knowledge to personal familiarity through regular practice. Because of this, you should find that the more you take part in group-work, the more comfortable you become.

During the group, learning takes place simultaneously in different ways in different parts of the brain, so the use of personal development (PD) groups covers many relevant aspects, such as theoretical influence, emotional responses, physical reactions, cultural differences and commonalities with professional practice. Discussion with previous students has identified an ongoing resistance to this less-formal method of delivery where considerably more responsibility lies with the student as there is a requirement for a deeper level of engagement. This widespread response has been well documented; see Further Reading.

The benefit to you as a counselling student taking part in what is essentially a non-assessed experiential activity is outlined by O'Leary et al. (1994: 133), who identified five significant components of growth resulting from involvement with personal development groups on counselling training courses. These components are self-awareness, congruence, spirituality, attention to positive and negative feelings, and the perception of growth as a dynamic process.

STUDENT EXPERIENCE 7.3   ERICA

Erica would have liked the lecturer to have remained in the role of educator and for the community group time to be spent examining student issues. She was of the opinion that the group was a waste of time as a result of this. Clear aims and goals would have made it a more positive experience. By comparison, the planned, organised and facilitated PD groups were of enormous benefit and encouraged reflection and self-questioning of both herself and others. Erica thought that this was as a result of the altered boundaries and more directive approach. Overall, she enjoyed and learned much from the structured PD groups but felt uncomfortable and withdrew from the unstructured community groups.

UN-STRUCTURED COMMUNITY GROUPS

The definition of a community group is not straightforward enough to characterise due to the very nature of being free-flowing, having no facilitator and being based on the remit of no agenda; in many groups, the agenda is formed by the group for the group. Loewenthal and Snell define the community group as:

> The large experiential group, which includes the tutors, is an opportunity for students to speak about and process experiences on and off the course, as well as being a forum in which members might reflect on their experience of being in a group, and on authority in the group and the programme as a whole. The experiential groups are often experienced as very challenging, by students and by tutors; at the same time they can function as the most important vehicles for learning. (2006: 66)

The most common difficulty experienced during community groups is often a general resistance felt by students or members. This shared experience of community group participants in relation to our practice is also of great interest; it is common that student counsellors often prefer the structured, facilitated and directed PD groups, but when asked, they prefer to work with a more person-centred orientation highlighting a dichotomy of methodologies. To sum up: when students adopt the role of client, they like to be guided and controlled, but when working as a counsellor with clients, they prefer a less structured, more person-centred approach (Amis, 2007).

Understandably, because of this there tend to be feelings of resistance, confusion and discomfort, which can continue until almost the end of the course. This interestingly appears to parallel a general client pattern within counselling sessions. Engagement is resisted until the end is in sight and the ensuing feeling of safety and a fear of missed opportunity motivates sudden participation and contribution. Group members are often aware of this phenomenon, which they find frustrating as well as enlightening.

STUDENT EXPERIENCE 7.4   JENNY

Jenny was a member of a full-time group, so attended non-facilitated groups for one year. As a quiet, thoughtful and reserved student, she was resistant to group work throughout. She felt that the community group was a 'waste of time with no point or structure that allowed free for all whingeing'. Jenny didn't feel unsafe or threatened, although certainly had some reservations in regard to trust and confidentiality with others in the group. She often felt the need to leave but didn't. Jenny felt that she gained personal benefit as it provided her with insight in to group work which she had no interest in previously and felt overt resistant towards. She identified real benefits for some members but not all, as she felt that the sense of repetition (through lack of structure) was not helpful.

Encouraging these new ways of communication (and therefore learning) is a valuable and educational process. With this consideration of new literacies, the emphasis is on value being applied to each student contribution and seeing all members and contributions as an active part in the process. You will find that counselling students tend to be mature and are, mainly, highly motivated and their systems of communication and dialogue are usually appropriate and valid, whether through discussion or text. Having been out of education for many years in most cases, mature students do not always work well within a culture of more traditional educational modes (chalk-and-talk classroom situations) which can often lead to alienation, disconnection and a breakdown in the learning process. However, to avoid this, the inclusion of group work does offer an alternative forum for discussion, hopefully bridging any potential divide. Any power imbalance can also have an impact if students lack confidence; trying to communicate with tutors but in a manner that is not always valued or validated by academia. A balance is necessary between the requirements of established systems (i.e. counselling course) and the alternative systems utilised by a potentially disempowered student. Especially with mature students, this can appear to increase the distance between themselves and education, resulting in possible marginalisation and isolation and then abandonment of the course. Maybe this is one role for the community group? To allow students to communicate in their own language without the constraints or rules imposed in personal development groups.

STUDENT EXPERIENCE 7.5   ANDREA

The components necessary for a safe community group, according to Andrea, were surrounding structure and instruction to begin with to provide an awareness of possibilities. She felt that there were trust issues that impacted upon the successful process, summing it up as a 'wasted opportunity'. Confusion in relation to 'what was expected' resulted in the group focusing on what Andrea classed as superficial issues at the beginning of the course; however, she was clear that at all times she felt completely safe within the group, felt no fear, and was confident that confidentiality was maintained throughout. She described it as 'flowering' at the end and that it was a shame that it didn't happen earlier. There was obvious progression 'from shallow to deep' which was 'nice' by the end.

The advantages of this self-determined model are condensed by Bion (1961), who conceptualises the group development as therapy *of* the group rather than individual therapy *in* the group.

STUDENT EXPERIENCE 7.6   DARREN

Darren faced confusion at the time of the first community group as he was unsure of the purpose and the feelings of 'I don't fit in'. Once this felt less intimidating he contributed, but was also aware of a sense of 'conforming to norms'. Darren resisted opening up in case he was judged by others. He considered that the community groups were not of benefit personally but there was an increase in the understanding of dynamics within a larger group. However, in retrospect, there was benefit in the long run. Darren felt that for a community group to be successful there needs to be setting of boundaries, and in a larger group there are less likely to be individuals who dominate, whereas in a smaller group some members so take over. Loose guidelines would be best. As the course progressed, Darren thought that the community group held 'more challenge and support'. There were 'subtle changes' that made it a 'less scary and more OK' experience. The structured group had more 'focus on activity' so was 'viewed as a task' so 'everyone was happy to take part'. They were 'good fun' and a 'great difference'. Darren identified the dichotomy in that although he preferred the structured personal development groups, he is very much person-centred and unstructured in current individual practice.

HOW THE COURSE ORIENTATION INFLUENCES PERSONAL DEVELOPMENT

When studying on a person-centred course, self-awareness is a central constituent of the course. It is essential to be comfortable with devoting yourself to the therapeutic relationship, and to recognise the fluidity and depth that are necessary for a warm and trusting bond to form. Lack of confidence can be an obstacle when first starting out; lack of confidence in self, but also lack of confidence in the power of technique. The client benefits from the counsellor being able to give themselves for the duration of the sessions, which can only happen if the counsellor has become sensitive to and worked through their own personal barriers. Within this approach, the role of expert is not apparent. As previously established in Chapter 3, the client is seen to be the expert in their own lives; the counsellor, although continuously alert and highly skilled, is immersed in the world of the client, is concentrating on their capabilities but is also consciously monitoring their own reactions. To be relaxed with this requires honest reflection upon our practice and the ability to be aware of any issues for later discussion within supervision.

However, on a psychodynamic counselling course the developmental emphasis is quite different. The role of personal therapy is viewed as a core element as it instils the need to explore transference and counter-transference issues to gain a better understanding of the process. This in turn can help from an analytical and interpretive perspective when working with clients. The constant search for meaning involves the counsellor relentlessly searching for meaning behind the surface, which demands moment-to-moment attentiveness. In addition to this, there is the continual risk of the counsellor exploiting their position as expert through unconscious or conscious manipulation. These aspects alone necessitate the counsellor having the ability to contemplate their own influence upon the therapeutic process.

A cognitive behavioural course is less likely to feature as many aspects of self-development because the awareness of self is not as important as the awareness of the client. Here the focus is very much on changing behaviours and challenging thinking; working with the outer (behaviour) framework at the same time as the inner (cognitive) framework. Specific plans and alterations are made which involves the counsellor adopting more of an educational role and looking to the future rather than to the past. This pragmatic approach places less relevance on how insightful the practitioner is, as that would be diverting attention away from the client.

PERSONAL THERAPY

There is no agreement as to whether personal therapy should be a require-ment when training to be a counsellor. In the past, it was a criterion of BACP-accredited courses, although now there is no requirement to have experience as a client to train as a counsellor. Dubiety exists to the point that some approaches such as CBT argue that it is totally unnecessary and would detract from work with the client, whereas psychodynamic courses maintain that it is a crucial aspect that can't be avoided. Other courses are divided in their view. It would be hard to deny that entering into a counselling relationship as a client allows one to experience the real fears, vulnerability and reactions from an alternative perspective, which in turn facilitates a more insightful and greater learning experience. The impact on personal development can be significant. However, the cost of therapy for the duration of the course can be prohibitive, in addition to the risk that issues may arise which cause such distress they may impact upon progress through the course.

HOW CAN PERSONAL DEVELOPMENT BE ASSESSED?

In some ways it is very difficult to assess personal development because:

- knowing that you are being assessed can prevent complete honesty and openness and can leave you feeling very vulnerable
- this is such a subjective and individual aspect of training
- how can a tutor make decisions regarding your internal framework and processing?

However, in other ways it is fairly straightforward because:

- tutors are able to monitor and evaluate the depth of reflection that is apparent, interpersonally within personal development groups and also intrapersonally within your journal if it is submitted
- many differing lists of competencies have been compiled over the years that cover a wide range of areas

- courses have set guidelines that are given to students to indicate exactly what is to be assessed (see learning outcomes listed by Connor earlier).

Depending upon the level and orientation of the course, it is not simply the tutor who makes decisions with regard to your personal development. Humanistic courses, in particular person-centred courses, place a greater focus on self-assessment based on self-actualisation, as opposed to CBT courses which take a more pragmatic approach and psychodynamic courses which place a greater emphasis on personal therapy. An integrative course might use a combination of methods depending upon the main underpinning theory and the stage of the course.

It is usual for focus to be turned upon the inner world of students right at the start of the course so that such in-depth reflection can become second nature – just another aspect of the learning on the course. Hopefully, this intimate process will become naturalised. Quite often, when looking back through a personal journal or discussing early PD groups, you might be embarrassed or uncomfortable with your first attempts at expressing your private thoughts and feelings, although this is actually very positive as it illustrates both an awareness of progression and the ability to assess your own work.

If you are still unsure of what you need to do, the simplest and safest route is to be direct and ask your tutor to be very clear about the exact criteria required and any additional expectations for you to pass this element of the course. It is in your tutor's interest that you are clear about the guidelines as clearly, if you know precisely what to do, it makes it a lot easier to do it.

As this is an authentic record of your journey during the course, if you don't achieve a pass for your reflective accounts in your journal on the first chance, remediation, reassessment or resitting can only realistically be attempted if you have missed out some of the assessable criteria (e.g. forgotten to discuss a particular specified area). Whereas if the issue is more esoteric, such as you are not being as open as you might in your writing or not recognising areas of yourself that others are aware of, it becomes very difficult for the tutor to challenge the content. A superficial and shallow style of writing that focuses more on the external framework than the internal one is clearly inadequate and can be difficult to work with. This is where the monitoring and feedback from your tutor is vital to ensure that not just your writing style develops but also that you develop the confidence in your reflection to be more true and genuine; seeing personal faults or questionable values as areas for examination and analysis rather than avoidance.

ACTIVITY

Take a piece of paper and a pen, and sit in a quiet place where you won't be interrupted. Allow yourself exactly two minutes and write down as many of your feelings and thoughts about your learning on the course as you can. Do not pause or stop – just keep writing until the time is up. This is a quick method that you can use at any time to prevent 'writer's block' and help refocus yourself. Simply include this in your journal as it is an alternative technique for encouraging unconscious honesty.

FURTHER READING

Connor, M. (1994) *Training the Counsellor: An Integrative Model*. London: Routledge.

Johns, H. (1996) *Personal Development in Counsellor Training*. London: Sage.

8

Personal Journal

The majority of counselling courses require students to be able to monitor their own progress using reflective writing, which is usually contained within a personal log book or journal. This chapter focuses on why this is considered necessary, how to document personal development in this writing style and when these accounts may be useful in the future, along with ideas to stimulate enthusiasm and overcome resistance to such sustained writing.

WHAT IS A PERSONAL JOURNAL?

As part of many counselling courses, you are expected to submit reflective accounts to demonstrate your understanding and learning, usually at the end of each module or unit. This is a different style of writing to other essays, so this chapter will provide you with some guidance as to how to structure these accounts. If you are working towards counsellor accreditation (BACP, CPCAB, COSCA, etc.) you are expected to maintain a reflective journal not just during your course but throughout your professional career as evidence of your personal development and learning. It then becomes an ongoing accumulation of progress and process rather than a single input as are other assignments. How you choose to present your reflective accounts depends very much on the guidelines provided by your tutor and also your intentions for the future.

AIM OF THE JOURNAL

One of the main purposes of the journal is to gather evidence to support the achievement of your learning outcomes throughout the course which can be requested by future employers. Your reflective assignments will ask you to provide specific information in the professional development journal. The journal also provides you with the opportunity to record any experience you may encounter during your course. This can be an aide memoir and an account of your progression through various stages of your classroom and/or placement experience. On some courses, the journal entries are assessed to ensure that there is an appropriate level of self-awareness being demonstrated. So there are several functions for the journal; is to not only record learning development but also to monitor personal, practical and professional development. A final aspect of the journal is that you can learn from your own writing within it. Rather than being a one-dimensional account, as you read back through it, elements of your personal growth and understanding will reinforce feelings of development, but the questioning process is very helpful in establishing the difference between what you know and what you don't know about the course, and more importantly, about yourself.

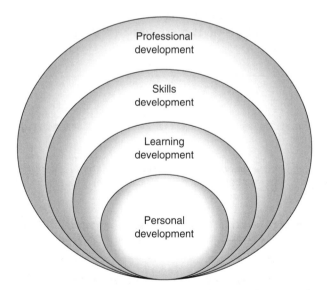

Figure 8.1   All learning experiences have significance for the trainee counsellor

THE CONTENT OF YOUR JOURNAL

Whatever experiences occur during your learning, they all have significance (see Figure 8.1). This may not be apparent at the time but can become relevant later. All experiences whether negative or positive will provide you with a learning opportunity. The aim is to determine what to learn, and to develop the ability to determine the difference between good and bad practice. Usually, several of your assignments are in the style of a reflective account and on some courses must be submitted for marking. An example of this type of assessment question is shown in Figure 8.2.

The marking guidelines that the tutor refers to can be as ambiguous as this:

> All aspects above should be covered. Candidate should identify how the concepts covered within this unit have increased their self-awareness, particularly in relation to their own experiences of loss. This should be inclusive of the wider issues and not focus solely on bereavement. Candidates should explain what insight the learning on this unit has provided them with in terms of their relationships with others. This response should be in relation to a range of loss issues. (SQA, 2007)

Hopefully, this demonstrates that the focus is very much on the viewpoint and perspective of the student; as long as the points in the

---

Learning Outcome 4

- Throughout this unit, document in your journal your self-awareness with regard to your own experiences of loss.

- Discuss any increased awareness of reactions to loss. This may relate to clients, friends, and family and course members. Include any insights this may have provided in respect of your relationships and reactions to loss.

- Ensure you consider a) the major theorists covered, b) any cultural considerations that may impact upon your future practice and c) knowledge and skills gained.

Figure 8.2   Example of a typical assessment question (from Scottish Qualifications Authority Higher National Certificate)

question are developed and explained in a personal context, it is highly unlikely that the content can be challenged. For example, a tutor would not be able to say 'No, you didn't feel that' or 'That experience is not true'. The question content is simply a prompt for the beginning of an internal process so the purpose is more about gaining insight into your inner world and being able to witness the way in which you document your many relevant encounters.

WHY DO WE NEED A JOURNAL?

To enrol on a counselling course, there are criteria that need to be met to ensure that you are able to develop the qualities and skills necessary to work with vulnerable clients. These are not just vague assumptions such as 'to be a nice person' or 'to care' but are stipulated by professional bodies such as the BACP. More is written about these requirements in the previous chapter on self-development, but the journal or log can provide a method for tutors to have a documented history to refer to when making crucial decisions such as passing the assessment or offering you a counselling position. Please note that although the majority of courses require a journal to be maintained, not all courses require it to be submitted.

WHAT IS REFLECTION?

Reflective practice can be described as developing ways of learning from experience which may help to modify and change approaches to counselling practice. Reflection is a way for counsellors to analyse experiences in order to develop new insights and understandings. This may involve changes in attitudes and values, skills and knowledge as the interpretations of experiences and events are evaluated and reassessed. Ultimately, reflective practice is a way of taking stock of events, experiences and outcomes and can be a means of learning from past actions and current situations. This is a method of CPD that is utilised within many professions such as nursing and social work with the aim of ensuring that all practitioners become reflective practitioners for the benefit of their patients, service users or clients.

HOW DO I WRITE REFLECTIVELY?

The journal is to help you to be positive and self-reliant in your learning by formally maintaining a record of all critical/significant events experienced throughout the course. These events may be educational, practice based or incidental, and may affect yourself and those you are close to. In this way, it is hoped to enable you to become a reflective practitioner. These written reflections will help you to:

- establish links between your understanding of the learning in each unit with the therapeutic relationship – don't forget to include other relationships, such as those with family and friends, as this shows your learning within different contexts
- try to set personal goals by identifying specific areas of need in your own learning
- explain your present learning, and link this with past knowledge and experiences which can be included if relevant to this section
- identify your strengths and be honest about your development needs
- evaluate your personal progress by critically assessing your own development.

Include a clear description of the knowledge and skills that you have developed during the unit you are writing about. Table 8.1 gives some helpful pointers as to what should and should not be included.

It will take time to gain confidence in developing the skills needed to assess your own knowledge and performance, but as you continue with the journal this would become easier. It can be helpful to view the journal as a close friend who is completely non-judgemental and very good at keeping secrets! You should feel free to write any personal thoughts, frustrations or any other feelings that you may experience. However, it may be difficult at first to disclose, especially those negative aspects which you identify, but

Table 8.1 The dos and don'ts of journal content

Inadequate content	Appropriate content
Description without exploration	A minimal description with the focus on exploration
Statements	Evaluation
Superficial observations	Deeper, more meaningful observations
Focus on others	Focus on self
Entries are separated	Entries are linked by themes
Self without connection to others	Self in relation to others

do give yourself time and remember that your tutor will endeavour to provide whatever support may be required. In addition, you will be able to share your thoughts, and talk through problems with your peers. Learning from personal experience is a continual process, which involves risk-taking, perseverance, personal attention and conscious effort. All counsellors need to learn from their professional experiences if they are to understand the issues and difficulties of the individuals they are working with.

HOW MIGHT YOUR JOURNAL BE USED IN THE FUTURE?

When reading the later chapters on 'Certification, registration and accreditation' and also 'Professional considerations' you will become aware that there is a requirement to record personal development, learning, feelings and self-monitoring of the process of learning to become a counsellor. To have such evidence of reflective writing addresses several areas. First, it gives the reader insight into your processing of experiences during the course and during practice. There tends to be a subtle change in writing style as you become more comfortable with writing and as you find your voice. This illustrates how you view your development and provides insight into values, qualities, understanding and encounters in training. A student who is able to acknowledge their weaknesses and areas for development alongside their successes and competencies is demonstrating the honesty and reflective skills necessary to be a successful counsellor.

It has been known for counselling journals to be requested during the interview process for employment as a counsellor (including voluntary work), so it is especially important to remember issues of confidentiality when it is not a tutor or assessor reading your accounts. As previously mentioned, your personal journal can also be requested when applying for accreditation prior to entering practice.

SUGGESTIONS FOR KEEPING YOUR JOURNAL

1 Keep it in a safe place.
2 It is your property, so any style will do. An A4 hardback book is one possible format, although it may suit you to maintain your journal on computer and print off particular sections that meet assessment criteria to be marked. Try to avoid using small pages as it can grow into quite a significant piece of work.

3   Record events regularly (preferably as they happen, so as soon after as possible) rather than allowing entries to accumulate into a chore.

4   Don't go back and alter previous entries. It should demonstrate the honest progress and development in your self-awareness and ability to document your reflections.

5   Remember to include reference to background reading so that you also have an accurate document of self-directed study.

6   Try to record all significant events, both positive and negative.

7   Read it at your leisure, you may find by looking back over the entries that you are resolving problems more productively, thereby identifying your own learning needs.

8   Be positive – if you find that you are experiencing any difficulties seek help sooner rather than later, before the problem becomes too difficult to cope with.

9   Reflection and support should not be seen as counselling or therapy. Professional support is available through the institution's student support services if the issues raised by reflection become overwhelming.

10   Don't forget to be systematic in recording the dates and times of your sessions and learning so in future you are able to identify exact moments when events happened.

SPECIFIC GUIDELINES TO WRITING REFLECTIVE ACCOUNTS

- Read the question carefully, noticing the key verbs that are used, such as 'discuss' and 'explain'.
- Always start with a rough plan that draws your memories together. This might be in list format but also may be as a mind map or other technique that you find helpful. Always be aware of the word-count or recommended length.
- What areas of skills, feelings, knowledge, learning process or experience are you being asked to write about?
- Reflect back over the course or the unit or module and consider specific areas of content.
- Don't forget about your background reading in this area – not just books but also websites and journals.
- Establish links between you learning and other aspects of your life to contextualise it, e.g. family, friends, placement, clients or colleagues on the course.
- Rather than simply identifying a point, remember to develop it to show the 'how' or 'why' it was relevant.
- Always read back though your work or proofread to ensure that you have included all the areas required.
- Finally, is it long enough – but not too long?

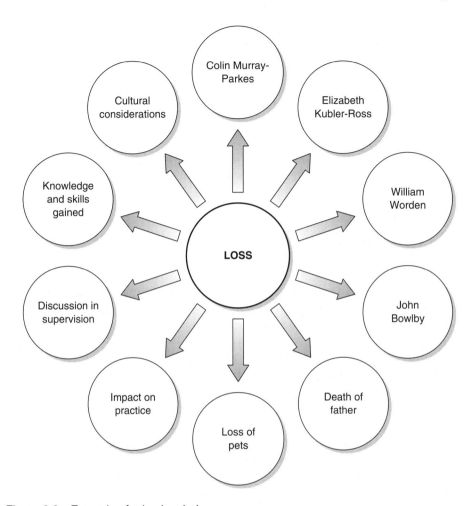

Figure 8.3   Example of a basic mind map

You may find that all your thoughts, feelings and memories are mixed up and you don't know where to start. Sometimes, learning tools such as a mind map (see Figure 8.3) might be of use to help you separate out your thoughts and allow you to document them in an order that makes sense to you.

Depending upon the guidelines provided by your tutor, there are many different ways that you can document feelings, experiences and learning. Recordings of music or drama can be acutely personal and can be used to encapsulate a moment. The use of poetry can be expressive in a different

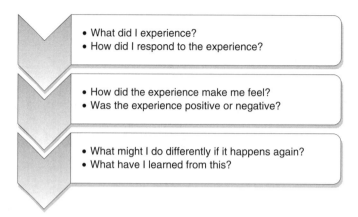

- What did I experience?
- How did I respond to the experience?

- How did the experience make me feel?
- Was the experience positive or negative?

- What might I do differently if it happens again?
- What have I learned from this?

Figure 8.4   Client-style questions that may aid your journal writing

way to prose if that is a comfortable medium for you. Even writing each page on a colour of paper that represents your mood at that time (e.g. yellow for happy or red for angry or green for serene) can add a different dimension to your account. If you tend to be expressive in a more fluid and artistic way, the use of drawings or graphics can be used to measure a very specific learning experience. Artists and other creative professionals usually maintain a notebook that they can enter ideas into to capture a moment or idea and prevent forgetting them. A counselling journal can be the equivalent. Alternatively, tools that we might use with clients can be put to good use here (see Figure 8.4). For example, you may find it challenging to write with such a lack of structure but find it easier to be specific and prefer a more scientific approach, in which case you could try using a rating scale of one to ten to show exactly how comfortable you were with learning a new theory or skill which helps you then progress onto justifying this through a more reflective narrative.

BOUNDARY ISSUES

Even within the boundaries of journal writing, issues such as confidentiality, ethics, orientation and level of course are very relevant. This is because they guide how we structure the content of the journal in relation to safety and professionalism. Here these will be addressed one at a time for clarity.

Confidentiality

The issue of confidentiality in this instance is two-fold: the writing within the journal and who has access to read it. First and foremost, when writing reflective accounts it is important to maintain privacy and respect the confidentiality of those you may be mentioning. You will be given guidelines by your tutor as to how your course deals with this. Usually, it is by being clear at the outset that you will be using pseudonyms or initials throughout for the protection of those you work and live with:

> Fiona (not her real name) appeared to be upset by this although last week she said that it was her choice.

or:

> Simon was so angry during the session today that I was quite taken aback by it.

Alternatively, you may be required to write only about yourself:

> I felt quite challenged when the client brought up such a sensitive issue although they were very open about it.

This style avoids overt confidentiality issues as you are only writing from your own point of view but there can be other identifying factors to be careful around, especially when writing about situations that happed within the class. To begin with, it is wise to read over your work objectively and ask yourself if you are able to recognise the individuals mentioned. Once you have developed a writing style that you are happy with, this is no longer necessary.

The second area of concern regarding confidentiality is to do with the book or computer files themselves. Find out at the start of the course exactly who will have access to read your journal, personal log or reflective accounts. Knowing this lets you know who should provide a good source of help if you should require it. Find a safe place to keep your journal so that it is easily accessible for you but secure from those you wouldn't want to see it.

Ethics

The use and content of a journal is often similar to the content of a session with a counselling supervisor. To be clear, the ethical guidelines that you adhere to with clients, in supervision and on the course also cover the writing within your journal. Although it is an environment where you can be honest with your feelings, this should be in a constructive manner that doesn't compromise or undermine your clients or colleagues. You will be provided with guidance and boundaries at the start of your course although this is such a personal method of documentation that self-direction is often encouraged.

Because of this, at the beginning of this process it is reasonable to ask yourself: 'How can I be honest in my journal if it is being used to assess me? If I identify my weaknesses, will I be judged and fail the course?' Luckily, this is not so. If anything, it is the opposite as if tutors are reading your account, they are looking for evidence of self-awareness, personal insight and self-questioning. Rather than being judged as a weakness, this is actually construed as a strength from the perspective that you can't change something if you are not aware that it needs to be changed. Clients are constantly questioning themselves, which we call 'therapeutic', so why shouldn't it be the same for counsellors?

Orientation

The orientation of your course may well impact upon your method of recording development. Although it will always be written in your own words and 'voice', the content may vary slightly depending upon the theoretical approach of your course. If you are studying a psychodynamic model, the focus may include your past, childhood and relationships prior to starting the course. Alternatively, if it is a person-centred course, you may find that there are fewer guidelines regarding what to include as the importance is more on your own interpretation of the course and for you to decide yourself which elements are important enough for you to include them. The tutor here would feel that you knew best; after all, you are the expert in your own world and therefore you know your internal framework better than anyone else. Cognitive and behavioural courses tend to be more pragmatic in that there is the added dimension of measurement (i.e. success, failure and rating scales). Solution-focused and time-limited courses do not always include a reflective journal. Specialised courses such as those concentrating on art therapy or working therapeutically with children may not have assessed reflective accounts, but individual students may prefer to maintain a journal as evidence of continuing professional development. Additionally there are numerous self-help groups that meet with the sole purpose of documenting personal narrative as a type of therapy on its own. There is no other dimension to this other than using self-expression as a cathartic process to examine your own issues or feelings.

Level of course

The level of your course may well influence the guidelines as to how you approach and present your journal in much the same way that the orientation can. Basic foundation courses, such as 'Introduction to Counselling' courses, can involve 40–120 taught hours and quite often introduce the idea of reflective practice and the importance of self-awareness, but may not all necessarily include an assessment on this area, especially if the focus is more on theoretical understanding than the practice of skills. However, courses which range between 120 and 480 taught hours will usually include the requirement to maintain a personal journal throughout the duration of the course. Once you have progressed and are studying at a higher level, the journal can become a central theme of your learning; students can become far more involved with this regular recording, and use it to keep up to date with the course content. It is a central depository for storing facts, feelings, content of supervision sessions, class interactions and background reading. By this level, you should be much more comfortable with this writing style.

STUDENT EXPERIENCE 8.1   HEATHER

The journal allows me to reflect and adapt what I have learned into my everyday life and realise the importance of having an open mind so that it becomes second nature to me.

POTENTIAL BARRIERS TO REFLECTIVE WRITING

At times, the journal can feel disconnected from the course, particularly after a period of time or if it is not assessed or monitored by the tutor. For there to be continuing input there needs to be a clear connection established with the course so that the personal writing becomes an integral part of the routine of attending the course. Finding the right time to put aside to concentrate on this more creative element requires ongoing motivation.

Motivation can be a barrier in itself, particularly if it is a course of a year or more when the impetus needs to be sustained. There is a danger of the journal turning from a cathartic pleasure into a chore that turns us into experts in procrastination. A test for this is if you are starting to negotiate with yourself, for example 'I'll write my journal when I have washed the dishes/dug over the vegetable patch/vacuumed the house.'

This shows a fall in enthusiasm that can stem from a lack of direction. One solution is to remind yourself of the purpose and value of the journal so that you can see it in context. View it as a professional document that is a necessary ticket to being a counsellor. Another solution might be to mention your struggle to your tutor and request journal workshops or discussion groups to re-stimulate an interest. You may wish to discuss it with your co-counsellor (see Chapter 9) or a partner you work with in the class. A facilitated group where students swap good practice and methodology that works for them can also plant seeds of ideas which may grow into renewed enthusiasm to help refocus on ongoing, regular input.

TO SUMMARISE YOUR JOURNAL

- This is an academic and professional requirement and not just part of your course and will be continued throughout your counselling career.
- It can be either an A4 book or a computer file.
- It is a single reflective log that documents your self-awareness, personal development and experience.
- It is also to document how you make sense of the theories and skills you are learning.
- This one 'book' gathers all this evidence together and can be requested by future counselling educators.
- It is can be a requirement for accreditation, depending upon the accrediting body's requirements.
- You should focus on thoughts, feelings and processing of information.
- It is necessary to include your experience of application of theories in placement or within relationships.
- It should not mention names or simply describe situations but focus on your personal development, interpretation and understanding.
- Learning outcomes covered within it should be identified clearly.

FURTHER READING

Bayne, R., Horton, I., Collard, P. and Jinks, G. (2008) *The Counsellor's Handbook*, 3rd edn. Cheltenham: Nelson Thornes.

Bolton, G., Howlett, S., Lago, C. and Wright, J.K. (eds) (2004) *Writing Cures: An Introductory Handbook of Writing in Counselling and Psychotherapy.* London: Routledge.

Johns, C. (2004) *Becoming a Reflective Practitioner.* Chichester: Wiley-Blackwell.

Johns, H. (1996) *Personal Development in Counsellor Training.* London: Sage.

Moon, J. (2006) *Learning Journals.* London: Routledge.

Schon, D.A. (1991) *The Reflective Practitioner: How Professionals Think in Action.* Aldershot: Ashgate.

Wheeler, S. (1996) *Training Counsellors: The Assessment of Competence.* London: Cassell.

9

Co-counselling

Here we examine the practice of co-counselling and the impact that it can have within a counselling course. We'll progress to consider the ethical and interpersonal implications before assessing its effect on both students and clients, and, finally, success on the course.

WHAT IS CO-COUNSELLING?

Although not included in all counselling courses, when used in training, co-counselling is a reciprocal counselling activity involving two counselling students who work together throughout their training on the course. Regular time is allocated by the tutor or, alternatively, negotiated between the students whereby the pair meet and take it in turn to be counsellor or client (Figure 9.1). The regularity and the length of the sessions may be different depending upon the course. It is usual for sessions to last for a therapeutic hour (which is 50 minutes), however, and how this time is divided is agreed by the couple involved.

Some individuals prefer to take it in turns so the client one week becomes the counsellor to their partner the following week. Alternatively, the sessions can run in succession with roles changing over in between the two sessions (Figure 9.2). Having this opportunity to be a client for the duration of the course can also be more convenient and considerably cheaper than buying personal therapy sessions if required for accreditation. Jackins claims that 'Co-counselling … requires awareness and persistence and

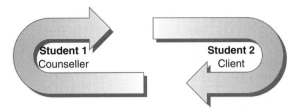

Figure 9.1   Co-counselling, whereby two counselling students alternate roles

willingness to apply counselling to difficulties as they arise. It can be very effective and become increasingly so. The interchangeable relationship is itself very rewarding and illuminating' (1994: 97) There are several other reasons for such an activity, which we will examine later in this chapter. Surprisingly, despite co-counselling being a fairly widely used activity in counselling training there is very little written about it. However, some additional reading is identified in the final section of this chapter.

Figure 9.2   The inter-related roles of co-counselling

THEORETICAL BACKGROUND

The original activity of co-counselling is rather different to that which is often utilised in counselling training. This shared activity evolved from the original movement of re-evaluation counselling (RC), which was developed in the USA by Harvey Jackins during the 1950s. RC communities meet regularly to share skills and monitor members whilst maintaining their disengagement with other counselling orientations, although RC shares similar assumptions to elements of person-centred therapy whereby it is non-directive and individuals are seen as being essentially good until life experiences present barriers and prevent such positivity.

However, a major difference is that 'the client is in charge of their work all the time. This makes the client role the expert one' (Evison and Horobun, 2006: 506), where as the relationship within person-centred counselling is more equal even though the client is still recognised as the expert in their own lives (Jackins, 1994).

The practice is designed to 'promote emotional discharge and catharsis' (Graham, 1986: 96) with considerable emphasis being placed on the role of emotions and the control they have over an individual. Some practitioners of RC led by John Heron formed an offshoot organisation called Co-counselling International (CCI UK) in 1974 which is more flexible in approach than the primary RC group.

Within these communities, co-counselling is not only a talking therapy but a more involved process that raises awareness of physical, emotional and cognitive processes, which is described by Evison and Horobin as 'best seen as a set of processes, ideas, and a special relationship which together comprises a toolkit for personal and social change in any setting– therapeutic, educational, in the home' (1999). Such breadth of technique and informality of structure differentiates the practice from that of other counselling models.

Heron condenses this difference by explaining that 'Co-counselling theory also holds that catharsis is a way of releasing distress from the mind-body. Keeping some attention in the place of the aware adult in present time, the client in co-counselling reaches down into the hidden place of the hurt child, honours and experiences the pain, and releases it' (1998). Other variations of the practice include the sharing within a group, with each member taking equal time in the role of client. As one individual takes the role of counsellor the other members are required to observe and support in silence (Figure 9.3). This provides demonstration of techniques so is a useful learning and development tool.

WHY DO WE DO IT?

Co-counselling is regarded by some to be a very useful activity to be involved in during training and there are numerous reasons why it is included in so many courses. Here we will consider some of the advantages and disadvantages of this type of therapeutic relationship within the context of training, including the opportunity co-counselling provides for bridging the gap between skills training and working therapeutically with a client. This link can make the progression to counsellor smoother by instilling confidence through previous experience within a safe environment.

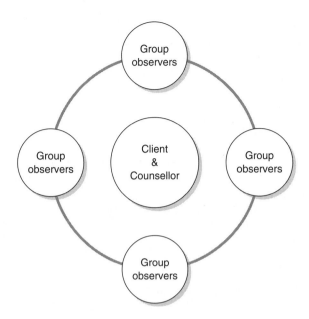

Figure 9.3   The re-evaluation counselling model including group participation

There are also reasons why co-counselling might not be included within a course. Many post-graduate courses would expect students to be in placement during the course and as such would be practising their skills directly with clients – the equivalent of jumping in at the deep end. It may also be that if a course is person-centred in orientation, the focus would be on the development of awareness surrounding attitudes and values, hence counselling is not a prescriptive activity but rather a natural evolvement of a supportive relationship and so such sessions might be of less value. Alternatively, if it is a short course or theory rather than practice based, there might not be the time or requirement for such a structured endeavour. Or it may simply be that co-counselling is perceived as being successful only in its uncorrupted form which does not fit in with the ethos of the course.

POSITIVE ASPECTS

Safety

To work in a therapeutic relationship – a controlled environment with guidance towards areas such as boundary setting with the knowledge that a tutor is available – can have a very comforting effect if you are not feeling confident or are just starting out in counselling. There is a balance between classroom learning and independent practice that can feel safer than working with a 'real' client.

STUDENT EXPERIENCE 9.1   JANE

My co-counselling partnership has, in my opinion, been an excellent working relationship which has gradually been built on trust, openness and a mutual understanding to both of us since we picked each other. We have a mutual understanding of what is required. It has helped both of us throughout the year and I can liken it to a solid foundation supporting the structure of a building but which can not be seen.

Available practice if not in placement

It is not easy to find a placement, especially if one is not provided by your college, university or trainer. There is also the possibility that one or both of the partners has not received counselling as a client. This is when co-counselling becomes a good compromise, allowing both students to encounter the responsibility of counsellor but also that of client, providing greater insight into the difficulties and strong emotions that can be experienced in both roles.

Non-threatening environment

Guidance is usually given regarding boundaries before the relationship begins so that both students are able to negotiate and confirm their own rules on a micro scale within the wider cocoon of agreed limits. This allows for an element of freedom and experimentation without the danger of damaging a vulnerable client. It may also be that sessions take place within the educational establishment so the task of finding a safe or private room is less stressful.

Mutual support and development

Another of the advantages of this undertaking is that of the potential for reducing any feelings of isolation which the responsibility of learning counselling can bring, such as fear, lack of confidence, uncertainty or self-doubt, which are common feelings during different aspects of training. The co-counselling relationship is a forum for allowing these feelings to be discussed when in the role of client or for regular skills practice to reduce them when in the role of counsellor.

STUDENT EXPERIENCE 9.2   MINNIE

I have personally found my co-counselling experience to be a positive, helpful step in my ongoing work with a trust issue. To be able to voice my innermost thoughts and feelings in a 100% trusting, warm and safe relationship, for me is a huge step for my own personal development.

'Real' situations

When first starting out, it takes a lot of courage to feel confident enough to work with a genuine client with real issues when there might be a risk of doing harm. Yet, when learning to drive, often our first lesson is on a real road with other motorists with every opportunity to crash! The co-counselling relationship allows for a middle ground where the client is opening up about issues in a trusting and warm relationship but with the knowledge that any mistakes that are made can be shared, discussed later and used as a learning tool for both.

Opportunity to practise skills in context

In Chapter 10 we will be looking at how we learn skills. Some courses teach skills in isolation (micro-skills; Ivey, 1971); others, particularly person-centred courses, prefer a gradual evolution and development of attitudes and skills within the student so they become instilled as part of the counsellor rather than tools used within a job. Co-counselling allows for these to be tested and evaluated so that strengths and weaknesses become apparent and can be focused on within sessions.

Co-counselling provides the opportunity to team up with another student and can offer a strong support mechanism with someone who understands the pressure and difficulties being experienced on the course. Co-counselling partners are often allocated by the tutor but occasionally students are allowed to choose their own partner, both of which can influence the culture of the relationship. However, the sense of comradeship that often develops can be highly beneficial, especially when it alleviates the feelings of 'it is only me that is worried about this' or 'I don't know what to do here', which can be quite alienating if not shared with others who may be experiencing similar reservations.

STUDENT EXPERIENCE 9.3   STEPHEN

Co-counselling was beneficial to myself. I would say that if a placement is not available, then it is essential. The co-counselling allowed the demonstration of learning and was helpful in the understanding of the theories. Over the course I developed an understanding with other class members, who were all displaying in a creative and sometimes negative way what the course had been teaching us. I feel that co-counselling is an integral part of the course and is a means of becoming more aware of yourself and of the needs of individuals. Without co-counselling you have no means of effectively measuring progress and knowledge. To a lesser degree I still have contact with students from the course and find that the relationships developed through this have been beneficial to my own sense of being.

NEGATIVE ASPECTS

Uncertainty about practice

If the participants in this insular relationship are new to counselling, there is the constant concern that each don't know if they are doing what they are supposed to. Uncertainty about technique is the most prevalent concern, although anxiety regarding boundaries can also be present. Co-counselling may well be the first opportunity individuals have of practising putting skills together in a non-supervised situation, which can foster self-doubt.

Dependency

Issues surrounding dependency may arise if co-counselling begins at the very start of a course when students are just beginning to get to know each other. It can be compared to children at a new school finding a 'best friend' on the first day so they have someone to sit beside to reduce any feelings of being alone. This may have certain advantages but it can result in a reduction in interaction with other students within the group. Finding such a seemingly protective sanctuary so soon can encourage both dependency on each other and the development of cliques. A good tutor will be aware of this and will ensure that measures are put in place to make the co-counselling relationship less of a friendship and more of a professional association.

Confidence

There is a link here between confidence and many other aspects that are identified as negative, especially surrounding uncertainty about practice. It is common to question yourself when learning something new, especially when it is not being closely monitored, and counselling skills and practice are no different. Fortunately, self-doubt has an outlet as it can be discussed in many forums, such as with your counselling supervisor, with your tutor or within a community group or personal development group (see Chapter 5). It is considerably preferable to question your abilities, allowing for improvement, than to arrogantly assume that you are good and be resistant to further learning.

Trust

The idea of immediately developing trust with an individual you might never have met before can seem daunting, but this is exactly what a counsellor expects a client to do in therapy. This is where the importance of boundary issues becomes apparent. If there is a mutually agreed contract in place for the first session, there is little else you can do except put your faith in your co-counselling partner to respect the guidelines as much as you do. It is also very good practice for the real thing.

Responsibility and accountability

When practising counselling in class within counselling triads (see Chapter 10), there is less opportunity for risk when being closely monitored or even recorded. The co-counselling sessions are different in that they are far more realistic due to the content being actual counselling sessions. The student who is in the role of counsellor is no longer able to hide behind checklists or observers but is in a position to take responsibility for their approach. If a technique or use of a particular skill is unsuccessful, it becomes a steeper learning curve.

Confidentiality

There is a difficult balance to achieve with confidentiality as, on the one hand, the sessions should be as realistic as possible so confidentiality is addressed within the contract setting at the start of the relationship. On the other hand, there is often a desire to discuss progress in class or ask questions relating to an issue that arose during a session. However, it is more appropriate to save this for counselling supervision even with the consent of your partner.

Difficulty in maintaining boundaries

Because of the dual role of counsellor/client as well as fellow student, there can be a blurring of the previously agreed boundaries if the roles become confused. The simple rule here is to remember that it is a counselling relationship and should be treated as you would a session with a client you didn't previously know. This should help the processes of respect, confidentially and trust to develop and reduce any potential for difficulties with boundaries.

Easy to develop into friendship and therefore an opportunity to develop into chit chat

Again, there are clear links here with the previous potential hazard. If boundaries are not maintained, sessions can disintegrate into a conversation with the practice of skills being forgotten. Although it is good that there is a closeness between the pair, it is totally inappropriate within this setting. Again, personal supervision or a discussion with a tutor would be of benefit in re-establishing the original purpose and underlying guidelines.

ACTIVITY

Consider your own experience and practice. Using a balance sheet technique, list the possible benefits of attending co-counselling sessions alongside the reasons not to. This will help you identify whether or not it would be a helpful activity for you to become involved in.

THE ROLE OF THE TUTOR

The role of the tutor is reduced here as there is more responsibility and autonomy placed on the student with respect of their personal and skills development, which in turn increases the role of the counselling supervisor for ongoing reflection on progress and self-awareness. The tutor is more likely to take a back seat and be more concerned with monitoring development if they are approached. This is more likely to happen only if there are difficulties that the student feels unable to manage, such as non-attendance or lack of focus by one or both partners. This additional responsibility can be freeing and exhilarating for those involved, as it is allowing a freedom to develop according to the individual's pace and style without direct guidance. So saying this, it is still important to feel that the tutor can be approached at any time and that to do so is no indication of failure in any way. Rather, it shows an active awareness of issues and the maturity to seek guidance or support which would be recognised by the tutor.

BENEFIT TO FUTURE CLIENTS

It may seem obvious, but the benefits to future clients are numerous. Because co-counselling allows you to gain direct experience before entering a placement or counselling environment, the practice ensures that each member is not beginning a counselling relationship with a client before they have any previous experience of the process. The benefit of this upon the client is that they are working with a more experienced counsellor than if you were not to have had the rehearsal. It you have or are attending a placement, co-counselling provides an alternative experience base. With this comes the confidence to focus more therapeutically on the client rather than being more conscious of one's own inexperience. This is evident in several ways, one of which is the maintenance of boundaries. It takes practice to be able to end a session at the agreed time when the client clearly wants to continue, or to have the insight to know when self-disclosure is definitely not appropriate. Such maintenance of boundaries develops with experience and confidence. Awareness of any potential difficulties tends to evolve alongside the ability to deal with them, and co-counselling is used in training courses to speed up this process. To have been involved in a placement as well as co-counselling provides a wider perspective for consultation with a counselling supervisor and may result in a well-established relationship even before starting work with external clients.

FURTHER READING

Evison, R. and Horobin, R. (1983) *How to Change Yourself and Your World Co-Counselling*. Sheffield: Phoenix.

Evison, R. and Horobin, R. (2006) 'Co-counselling', in C. Feltham and I. Horton (eds), *The Sage Handbook of Counselling and Psychotherapy*. London: Sage.

Heron, J. (1974) *Reciprocal Counselling Human Potential Research Project*. Guildford: University of Surrey.

Jackins, H. (1994) *The Human Side of Human Beings: The Theory of Re-evaluation Counselling*. Seattle, WA: Rational Island.

Kauffman, K. and New, C. (2004) *Co-Counselling: The Theory and Practice of Re-evaluation Counselling*. London: Routledge.

10

Working on Counselling Skills

The distinction between 'counselling' and 'counselling skills' is often blurred, so this chapter will focus on defining the usage of each and their role in counselling training courses. We will also identify and discuss a range of commonly used skills emphasised within different counselling approaches. The chapter ends with methods used to show evidence of skills development in counselling courses.

COMMUNICATION SKILLS

By reducing this area down to its most basic definition, counselling skills are simply developed communication skills. Everyone communicates in some way, through behaviour, movement, actions or speech, as humans are rarely solitary beings. How we integrate with others is learned from our family, peers and previous experiences and continues to evolve throughout our lives. Slightly more developed communication skills are core tools that are used widely in most professional roles.

ACTIVITY

Imagine that you carry a large invisible bag into class with you and, every time you learn a new skill and move along the learning continuum, you add that skill to your bag. When you are working with clients, you can have the bag open beside you and the skills within easy reach to choose which ones are appropriate at that time.

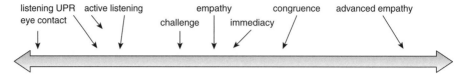

Figure 10.1   An example of a personal counselling skills continuum

For example, you might expect a vet to know how to support a customer whose pet has just died or a GP to understand a patient who is describing signs and symptoms experienced. Such basic understanding and eye contact are hardly complicated but can make a great difference to how well we feel listened to, supported or heard. These examples show us that it is necessary to have appropriate values and attitudes in place beforehand so that there is a foundation for skills to embed into. Egan (2009) has written extensively about skills necessary within the counselling relationship and the impact that we can have on others. When trying to master such ways of being, it can help to think of communication skills as sitting on a continuum with very basic skills that are used daily leading up to more advanced techniques that require the counsellor to be highly trained and experienced (Figure 10.1). When starting out on a counselling course, whether it is a basic introductory course or a post-graduate qualification, we are trying to move along the continuum gathering as we go and adding new skills to our repertoire. As with all developments, sometimes the journey doesn't necessarily progress as we would like it to as it is natural to struggle with mastering different ways of working and even to lose skills occasionally, particularly if they are not being regularly practised. The acquisition and development of a wide range of skills is necessary to work flexibly and competently in an intensive therapeutic environment with potentially vulnerable clients.

ACTIVITY

Draw your own personal continuum and place counselling skills on it according to ease and difficulty for you. Feedback, assignments and how comfortable you feel all indicate where they should sit in relation to each other.

WHAT ARE COUNSELLING SKILLS?

There are a huge number of interpersonal skills that are used in counselling and they all relate to the method in which we choose to communicate with others. Different counselling approaches use some more than others, and along with underpinning theory, our choice of counselling skills are a principal method of differentiating between the models. (There is a relevant chapter by Francesca Inskipp on generic skills in *The Sage Handbook of Counselling and Psychotherapy*, edited by Colin Feltham and Ian Horton.)

Here is a selection of some of the most well used skills:

- *Active listening*: a fundamental focusing skill that is necessary in almost all talking therapies. It is not simply the hearing of words but also noticing how they are said and what the client does when they say them. Understanding why and how something is said improves knowledge on both sides.
- *Attending*: goes together with active listening as there is also the need to concentrate as fully as possible on the client during a session, to notice the additional communications that accompany speech, for example, when the client doesn't speak or when they pause.
- *Empathy*: the ability to understand and confirm one's understanding of the client's inner world, to accurately see the client's life through the client's eyes.
- *UPR*: unconditional positive regard refers to the acceptance, warmth and non-judgemental attitude expected of those in the helping professions. Acceptance of the client but not necessarily of their actions or choices.
- *Congruence*: complete openness, genuineness and honesty, sometimes to the point of transparency, which can feel uncomfortable to begin with.
- *Summarising*: the ability to recap the main points that have been raised. This is very useful for helping the client see things from a slightly more objective perspective.
- *Paraphrasing*: rewording or rephrasing what has been said to highlight meanings or inaccuracies.
- *Challenge*: is not confrontational or aggressive but rather gentle and supportive. Challenge is used to highlight distortions, projections, misinformation or self-defeating attitudes. It can be as basic as 'you say that it makes you angry, but I see that you smiled rather than looked angry when you said that.'
- *Advanced empathy*: taking the deep understanding of empathy to the next level whereby the counsellor picks up on what is unsaid by the verbal and non-verbal clues given by the client. There is an element of working with hunches and intuition, but it is all firmly bedded on the client's story.
- *Encouraging strengths*: helping a client identify areas that they are competent or strong at can be very empowering.
- *Highlighting conscious and unconscious interactions*: the counsellor may see the client's interactions in a different context to the client and is able to identify

actions that are intended or unintended, and also whether they are within the client's awareness or not.

- *Reflection*: looking back over what has previously been said or done can encourage new responses and feelings.
- *Exploration*: this can be approached in different ways, although questions (open or closed, depending upon model being practised) are often over-used when first starting counselling training. Almost all of the other skills listed here can be used to encourage the client to delve more deeply into their issue.
- *Non-verbal*: it's not just what the counsellor says but also what they do or are perceived to do that can also have an impact upon the therapeutic relationship. Maintaining comfortable eye contact, avoiding fidgeting, or being aware of open body language can encourage or discourage dialogue.
- *Silence*: when first learning counselling, silence can be seen as uncomfortable and a sign of failure, but is actually a crucial element of a positive session. It allows the client time to think but is also a tool to stimulate talking. Silence is not often used comfortably in general conversation.
- *Focus*: remaining fixed on the client's story and purpose avoiding diversions and tangents can be demanding but is ultimately very beneficial.

'COUNSELLING' VERSUS 'COUNSELLING SKILLS'

There is understandable confusion between these two terms due to the overlap between the two activities and also the common and often incorrect use of the terminology. Distinction should be made between the activity of counselling as opposed to the general use of counselling skills. As previously established, counselling skills such as active listening, challenge, summary and focus can be used in any interpersonal exchange, whereas counselling is a far more rigid term that covers a range of specific activities but confusion arises as it also involves the use of counselling skills (see Figure 10.2). Counselling sessions are only carried out with the agreement of the client and adhere to ethical and procedural guidelines.

COUNSELLING COURSE OR COUNSELLING SKILLS COURSE?

When learning counselling, a choice has to be made between a counselling skills course and a counselling course. Considerations may involve interest level, CPD, career plans, availability, cost and self-confidence. A certificate in counselling skills shows evidence of transferable proficiency

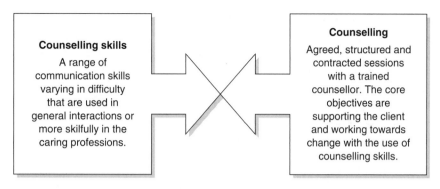

Figure 10.2   Counselling skills versus counselling

and is useful in all manner of employment; a counselling qualification is different as it indicates an ability to work intensively with people in a therapeutic manner. Generally speaking, the lower the level of the course, the more likely it is to focus purely on skills development. How you intend to use the course content is a fair indicator of which should be most appropriate. How we learn these skills depends upon a number of factors, namely our starting level of communication, awareness of others, level of the course in relation to own experience, opportunity to practise and the quality of the teaching, but of course there are many more.

HOW COUNSELLING SKILLS TRAINING SITS WITHIN COUNSELLING COURSES

Not all counselling courses teach skills in isolation as there are several, often opposing views as to how such skills can be taught, learned or integrated into a course, or even if they should be at all. Ivey (1971) believed strongly that skills (or micro-skills) should be taught explicitly one by one, so that the student builds up their repertoire gradually over time and allows understanding and practice of each before progressing onto the next. This can involve demonstration, video and checklists. Once the list had been completed, then the student was ready to combine them together for therapeutic practise. However, this structured and methodical approach is disputed by others who believe that the practice of integration is more beneficial. Geldard and Geldard

(2005) note that competency can reduce when learning in this style as the student concentrates on a single skill rather than the overall relationship, and behaviour isn't natural until the new skill is mastered. Conversely, here is also an argument that skills are considerably more attitudinal and should come from within, in response to the client, an example being Legg and Donati who argue that 'confidence can never come from mastery of technique alone, it is a question of "being" rather than "doing"' (2006). s

The style of instruction and the context in which the training of counselling skills is placed depends very much upon the orientation of course. The theoretical model underpinning a course dictates which skills will be most commonly employed. A person-centred course may concentrate more on a foundation of attitudinal qualities and the core conditions as a foundation, whereas CBT values focus, objectivity and challenge. Putting the basic building blocks in context helps develop a clear and specific approach to working with clients. Once competent in a particular model, it is possible to move on to another to enhance or complement current understanding. Integrative or eclectic therapies often combine one or more approaches, allowing the counsellor to choose the most appropriate skills to be used with each individual client.

SKILLS USED WITHIN DIFFERENT ORIENTATIONS

Egan's 3-stage approach to helping

Gerard Egan's model of helping skills (see Chapter 3) is somewhat more structured as particular skills are clearly drawn on at each stage, which makes learning the process and progress a matter of advancement, and this order can be satisfying. Stage I utilises a very humanistic approach, so the skills are the three main core conditions from person-centred therapy. This allows for a gentle introduction for both client and counsellor to become aware of the client's perception of the issue. Stage II moves this on to be more focused by establishing current cognition, feelings and attitudes to the situation by the use of immediacy, advanced empathy and challenge. Finally, a more behavioural influence in Stage III ensures the counsellor instigates tools for action and evaluation. Interestingly, Egan (1994) suggests that each stage should also integrate the previous skills, so that by Stage III the skills from all three stages are being employed. Table 10.1

Table 10.1   The 3-stage approach to helping (Egan, 1994)

Stage	Skills employed
Stage I **(Exploration or story telling)**	• Empathy • Congruence • Unconditional positive regard
Stage II **(Goal setting)**	• Stage I skills • Immediacy • Challenge • Self-disclosure • Advanced empathy
Stage III **(Action and evaluation)**	• Stage I and II skills • Quickthink • Forcefield analysis • SMART • Evaluation

highlights the different skills used within each stage of the therapeutic process.

Person-centred practice

Rogers' person-centred approach is founded on the assumption that the client is the expert in their own lives, and as such the role of the counsellor reflects this premise (Rogers, 1951). This balance or equality is reinforced if the counsellor is to remain totally honest and open throughout the process to the point of transparency, managing a balance between what is said and what is thought.

Rather than being simply the demonstration of skills that brings around change in the client, Rogers also places credence on the qualities and attitudes of the counsellor, or their 'way of being' (Rogers, 1980). The relationship between those involved in the therapy is at the heart of the sessions so the skills, qualities and attitudes are expected to be integral (see Figure 10.3). Fundamental elements such as the ability to remain empathic, genuine and accepting throughout are to be accompanied by active listening so that the counsellor is able to enter the inner world of the client. To be empathic is to gain a deep understanding of the client's perspective and their view of the world and requires considerable concentration. Genuineness and honesty, referred to by Rogers as 'congruence', is also necessary to reduce or eradicate barriers and ensure both client and counsellor are able to develop a trusting and warm therapeutic relationship. A vital element of this relationship is a safe environment whereby

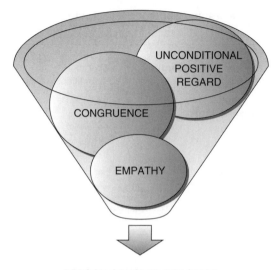

PERSON-CENTRED PRACTICE

Figure 10.3   The person-centred approach (Rogers, 1951)

there is permission for the client to discuss anything they choose without fear of reprisal.

Rogers suggested separating the client as a person from their choices and behaviours if this helped to establish acceptance and avoid judgement (Figure 10.4). The skills of summarising, reflection, focus and paraphrasing all aid with this process as they can help the client to identify and examine the issues that brought them to counselling. There is an equality between the counsellor and client that is not always present in other therapeutic models.

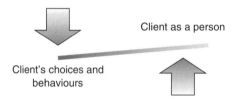

Figure 10.4   The client as a person should be seen as separate from their choices and behaviours (Rogers, 1951)

Carkhuff (1969) developed a five-point scale for measuring the main core conditions in interpersonal communication. First, let's consider congniene (genuineness, honesty or transparency):

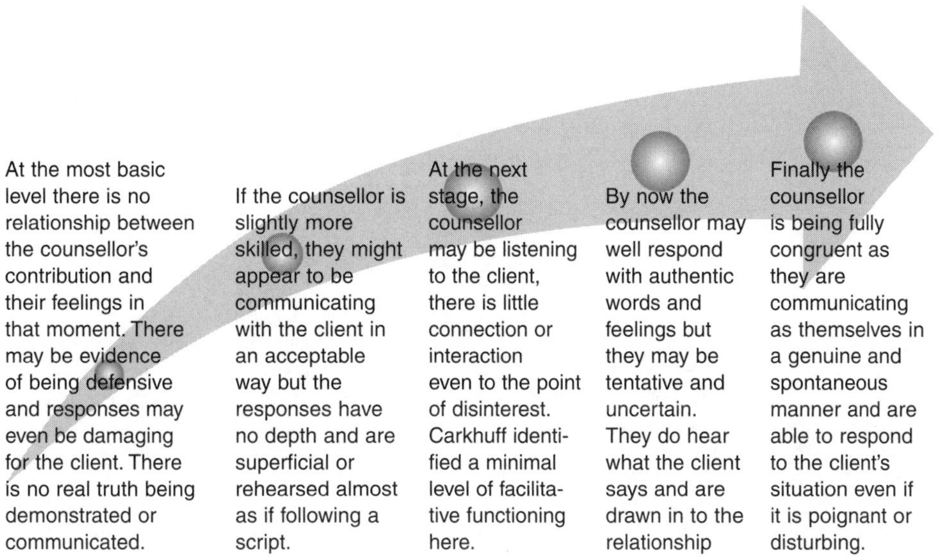

At the most basic level there is no relationship between the counsellor's contribution and their feelings in that moment. There may be evidence of being defensive and responses may even be damaging for the client. There is no real truth being demonstrated or communicated.

If the counsellor is slightly more skilled, they might appear to be communicating with the client in an acceptable way but the responses have no depth and are superficial or rehearsed almost as if following a script.

At the next stage, the counsellor may be listening to the client, there is little connection or interaction even to the point of disinterest. Carkhuff identified a minimal level of facilitative functioning here.

By now the counsellor may well respond with authentic words and feelings but they may be tentative and uncertain. They do hear what the client says and are drawn in to the relationship

Finally the counsellor is being fully congruent as they are communicating as themselves in a genuine and spontaneous manner and are able to respond to the client's situation even if it is poignant or disturbing.

Figure 10.5a

The second is unconditional positive regard (acceptance, warmth and respect):

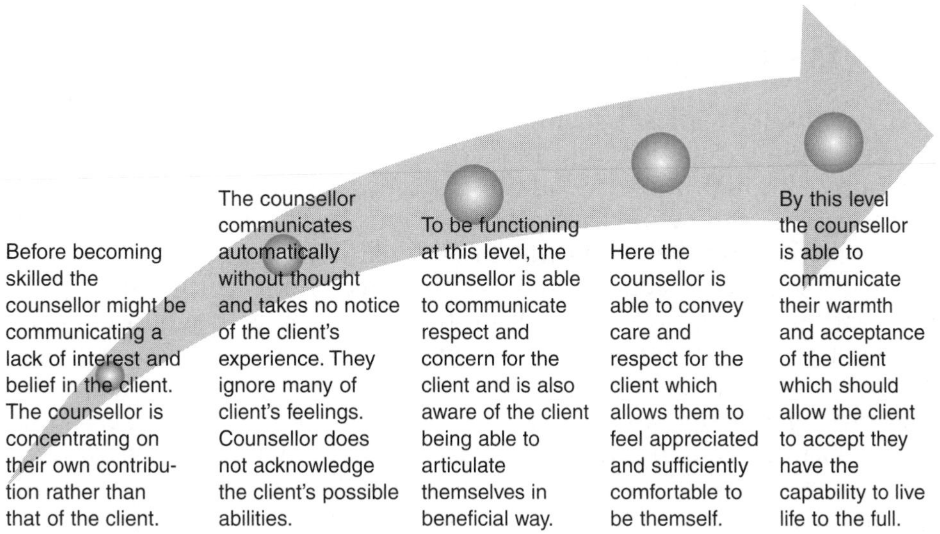

Before becoming skilled the counsellor might be communicating a lack of interest and belief in the client. The counsellor is concentrating on their own contribution rather than that of the client.

The counsellor communicates automatically without thought and takes no notice of the client's experience. They ignore many of client's feelings. Counsellor does not acknowledge the client's possible abilities.

To be functioning at this level, the counsellor is able to communicate respect and concern for the client and is also aware of the client being able to articulate themselves in beneficial way.

Here the counsellor is able to convey care and respect for the client which allows them to feel appreciated and sufficiently comfortable to be themself.

By this level the counsellor is able to communicate their warmth and acceptance of the client which should allow the client to accept they have the capability to live life to the full.

Figure 10.5b

Finally, empathy (understanding the client's world):

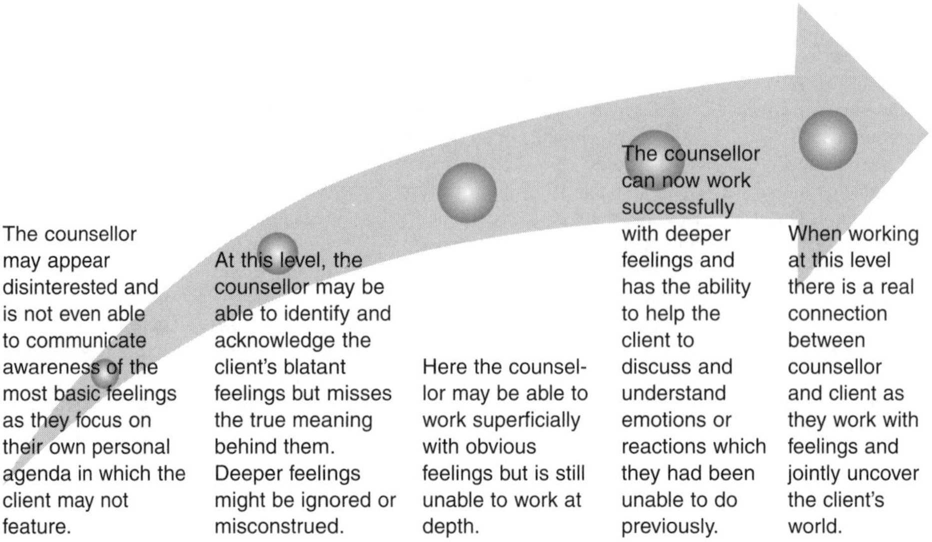

The counsellor may appear disinterested and is not even able to communicate awareness of the most basic feelings as they focus on their own personal agenda in which the client may not feature.

At this level, the counsellor may be able to identify and acknowledge the client's blatant feelings but misses the true meaning behind them. Deeper feelings might be ignored or misconstrued.

Here the counsellor may be able to work superficially with obvious feelings but is still unable to work at depth.

The counsellor can now work successfully with deeper feelings and has the ability to help the client to discuss and understand emotions or reactions which they had been unable to do previously.

When working at this level there is a real connection between counsellor and client as they work with feelings and jointly uncover the client's world.

Figure 10.5c

Psychodynamic practice

Many of the skills already mentioned within other orientations are incorporated into psychodynamic practice such as clarification and active listening, although there are additional specific characteristics which we will consider now. Before therapeutic sessions begin, there is great importance placed upon the establishment and maintenance of boundaries and the counselling contract. Working within agreed limits adds a structure to the relationship that is valued within this approach as the counsellor can interpret additional information about the client when observing their adherence to these agreed boundaries. Behaviours and actions that break previous agreements can be a result of conscious or unconscious impulses that indicate an underlying issue or past experience which can be explored during the therapeutic sessions (Figure 10.6). The counsellor places this within the context of the current issue so that they can search for meanings

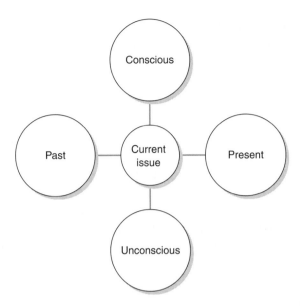

Figure 10.6   Reflection on essential influences in psychodynamic sessions

together, which may also involve dream analysis to identify possible unconscious influences. This theme of interpretation is commonly used as a method of determining links that are established between past events and present behaviours and feelings. Sometimes these can only be identified by observing the client carefully to notice behaviours and responses that might otherwise go unnoticed. If the client appears resistant to exploration of areas, and observations, or if they display responses characteristic of defence mechanisms to areas that are introduced, this can have meaning. There may be evidence of transference between client and counsellor or vice versa, so any of the implications of these would be investigated. Essentially, a core skill of the counsellor which differs from other approaches is the ability to identify and reflect upon any feelings that the client projects onto them and be able to find meaning in it: 'Revelation is the goal' (Klein, 2006).

Cognitive behavioural practice

Cognitive behaviour therapy has many differences from the non-directive style of person-centred counselling. To begin with, there is not so much focus on the relationship but more on actions and change. Although it is directive in nature, there remains a requirement for honesty and trust, but admittedly there is more emphasis on the client to demonstrate these rather than the counsellor. The counsellor establishes links between the triggers of negative behaviours and the response that the client has developed, which is why it is so commonly used with reducing phobias and freeing myself from bad habits and addictions such as smoking. There may be use of rewards to reinforce positive changes in entrenched behaviour patterns, but the main significance is to do with the focus on and process of change. Behavioural methods such as improving assertiveness and social skills, desensitisation and relaxation techniques are frequently used to help the client to develop an awareness of alternative responses and reactions. Training and re-training can be central to the sessions, as can the setting of homework which transfers responsibility very much onto the client who takes on the role of monitoring themselves honestly. The counsellor must remain objective and use specific tools such as rating scales to measure the effect on the client to ascertain a baseline so that future change can be accurately calculated, thereby making it a quantifiable process. A relationship is established between trigger and response, so sessions are used to break old habits and through training develop new, healthier ones.

Group work

So far, all the skills and session management that we have looked at have been working with an individual, which has a very different dynamic to working with more than one client at the same time. In group work, the counsellor must be able to balance the needs of the unique members of the group with the needs of the group as a whole. This requires a whole new skill set in addition to the skills that are already employed within the theoretical orientation of the facilitator.

ACTIVITY

Consider which theoretical orientation is of most interest to you, then list the skills that are used within it and rate which you are:
✓ skilled in,
½ competent in, or
X requiring practice in.

First and foremost, members should feel they are in a safe environment where they can trust the group. The facilitator or counsellor will still be using skills such as active listening, clarification, focus, generating discussion and summary, but in addition to that they will be observing individual members of the group to take cognisance of evident behaviours such as avoidance, distrust, rescuing, anger, irritation. Clearly this is not a comprehensive list as there are so many interactions, behaviours and responses that may be present, it would not be possible to include them all; suffice to say that a group facilitator must remain aware and alert at all times and have confidence in both their therapeutic modality and management skills. These management skills can become crucial if there is disagreement within the group or breaking of boundaries, such as talking over others, punctuality or confidentiality. The ability to be seen as fair and competent by all members of the group can be very challenging.

THE USE OF DEMONSTRATION

All of us have preferred ways of learning, and course lecturers and tutors usually try hard to meet the needs of a wide range of students. One of the most straightforward methods of introducing and explaining skills may seem to be demonstration, but how this is achieved can be ethically or practically problematic. Some tutors are more than happy to demonstrate skills within the classroom, whereas others prefer to use video or other examples to pass on information. There are four key issues here, the first being that the tutor has to be competent themselves to be able to demonstrate accurately or successfully and how might this be monitored. Second, is there an expectation for the tutor to be in practice during the time that they are delivering the skills element of a course? Third, is there an expectation for students to volunteer to be a client for the purpose of demonstration, or does the tutor invite an external volunteer? Fourth, during the demonstration, is the client expected to use current issues for realism, past issues for safety, or role play depending upon the experience level that the student group are at? There is a certain symmetry to this 'I do/you' do method which is not representative of practical work with clients and as such can only be viewed in isolation as opposed to being representative of a model of intervention. Practical skills demonstration is also dependent upon the theoretical orientation of the course, as a person-centred course may rely more on

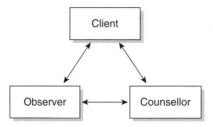

Figure 10.7   A typical training triad

an individual evolutionary approach whereby the student gradually interprets what is learned and synthesises it into their own personal framework of skills.

In summary, demonstration of skills can be performed in several ways dependent upon the theoretical orientation and level of the course, the skills of the tutor and the reason the skills are being covered. This leads on to the turn of the student. It is usual for practice to be carried out in triads which consist of a counsellor, a client and an observer. The counsellor is the student being assessed and the observer is the record-keeper who completes any necessary checklist and provides feedback at the end (see Figure 10.7).

METHODS AND USES OF GATHERING EVIDENCE

Whilst engaging with learning and developing skills on a counselling course, there needs to be some form of measurement of progress or success either for assessment or a sense of competence to build confidence. Clearly, it is difficult to determine such an intangible element, but there are different approaches to making decisions about ability.

Recording demonstration

Carl Rogers is recognised as the first practitioner to acknowledge a role for recording and monitoring sessions to increase transparency and encourage objective, constructive feedback. For this purpose, evidence for assessment or evaluation can be taken as an audio recording, video recording or by an assessor witnessing the session in real time. The main advantages of audio recordings are that it is unobtrusive and allows listeners to concentrate on speech. This is used mainly when training is for environments where speech is the main link with the client, such as telephone counselling, whereas video recordings allow viewers to make links between verbal and non-verbal communication and place the skills in a wider context; in other words to see the whole picture. Clearly, the recording of sessions introduces ethical issues too (Horton, 1994). Prior to commencement, the client must give permission for the recording to take place and the subsequent use and distribution. There has since been debate surrounding the ethical issue of informed consent and the dissemination of recorded sessions, including debate surrounding the well-known and often used sessions with Carl Rogers, Fritz Perls and Albert Ellis working with the client 'Gloria' (Shostrom, 1965). Excerpts of these educational sessions are widely available, even accessible online.

The next choice is that of whether to remain within the safety, manageability and control of role play or to require evidence to have been generated from real counselling sessions with genuine clients to provide a far more accurate picture of the counselling student's abilities. It is often the level of the course, assessment criteria and liability insurance that dictates which it should be. Role play tends to be used in basic, introductory courses when skills have yet to be developed to ensure a safe environment for practise, whereas the recording of real sessions is used to evaluate students on higher level courses when it is the appropriateness of use and the impact of the developed skills on the client that is being assessed. Both role play and real sessions are valid learning tools depending upon the situation.

Checklists for demonstration

Whilst engaging with learning and developing skills on a counselling course, there needs to be some form of evidence for measurement of progress or success, either for formal assessment or to promote a sense of competence to build confidence. Clearly, it is difficult to determine such an intangible element but there are different approaches to making decisions about ability. Figure 10.8 gives an example of a simple checklist which shows how comments can be made on a list of basic skills that are required to be demonstrated appropriately within a session for the student to pass the assessment.

SCHOOL OF HEALTH, COUNSELLING AND SOCIAL CARE

COUNSELLING PRACTICE CHECKLIST

Counsellor: _____ Date: _____

Client: _____ Observer: _____

Role-play situation _____

Counselling skill	Comments
Opening	
Confidentiality	
Empathy	
Unconditional positive regard	
Congruence	
Summarising	
Reflecting	
Method of exploration	
Body language	
Eye contact	
Use of silence	
Focus	
Open questions	
Internal framework or situational	
Ending	
To work on:	

Pass		Remediate		Fail	

Tutor's Signature: _____ Date: _____

Figure 10.8 A simple checklist allowing for observer's comments

Source: based on SQA National Certificate module unit specification: Introduction to Counselling, module no. 7330006, 1996–7.

GENERAL GUIDANCE FOR FIRST PRACTICAL SESSION

- Remember to be yourself – be friendly. Remain professional but don't lose your personality or be false.
- Privacy is an issue! If you are in a classroom, do not to disturb other groups.
- Your main task is to really *listen*!
- Use open rather than closed questions as you tend to get a more in-depth response.
- 'You have obviously ...' Nothing in counselling is 'obvious', so avoid the word.
- Remember to be empathic: 'It sounds like you're feeling ... '
- Avoid 'I think ...' and 'in my opinion ...'
- Don't give advice – you'll be blamed if it's wrong!
- Concentrate on demonstrating core conditions, not solutions.
- Don't be scared of silences – they are just spaces for thought.
- Make sure that the seating is appropriate – no desk or barriers.
- Remember that you are focusing the client's internal framework; on their feelings and emotions rather than just the situation/facts.
- Observation is useful – what do you see?
- The client is the person to be discussed, the focus, not others that aren't present.
- Don't talk about your own experiences – you are not the client!
- It is not appropriate to refer your client elsewhere or give them practical information at this stage.
- A sense of humour (when appropriate) is often a mutual relaxant.
- When beginning, you are simply building a trusting, warm relationship and hearing the client's 'story'.
- Verbal/non-verbal encouragers are often more useful than lots of questions. It is not an interview or an interrogation!
- Keep going for the full length of your session.
- Summarise situation and feelings at end.
- Use the feedback time to learn how others perceive you.
- Be honest but kind in your feedback.

FURTHER READING

Aldridge, S. and Rigby, S. (eds) (2001) *Counselling Skills in Context*. London: Hodder & Stoughton.

Burnard, P. (2005) *Counselling Skills for Health Professionals*. Cheltenham: Nelson Thornes.

Geldard, K. and Geldard, D. (2005) *Practical Counselling Skills an Integrative Approach*. Basingstoke: Palgrave Macmillan.

Hough, M. (2006) *Counselling Skills and Theory*. London: Hodder Arnold.

Joyce, P. and Sills, C. (2001) *Skills in Gestalt Counselling and Psychotherapy*. London: Sage.

Lindon, J. and Lindon, L. (2008) *Mastering Counselling Skills*. Basingstoke: Palgrave Macmillan.

McLeod, J. (2007) *Counselling Skill*. Maidenhead: Open University Press

Nelson-Jones, R. (2009) *Introduction to Counselling Skills: Text and Activities*. London: Sage.

11

Academic Assignments

Academic assignments can be daunting if you are returning to education after some time. Here we will investigate different methods of assessment, why they are used and also include guidelines on how to embark upon them.

Students on counselling courses are often mature adult returners to education so the thought of writing an essay to be submitted for assessment can be considered a challenge at least and a barrier at most. Luckily, the majority of lecturers and tutors are aware of this and additional guidance is usually provided at the beginning of a course until everyone becomes more comfortable with what is expected of them. Just like any other part of the course, the assignments are a learning curve in themselves, making the beginning of any course harder as you are not only having to learn the course content, but also learn how to present it in a format to succeed. Luckily, there are several simple techniques that can help you get it right from the start.

FINDING YOUR BEST TIME TO STUDY

Before putting pen to paper or finger to keyboard, it makes sense to establish the way in which you study best so that you are more likely to be able to focus on your work. Choose the time of day that you find it easiest to concentrate and design a regular study plan around that. For example, most of this book was written between 6.30 and 8.30 in the morning as I am definitely a morning person! If charts or lists help you, use them so that you can keep an accurate record of what you have completed and what is still left to do. Find a private area where you can leave your course work knowing it won't be disturbed when you are at university or college. Where this is will depend upon whether you require a quiet environment on your own or prefer noise and the company of others. If you prefer to use a computer, you need to ensure that a desktop is in the best place for you, whereas a laptop allows freedom to move anywhere. Is it for your sole use or do you share it with others? How you safely store your work may be an issue, so always back up your work. Using a memory stick for this allows you to take a backup of assignments into university or college with you so that you can access them if there is an problem with your paper copy. Another tool that can help with learning is use of a virtual learning environment (VLE) if the course has one. This is an online forum (e.g. Moodle, Blackboard) that students on the course have access to which may have assessment materials, handouts, presentations, etc., along with a communications area where you can e-mail other class members, pose questions, answer questions and generally discuss elements of the course when you are not in class. Although daunting at first, this can be a highly successful way of motivating yourself when at home or feeling isolated. Another method of motivation is to stick an advert for your dream job in your study area so that you are constantly reminded of why you are enrolled on the course. Being aware of the end product or bigger picture helps you keep going by placing each essay in the context of your life plan. Once you have established a support network that you have tailored to meet your study needs, it becomes a lot easier to focus on your work.

ACTIVITY

- Which is your best time to study – morning, afternoon or evening?
- Do you prefer silence or background noise as you work?
- Do you work better surrounded by personal resources or in an isolated environment with fewer distractions?
- Do you type or handwrite notes and assignments?
- Are you able to concentrate more when working alone or with others?

WRITTEN ASSIGNMENTS

There are numerous styles of written assessment such as:

- Essay – answering a set question in detail within a word count
- Report – providing specific information based on facts
- Project – producing collated research on a given topic
- Restricted answer questions – short answers
- Extended answer questions – longer answers
- Reflective account – explaining your personal perception
- Thesis/dissertation – putting forward a theory for extended discussion an extended, structured essay used particularly in higher level courses
- Case study – an in-depth observation and often analysis of a client
- Analysis of recording – either audio or visual (e.g. DVD).

The ability to pass first time is two-fold; first, to be clear as to exactly what the question is asking of you; and second, to ensure that your answer covers all of the points required. The first part is fairly straightforward as you can always ask your tutor to clarify any confusion if necessary, made easier as the majority of courses make the criteria for assessment available beforehand. The second part is your responsibility as a student, although we will look at some useful tools and tips later on to help with this.

Establishing exactly what the question is asking can be one of the most challenging aspects of beginning a written assignment. The most common instructions include the following:

- *Identify* is the briefest request, as you are only asked to ascertain or isolate characteristics of the topic in question. This can sometimes be covered in list format. No detail is required.
- If asked to *describe* you are required to include details of the subject almost as though you are looking at it, so you need to remain objective.
- The request to *examine* an aspect is the equivalent to placing it under a microscope and identifying the details of it. This is often used if more detail is required than simple description.
- *Investigate* involves systematic study, even asking for new aspects of a topic to be considered.
- To *discuss* a topic is to consider different aspects of it. The inclusion of examples is particularly relevant here to demonstrate understanding and application.

- *Evaluate* is to consider two or more aspects of the subject, including the positives and negatives of each.
- *Analyse* is a more advanced skill, as there is a need to dissect the topic and examine it in relation to the context or situation it is placed in.
- *Compare and contrast* expects you to focus on the similarities and differences between two or more elements, which may include positives and negatives of each in relation to the other.
- The *focus* of the theorists relates to the central or most important aspects of the school or approach. This includes the fundamental basis or core beliefs and assumptions within a theory.
- Reference to the *application* is referring to when the approach might be most appropriately or successfully used, e.g. within particular situations or client experiences.
- The *counsellor–client relationship* is asking about the interpersonal interaction and any power issues surrounding those involved; the potential unconscious interactions taking place between individuals within sessions.
- The *counselling process* relates to what actually happens within the sessions; the methods and skills implemented and any stages or progression that may be worked through.
- *Analysing theories in terms of clients' needs* is asking for both the positive and negative aspects of the theory to be assessed in relation to clients' requirements. This may relate to boundary issues and settings or other theoretical or practical issues that might impact upon clients' needs.

So to put this into practice, an example of an essay question might be:

QUESTION:

'The humanistic tradition emphasises the uniqueness of the individual human experience.'

   Explain the historical development of this tradition in relation to main theories, values and assumptions. Within this, you must identify the boundary issues with regard to both settings and models.

2,000 words

Read through the question very carefully. It can be helpful to use a highlighter or underline specific areas to make sure that you focus on them so the question might then look like this:

QUESTION:

'The humanistic tradition emphasises the uniqueness of the individual human experience.'

Explain the historical development of this tradition in relation to main theories, values and assumptions. Within this, you must identify the boundary issues with regard to both settings and models.

The next stage is creating the skeleton for a plan taking cognisance of any word count. There are different methods of doing this, but a simple example would be:

Introduction – 100 words
Historical development of main theories   4 theories for each
Historical development of values   125 words each
Historical development of assumptions   = 500 total each
Boundary issues – settings 100 words
Boundary issues – models 100 words
Conclusion – 100 words

By using the word count as a guide to length of content, it allows you to divide up the content into easily manageable sections, prevents 'waffle', and ensures you remain within the word count from the start. Your plan can be developed into a table (see Table 11.1) so that detail can be added ready to turn into sentences.

Table 11.1 Writing plan in relation to word count

4 main theories:	PCT	Gestalt	TA	Existentialism
125 words on each	Main theories	Main theories	Main theories	Main theories
125 words on each	Values	Values	Values	Values
125 words on each	Assumptions	Assumptions	Assumptions	Assumptions
100 words on each	Boundary issues – settings	Boundary issues – settings	Boundary issues – settings	Boundary issues – settings
100 words on each	Boundary issues – models	Boundary issues – models	Boundary issues – models	Boundary issues – models

Alternatively, mind map techniques are useful if you are more comfortable working with a more graphic or fluid plan. An example of a mind map is shown in Chapter 8, although for this essay title it might resemble Figure 11.1.

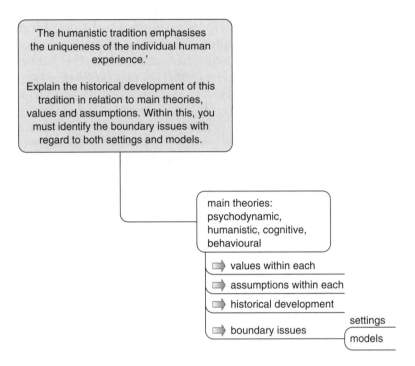

Figure 11.1   Mind map relating to example question

ESSAY STRUCTURE

When the plan is complete and all aspects necessary have been added to it, the content needs to be converted into the essay format using sentences and paragraphs which provide a fluid and connected structure. This is where connecting or linking words and phrases are used which ensure that your sentences are tied in with those before and after to make sense. Words and phrases such as *however, on the other hand, considering this, alternatively* and *with this in mind* can all add a sense of connection to your work and make the difference between a collection of disconnected words and an articulate, structured answer. This applies to paragraphs too.

It is good practice to ensure that the first sentence of a paragraph links in some way with the last sentence of the previous one.

The introduction should 'introduce' the reader to your essay, touching on how you intend to approach or answer the question asked, and at the end your conclusion should reiterate the main points made and tie up any loose ends. It is usual for work to be submitted in 12-point font, justified text, and double spaced to allow for plenty of feedback. Following the conclusion should be the reference section or the bibliography presented in the correct format. These should not be justified or double spaced. Look at the reference section at the back of this book to see how they should be presented, although there are various styles that could be used so do check which one you should follow. Remember to always save a copy (a photocopy if it is handwritten) just in case the original goes missing. This can save a lot of stress in the event of a mishap!

An alternative to an essay question is restricted or short-answer questions, which tend to be used for the identification of specific information and are usually very basic, such as in Figure 11.2

Answer the four questions below:

1. Identify five chemicals or substances that can become addictive:
   a)
   b)
   c)
   d)
   e)

2. Describe each of the five chemicals or substances identified using no more than 100 words each.

3. Identify three behaviours that can become addictive:
   a)
   b)
   c)

4. Describe each of the three behaviours identified above using no more than 100 words each.

Figure 11.2   Example of restricted or short-answer questions

REFERENCES AND BIBLIOGRAPHIES

In academic writing, it is important to ensure that the content of your submissions is in your own words and not copied from another author (which includes from the Internet). Plagiarism, as this is known, is a serious accusation and you can be asked to leave the course if it is believed that you cheated (even unknowingly). Confusion can occur because a balance needs to be achieved between answering a question in your own words but making sure that the content portrays the views, theories and approaches of significant or published theorists. The only exception to this is if you are asked specifically for your own opinion, as in a reflective account. This needs to be balanced with demonstrating your knowledge of the subject through background reading.

Below is an exemplar of a small reference section which includes examples of references sourced from a book, journal, newspaper and website. You will notice that it is listed in alphabetical order according to the surname of the author and adheres to the following formula:

Surname, Initial(s). (date) *Title in Italics*. Place: Publisher.

You may also notice that if it is taken from a book, the *title* is in italics, although if sourced from a journal, the *journal* name is in italics:

Book:
Shapiro, E.R. (1997) *The Inner World in the Outer World: Psychoanalytical Perspectives*. New Haven, CT: Yale University Press.

Chapter in an edited book:
Mearns, D. (1993) 'The Core Conditions', in W. Dryden (ed.), *Questions and Answers on Counselling in Action*. London: Sage.

Journal:
Chu, J.A. (1988) 'Ten Traps for Therapists in the Treatment of Trauma Survivors', *Dissociation*, Vol. 1, No. 4, pp. 24–32 [*or* 1(4), 24–32].

Newspaper:
McLeod, J. (2007) 'Help is Order of the Day', *Herald Society*, 19 June, p. 11.

Website:
Young, R.M. (2002) *How Are We to Work with Conflict of Moral Standpoints in the Therapeutic Relationship?* www.psychoanalysis-and-therapy.com/ human_nature/free-associations/young.html. Accessed 14 May 2007.

There are some excellent websites that will allow you to copy and paste the correct format once you have added the necessary detail required (e.g. www.neilstoolkit.com). Just use a search engine to find others. Otherwise, if the book is taken from the course recommended reading list, simply copy the format from the list you were given.

Summary of main points

- Include evidence of background reading.
- Use the correct format for listing references.
- Write in your own words unless citing a referenced quote.
- If in doubt, ask your tutor.

PRACTICAL DEMONSTRATIONS – ROLE PLAY OR REAL?

As counselling is such a practical and dynamic activity, there is more to training than simply understanding the theoretical foundation behind it. Putting the theory into practice is an equally vital aspect of all courses, and one that can cause anxiety to begin with. If your course demands that you are in a placement and working with clients, it is usual that your practice sessions in class will involve working with your own current and personal issues. However, if your course does not involve an assessed placement, such as a certificate course, practical sessions in class will more likely involve elements of role play where you are given scenarios to work with. An ongoing debate surrounds which is the most appropriate for trainees but there are very clear reasons for both, some of which are provided in Table 11.2.

Hopefully it is becoming clear that there are ethical and safety concerns surrounding both scenario options. The orientation of the course comes into play here too, as a person-centred course may expect the students to develop the theory into their own practice whilst working with real situations. A CBT course may involve the tutor demonstrating specific skills which are then replicated by students to ensure that the methodology is correct and proficient. On any course, a tutor should not ask you to do something that they are not prepared to demonstrate themselves. You should feel supported and guided throughout the course but still recognise that there are elements that you need to work on yourself which the tutor can't provide, such as confidence, experience and placing the learning in the context of your own life. An example of a basic checklist for practical sessions can be found in Chapter 10.

CASE STUDIES

Similarly to the previous section, there are two types of case study; one you are asked to provide on a client you are working or have worked with, the other a written case study you are given and asked questions on. If

Table 11.2 The value of actual versus role-play scenarios

	Reasons for
Actual scenarios	• It is as realistic as possible for a classroom. • The trainee being counsellor witnesses the direct effect their choice of words can have. • Counsellors are working with real clients with real situations, so role play would be a backward step. • Excellent experience of being a client if personal therapy is not a part of the course. • Confidentiality policy must be understood and strictly adhered to.
Role-play scenarios	• Very good for avoiding upset when starting out as not working with potentially upsetting concerns. • No issues surrounding confidentiality. • No indemnity insurance necessary for university or college. • Allows focused practice of specific skills without worries of boundary issues. • The whole class can work with the same scenario, facilitating the opportunity for group discussion.

you are working in placement, you are ethically obliged to ask the chosen client to give their consent to being used in such a way. Once permission is granted, remember to allocate them a fictitious name and don't include any associated information as a safeguard to ensuring their identity is protected. An example of the second method, being given a written case study to answer questions on, is provided below. The purpose of these is to provide an opportunity for assessing the ability to link theory with practice. You may be good at theoretical essays or practical work, but case studies are an excellent tool for connecting these together at the same time as providing evidence that can be marked.

EXAMPLE OF CASE STUDY WITH QUESTIONS FOR TRAINEE

Natalie Parker is 19 and lives in the family home with her mother, father and younger brother, Dominic. Both parents are teachers and work full-time. Natalie started smoking cannabis at the age of 15 just prior to sitting her standard grades. She was expected to be a high achiever and progress to university but started mixing with peers who had a negative effect upon her life. She stopped attending school around this time. On a regular basis, Natalie returns home stoned and Dominic has been covering up for her to prevent the inevitable arguments that would follow.

Brian Parker, Natalie's Dad, is 47 and teaches physics at a private school several miles away. Brian is fairly relaxed about Natalie's use of drugs, seeing them as 'recreational'

(Continued)

(Continued)

and saying that it reminds him of his own behaviour when he was an adolescent. He is convinced that Natalie will grow out of this phase soon and complete her education.

Natalie has only had occasional part-time jobs since dropping out of school, having been dismissed for poor time-keeping and regular sickness days. She is not currently receiving benefits because of this and relies on her parents for financial support, which has also caused problems as Angela, Natalie's mother, constantly questions her about how she spends her money. Occasionally, Brian has given Natalie additional money despite Angela forbidding it.

Angela is 46 and is an Assistant Head Teacher at the school Natalie was attending. Despite expectations, Angela was not awarded the Head Teacher post when the previous Head retired, and feels this is a direct result of Natalie's behaviour and reputation.

Dominic is 15 and is doing fairly well at the school his Mum works at, yet feels neglected at home. He has been lying to protect Natalie and feels ignored and rejected by his mother, who is constantly in a state of high anxiety about Natalie. He is growing resentful of Natalie's behaviour but continues to cover for her and collude in the hope of them establishing a co-conspiritorial relationship. Natalie is no longer the best friend he once saw her as when they were younger; instead she is withdrawn, distant and irritable. He knows that she often steals his earnings from his paper round but hasn't mentioned it to her yet as he is scared she will be even more horrible towards him. When he has the money, he buys Buckfast to drink with his friend Joe at the local swing park, but because Natalie is taking his money, he has started stealing vodka from the drinks cabinet in Brian's study.

Yesterday, Natalie was arrested whilst shoplifting.

READ THE ATTACHED CASE STUDY AND:

- Discuss the family systems approach with regard to substance- and alcohol-related issues.
- Examine the debate surrounding co-dependency.
- Apply the family dysfunction model to the client situation.
- Apply the theory of family adjustment to alcohol and substance misuse in the client situation.

[*This assignment should be approximately 2,000 words in length.*]

INTERPERSONAL CONNECTIONS

Counselling is based on relationships and it is hoped that a successful counsellor is more likely to have successful relationships. This is due to the importance of communication and understanding of others, which is inherent to the process. How we communicate with others can be hard to assess, which is why tutors monitor classroom interaction. We are not studying in isolation on counselling courses but have colleagues or fellow students who are working through the process with us. Many course tutors are very vigilant of inter-student relationships and weave classroom interactions into assessment of personal development. Examples of such activities are discussed in Chapter 7, but how these are evaluated is interesting. Reflective accounts are used to encourage discussion of your internal world, to provide insight into your learning process. Personal development groups can demonstrate interpersonal behaviours but are harder to assess. Examples of criteria for assessment are:

- Communication of core conditions
- Offer constructive feedback
- Distinguish between enabling and rescuing
- Maintain appropriate boundaries, especially confidentiality
- Adhere to agreed group rules
- Personal development
- Relationship with other members
- Relationship with group facilitator
- Feedback input
- Own participation
- Taking responsibility
- Openness to learn
- Openness to feedback
- Resistance
- Relationship with group
- Reaction to conflict
- Reaction to emotion
- Collusion
- Fear of rejection
- Scapegoating
- Dependence.

PERSONAL DEVELOPMENT

Chapter 7 deals with personal development as a concept, so the focus here is on the dilemma surrounding the use of personal development as an assessment tool; is it ethical to evaluate an individual on this element of a course as opposed to purely their academic ability and practical demonstration? Initially, the fear of being 'marked down' can impinge on students' decisions surrounding levels of honesty and openness. A fear of 'if they really knew what I was thinking/feeling, there is no way I would pass', the logic of which is completely understandable. However, this doubt and questioning is one of the core components of personal development; if you don't do it, you aren't developing. Tutors are observing and encouraging levels of openness, genuineness and awareness which, by definition, must include uncertainty, scepticism and misgivings at some point. This is a natural process and what you may perceive as negativity is often viewed by tutor, supervisors and peers as self-questioning leading to self-discovery – a negative turning into a positive. Consider learning to drive: if you tried to pretend that you knew everything already, the instructor would be bound to notice – it would be obvious when you struggled with gear changes or forgot to look in the mirror. In counselling training, we are going through the same process of learning except it is internal, so by talking about our struggles, the instructor (tutor) can help.

WHO ASSESSES?

If assignments are designed to measure your level of skill or knowledge, who is qualified to make that decision? This depends on the orientation, level and approval body of the course you are on. For example, self- and peer assessment are more common on person-centred courses where the perception of the individual themselves takes more of a centre stage. Universities have more flexibility and so are more able to utilise these approaches, whereas colleges are more likely to use tutor assessment. This is because the approval bodies who verify counselling awards are more traditional in their requirement for evidence of standards (i.e. essays and checklists). Decisions are made by staff, peers, placement supervisor, counselling supervisor or self, and each has its strengths and weaknesses:

- *Staff* are able to make an objective evaluation based on comparing standards to set criteria.
- *Peers* are able to provide an interpersonal, subjective, sometimes challenging viewpoint.
- *Placement supervisor* is able to evaluate from the context of a working relationship, a totally different angle, including feedback from clients, colleagues, etc.
- *Counselling supervisor* is controversial in the same way that assessment of personal development can be; however, it can also provide excellent insight into both internal and external frameworks of the student.
- *Self-assessment* allows for self-awareness, honesty and the valuing of personal opinion.

In conclusion, academic assignments might be daunting but unless you are drawn out of your comfort zone and put to the test in different ways, you will remain at your previous level of ability. Once you fathom out the requirements, have a go and receive some feedback from your tutors and lecturers, you may well surprise yourself!

FURTHER READING

Bor, R. and Watts, M. (eds) (2006) *The Trainee Handbook*. London: Sage.

Cottrell, S. (2003) *The Study Skills Handbook*. Basingstoke: Palgrave Macmillan.

Rose, J. (2007) *The Mature Student's Guide to Writing*. Basingstoke: Palgrave Macmillan.

Sanders, P. (2003) *Step in to Counselling: A Students' Guide to Learning Counselling and Tackling Course Assignments*. Ross-on-Wye: PCCS Books.

12

Ethical and Legal Issues

Here we will start by looking at the dos and don'ts or ethical issues within the counselling relationship, particularly the maintenance of boundaries, before moving on to consider the wider legal implications. The value of ethical practice within the course group will also be discussed. Ethical considerations within research practice are covered within Chapter 16.

This is a far-reaching topic which is much discussed, debated and updated. As such, many books are available on the different aspects, so this will be a broad overview of some of the major issues. Checking with your accrediting body, course tutor, supervisor and placement policies and procedures should provide you with answers concerning any specific issues that you would like to be clarified.

WHAT DO WE MEAN BY 'ETHICS'?

At the heart of sound counselling practice must lie a framework of respect, care and sensitivity toward others to ensure that we are working to the highest professional standard. This guarantees that care of self, care of client and care of colleagues are all part of this structure, based upon personal and professional moral values, principles and qualities. Rowson explains ethical principles as being 'the rules which people are committed to because they see them as embodying their values and justifying their moral judgements' (2001: 9).

THE ROLE OF ETHICS IN PRACTICE

So that we protect our self and our client, we need to adhere to a set of guidelines that are designed specifically for the therapeutic relationship to ensure that we are accountable for our actions. If we are challenged, we then know that we behaved in a professional and considered manner that we are able to justify. The ongoing self-questioning of our actions, decisions and feelings in this area is a continual process, and a very healthy one. The attitude of 'I am absolutely right and you are absolutely wrong' would sit comfortably in few counselling approaches.

ESTABLISHING BOUNDARIES

Whilst working therapeutically with a client, trust is a crucial element of the relationship; without trust there can be no true opening up of feelings, and congruence would not be present. Although there is no exact formula to gain trust, being able to demonstrate honesty and openness are key aspects which are guided by our ethical guidelines.

Rather than simply being an abstract concept, a combination of ethical guidelines and clear boundaries provide the framework in which to work in safely. 'Boundaries' simply relate to the external or the management aspects of the counselling relationship. Ethical guidelines instruct us in respect of this as well as in the practice of counselling itself. Being transparent and explaining this right at the start so that the client is aware of our boundaries will impact upon both the retention of the client in the service and increase their understanding of the process. The major aspects include:

- *Contracts*: Depending on the theoretical orientation you are working within, contracts can take on different roles. For example, if you are working with transactional analysis, or in some instances CBT, then contracts may be a fundamental aspect of your relationship with your client. However, the vast majority of counselling relationships begin with some form of contract, even if it is just negotiating the number of sessions with your client. Often this process is referred to as an 'assessment' or 'first meeting'; no formal counselling takes place but information is exchanged. The counsellor may provide information on the service that they provide, explaining several relevant boundary issues, and the client may give a brief overview of their situation. At the end, both either agree to work together or consider alternatives.
- *Confidentiality*: This is not as straightforward as you might think, and much has been written about its use when working with vulnerable people. Basically,

there are several different types depending upon the service, mainly total, agreed and shared. Total confidentiality may sound appropriate at first glance, but is not used in counselling in case a client divulges information that indicates they are a risk to themselves or others. If you have already promised to keep the session totally confidential, you are placing yourself in a difficult position with regard to the law. Agencies have their own policies and procedures about how to deal with this, but legally this information cannot be kept confidential and must be passed on to the appropriate person or service. Usually this is with the knowledge but not always the agreement of the client, and is referred to as 'agreed confidentiality' and is commonly used when working in a voluntary or private practice. Alternatively, shared confidentiality is usual practice when working within a care team where other professionals who are also involved with your client have access to case notes and are present at case conferences when treatments and progress are discussed. The client should always be made aware of the confidentiality policy within the initial contracting session.

- *Beginnings and endings*: This can refer to either the beginning and ending of a session, or alternatively the beginning and ending of a course of sessions. Both can be sources of concern for a client, so clarity, discussion and openness are important to reduce potential worries, dependency or avoidance (see Further Reading).
- *Referral*: The ease of this depends upon the setting in which you work. Within the statutory sector, referral is quite common, and within the voluntary sector, slightly less so. Use of the core conditions and CPD should reduce the need for referral to another counsellor. The sensitivity with which this is discussed is crucial when the difficulty is exacerbated by the fact that whilst you may feel you are doing your best for the care of your client, their perception of referral might be 'my situation is so difficult that even my counsellor can't work with me', which has the potential of causing significant harm.
- *Monitoring and evaluation through reflective practice*: Almost all care professions require practitioners to contemplate their day-to-day routines, evaluate their success and understand their impact upon those around them; both colleagues and clients. A range of techniques or tools are used for this including reflective accounts, personal journal, attending peer support groups, encouraging feedback, 360° reviews and supervision.
- *Supervision*: This is crucial in the monitoring not only of the counsellor and their practice but also as a sounding-board for clarification of boundary issues. Apart from you and your client, your counselling supervisor is closer to your client relationship than anyone else and is the appropriate person to open up to with regard to your concerns. Chapter 14 includes more detail.
- *Education and training*: Your period of study, qualifications and experience are all relevant to your ability and confidence when working with exposed clients.

Some organisations insist on certificates being on show to reinforce the professionalism and training standards of counsellor, although this is challenged by more humanistic models where the client is very much seen as the expert. Historically, when counselling was more medicalised, having certificates on view was to be expected to give peace of mind to clients. CPD is good practice and a necessary aspect of being a counsellor for several reasons: first, along with other professions, it is essential to keep up to date with new approaches, research findings and developments within the sector. Second, a wider understanding directly improves client work. They offer networking opportunities which are of particular value to counsellors working in isolation, and the experience of progressing knowledge and understanding is a core element of personal development.

- *Number of sessions*: This often varies depending upon the orientation you are working within. For example, counsellors working within a person-centred model are more likely to discuss openly and negotiate the length of the therapeutic alliance, whereas other approaches, such as CBT, might be clearly defined at the start due to referral, funding or service options. The analytical manner of many psychodynamic methodologies are significantly more intensive and, as such, can last for a considerably longer period; clients attending sessions for up to 20 years has been known. However, financial considerations play a part and many GPs fund 6–8 general counselling sessions initially, with an option of evaluation and extension at the end. The length of time working with a client can raise ethical issues for several reasons, such as who makes the decision that the client is ready to finish, what if the client develops a dependency on the process, or if a counsellor in private practice is relying on the financial income. This is another area in which regular supervision becomes invaluable.

- *Timing of sessions*: Much like above, the frequency of sessions is dependent upon the orientation of the counsellor. Once or twice weekly are the most usual, but psychoanalytical therapists can work with clients up to five sessions weekly. Non-directive counsellors are more likely to negotiate this with a client during the contracting session at the start, whereas counsellors working within directive models tend to be more prescriptive.

- *Orientation*: The theoretical basis on which you base your practice is included as a boundary issue because, during the first meeting, there is often a matching exercise taking place between counsellor and potential new client. This process involves the client considering whether the modality within which you work and the methods implemented sit comfortably with them, and if they sound as though they might work. For example, a very structured and methodical client might prefer to work within a clear framework of directive therapy, whereas a client who is more introspective and is searching for understanding might opt for an approach that is reflective and non-directive.

EXAMPLE

Fiona and her husband Sam had been married for 22 years but divorced over two years ago. Fiona felt extremely betrayed and still talked constantly of her hate for Sam. As this continued without sign of abating, Fiona's friend suggested she attend counselling. Fiona made an appointment with a cognitive therapist in private practice and attended the first session willingly. When the therapist suggested that they progress without mentioning Sam but concentrated purely on Fiona's inner world, she refused to accept this and failed to make a second appointment. (*Fiona viewed herself as a victim and this directive approach was moving her on before she felt ready to acknowledge her independence. A more reflective approach might have had a different outcome.*)

- *Settings*: Whether you are working within the voluntary, statutory or private setting dictates the flexibility of negotiation regarding boundary issues in numerous ways depending upon the policies, procedures, staffing and funding in place. Chapter 5 discusses this in detail.
- *Dual relationships*: This is almost unavoidable if you are based within a rural location or are one of few local counselling services. It is unacceptable to work therapeutically with a client who you know, such as a friend, colleague or family member. Because of this, issues surrounding dual relationships tend to only emerge with current or past clients – not future ones, as they can't be clients if you already know them.

  Examples of ethically problematic relationships might include bumping into a client who is involved with the same school or church or they may work in a local shop. This can be dealt with successfully if potential awkward situations are discussed during the contracting session or are included in the counselling contract (see Figure 12.1). This ensures that you do not feel compromised and the client does not feel ignored or rebuffed should a meeting happen. More prolonged contact such as sitting on the same public committee or some other community setting should be openly discussed with the client at the next session, and also taken to supervision. Balancing professional boundaries whilst maintaining a secure and positive working relationship can be very difficult.
- *Record keeping*: Not always classed as a boundary issue, but ensuring you use and update appropriate paperwork is a crucial element of practice. This might involve an initial contract, some form of evaluation tool (such as CORE-OM) and regular case notes. These maybe accessed by other members of the care team (see *Confidentiality*) or in an extreme case maybe requested by a court. Therefore, they should be current, accurate, detailed and professionally appropriate.

Our relationship

To maintain privacy, if we meet outside the sessions accidently, I will not acknowledge you unless you acknowledge me first.

You will only be contacted by your chosen method. You have chosen

<u>texting your</u>
<u>mobile number</u>

It would not be appropriate to discuss any issues outside the arranged sessions.

Figure 12.1   Example extract from a counselling contract

- *Storing notes*: When notes are kept on clients, secure storage and restricted access are both issues on which the client may require clarification. It is usual for notes to be identifiable by code rather than name, to be stored in a locked cupboard and often within a locked room. Many organisational policies only allow staff with direct therapeutic involvement with that client to access the notes, which may have to be signed for. More specific guidance regarding data protection can be found within the texts listed in Further Reading at the end of this chapter.
- *Competence*: As a counsellor, you need to be able to prove that you are proficient in the role. This is not simply evidence of your certificates from training but also requires regular review to ensure that you are keeping up to date. Maintaining a CPD log, where you collate all your ongoing learning activities, is the most common method. There are further suggestions for a range of methods to update your knowledge and skills in Chapter 19.

If you are unsure of any of these boundaries, discuss your questions with your course tutor, supervisor or line manager, who should be able to clarify the situation and explain the reason for this.

ACTIVITY

- Why are confidentiality, referral, supervision and ethics necessary boundary issues within counselling environments?
- Why, in your opinion, is training so important before working with clients?
- How can the setting and orientation influence the client's needs? Think of two examples of each to illustrate your point.
- How do you intend to maintain your own professional development?

THE LAW AND COUNSELLING

A detailed inventory of the legal responsibilities of counsellors are provided by most accrediting and professional bodies within their ethical framework. To give an example, the BACP ethical framework states clearly that the practitioners should adhere to the following ethical principles:

- *Fidelity:*   honouring the trust placed in the practitioner.
- *Autonomy:*   respect for the client's right to be self-governing.
- *Beneficence:*   a commitment to promoting the client's well-being.
- *Non-maleficence:* a commitment to avoiding harm to the client.
- *Justice:*   the fair and impartial treatment of all clients and the provision of adequate services.
- *Self-respect:*   fostering the practitioner's self-knowledge and care for self.

(BACP, 2009a)[1]

In addition to this, they identify three areas that complaints can be raised against: professional misconduct; professional malpractice; and bringing the profession into disrepute (BACP, 2009a), which leads nicely onto the next focus!

INSURANCE

Professional indemnity insurance is recommended for all practising counsellors and counselling services. This may be provided by your employer if you are working within a counselling agency or organisation.

---

[1] © BACP (www.bacp.co.uk/admin/structure/files/pdf/566_ethical%20framework%20feb2010.pdf). This information is regularly updated and all up-to-date material can be found on the BACP website.

As you may be starting to realise, the purpose of insurance cover is to increase safety of your working practice, both for you and the client, so that if the worst did come to the worst, you would have legal and financial backing. Such insurance provides highly valuable security that will hopefully never be required. There are numerous companies that offer such cover, and their adverts are often placed in professional journals.

POLICIES AND PROCEDURES

If you are working within an agency or organisation, the importance of their policies and procedures documentation can't be emphasised highly enough. Take time to read them carefully and understand them, as it a luxury to have these provided for you. However, don't forget that you are still ultimately responsible for your own actions. They will cover complex issues such as shared confidentiality, complaints procedure and appropriate referral. Most organisations require a very clear course of action in the case of a complaint (either by a client or by a colleague), and these need to be followed exactly.

MAINTENANCE OF BOUNDARIES

Or how the 'rules' are adhered to. One of the great strengths of professional boundaries is that they are always an ongoing process, a work in progress, so needs to be regularly reviewed and updated if necessary. This is due to circumstances such as regular changes in the law, new discoveries and developments in practice and organisational changes.

It's not so much a case of managing boundaries but being very aware of what they are, where they are and making sure that we remain within them. If we overstep a boundary, as with any spectrum, the consequences depend very much on the circumstances. To one extreme, we may feel unsure or uncomfortable with our actions (or those of the client), which we then discuss in supervision and then feel supported and eventually a sense of relief. At the other end of the scale, we might find we lose our accreditation or even that a legal case ensues, although that would usually result from gross misconduct.

THE ROLE OF ETHICS ON YOUR COURSE

First, we need to determine the difference between learning about counselling for professional or personal interest as opposed to enrolling on a class as an

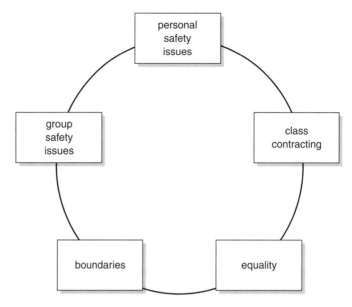

Figure 12.2   Safety aspects for consideration

alternative to attending counselling. A professional counselling course is an educational process which should include personal development and in insight into therapeutic change, but is not a substitute for personal counselling. Before being offered a place on a counselling course, the interview process, whether individual or group, is designed to establish your motivation for wanting to study counselling. Although most interviewers strive to avoid the role of 'gatekeeper', they do have a responsibility to ensure that applicants are wanting to learn about counselling and not actually substituting the course for attending counselling. This can be a fine line but it is imperative that it is recognised to ensure the safety of the group (see Figure 12.2).

As previously mentioned, having a clear understanding of the balance between the educational and therapeutic aspects of your course can be challenging. Just like therapeutic sessions, training courses are also required to adhere to ethical guidelines.

These are maintained in a range of ways, an obvious example being that if you are studying an introductory course, you may be required to use role play in your practice sessions until your skills are proficient enough to deal with any issues that arise (sometimes this can also relate to insurance requirements). This is designed for protection: to allow you to develop your skills without the fear of saying something that might deeply hurt or upset your 'client'. Essentially, you are both protected until you or your tutor feel you are ready to engage with genuine issues.

WHAT BOUNDARIES ARE THERE IN THE CONTEXT OF A COUNSELLING COURSE?

Clearly, the most important boundary is with regard to safety issues (e.g. confidentiality), to be in no doubt that the learning environment is safe and that no damage is done in the confines of the classroom or student group. This is often achieved through class contracting, whereby the group negotiate and establish their own group rules at the start of the course. This allows for a discussion regarding the equality and culture within the course group and provides a negotiable boundary in which to work comfortably in much the same way that initial contracting with a client does. This should cover both major and minor boundaries, although there might be future changes once everyone becomes better acquainted and possibly discover better ways of working together.

ACTIVITY

Finally, what might you do if you were faced with any of these challenging scenarios? They all include issues that might challenge your personal moral or ethical code to varying degrees:

- You are in your fourth session with 17-year-old Sofia when she discloses that she has been self-harming by cutting her arms with a razor blade. She says that she has told her mother, who is monitoring the situation at home.
- Jim, an elderly client is the main carer for his spouse who is terminally ill. He wants to discuss with you how he could help relieve his partner's pain. You suspect he is referring to assisted suicide.
- Sarah, a client who you have just started working with, tells you that she is registered as unemployed to receive DSS benefits, but you know she is also working in a pub.
- You have been working with Jean for three months when she starts to talk about her sister. Her sister sounds very like your mother's cousin who you have only met once, shares the same name as her and lives in the same town.
- The large counselling practice that has just offered you a job has a communal waiting room where clients sit together before their sessions.

The decisions you have to make in the above Activity should be influenced by legal rules and moral guidelines. Hopefully, your answer involves an open and honest conversation with the client before making a decision and includes a discussion with your counselling supervisor.

FURTHER READING

Bond, T. (2009) *Standards and Ethics for Counselling in Action*, 3rd edn. London: Sage.

Bond, T. and Mitchels, B. (2008) *Confidentiality and Record-keeping in Counselling and Psychotherapy*. London: Sage.

Dryden, W. and Reeves, A. (eds) (2008) *Key Issues for Counselling in Action*. London: Sage.

Palmer, F. and Murdin, L. (eds) (2001) *Values and Ethics in the Practice of Psychotherapy and Counselling*. London: Open University Press.

Sills, C. (ed.) (2006) *Contracts in Counselling and Psychotherapy*. London: Sage.

Also, accrediting bodies such as the BACP have their ethical guidelines available online.

13

Relational Issues

Counselling is fundamentally about communicating positively with others so this chapter will consider counselling relationships within two distinct contexts; first, with our colleagues on a counselling course and second, within the therapeutic relationship.

ARE FELLOW STUDENTS FRIENDS OR COLLEAGUES?

Being part of a counselling course can introduce some issues that you might not have considered before. Many of the issues and circumstances that often arise in a counselling course are actually similar issues and circumstances that may arise in a counselling relationship. Such parallels mainly include the boundary issues, interpersonal or relational aspects and how you perceive yourself in the relationship. There are both advantages and disadvantages of being part of a course where relationships are more important than when studying other subjects, such as computing or maths. The level of disclosure and depth of discussion has the potential to lead to blurring of both boundaries and interpersonal connections. Finding the appropriate balance on the course between it being an educational experience and also a personal journey can be a source of anxiety for some people for many reasons; a selection of the main ones are outlined below (see also Figure 13.1):

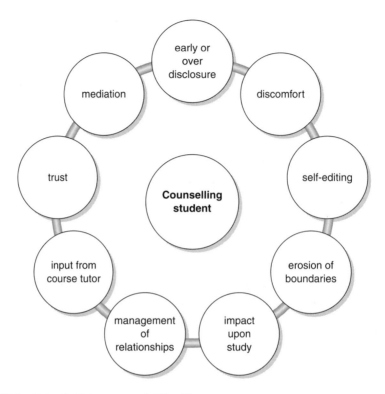

Figure 13.1   Potential interpersonal difficulties

- *Early or over disclosure*: sharing personal information before establishing whether the group is safe or not and, of course, not being able to retract it.
- *Discomfort*: either with own contribution or with that of others.
- *Self-editing*: the ability (or lack of) to control what you say as a result of an internal decision-making process.
- *Erosion of boundaries*: such as confidentiality if group content is discussed during breaks or lack or trust if cliques develop.
- *Impact upon study*: emphasis upon the personal and interpersonal can be uncomfortable for a student who is used to more mainstream methods of study.
- *Management of relationships*: there is considerable overlap here between the roles of friends, colleagues, co-counsellors or fellow students.
- *Input from course tutor*: may initially sound positive but can actually prevent self-management and development by inhibiting members taking responsibility or having to negotiate appropriate solutions.

- *Trust*: is an essential component of a course if the experiential elements are to be used as a learning tool.
- *Mediation*: who is the mediator? Is this expected of the tutor or lecturers or is it a shared responsibility? Acknowledging that accountability and responsibility need to be developed and cannot be taught is a valuable lesson in itself.

ACTIVITY

Identify within your journal your reflections upon your learning group and personal development group, and your thoughts and feelings regarding members, roles adopted and your personal roles and contribution. You might also consider issues such as power balance, confidence, trust and dominance.

What if we fall out?

All of the points identified above can make the experience of attending university or college uncomfortable and, in some cases, lead to withdrawal from the course. However, if they are viewed as a learning experience and the resolution comes from the group and not from input from the course tutor, there is enormous learning potential. If one is unable to negotiate or mediate with co-students, there is little evidence to support them being able to do the same with a client, never mind when facilitating a group. Being able to handle the downs as well as the ups shows a more rounded character who is able to contextualise situations rather than simply personalise them – a valuable skill. It could even be argued that a smooth, harmonious course with no disagreements or disputes would not provide the opportunity to experience conflict in a safe and controlled environment to practise responses.

How does this help me become a counsellor?

The experience of managing or witnessing the development of relationships throughout the course provides a wide range of encounters accompanied by a greater depth of understanding. This knowledge provides insight into the workings of interaction and associations that inform our practice as counsellors. The course is, in essence, a practice run for understanding, supporting and working with others. Along with our value base, attitudes and ethics, this underpins our professionalism. Of course, it isn't all interpersonal development as your intrapersonal reflective journal plays a significant role here too. Experience and insight help us make sound decisions and judgements in situations that involve boundary, ethical and safety matters.

Formal or informal

Now that we have established that the class is a group in which to practise positive communication and supportive relationships, there are some additional aspects to consider. Although most of your time together is timetabled, structured and therefore fairly formal, there is also a significant proportion that is informal, for example during breaks, study groups and also social occasions. This is where the impact of cliques and factions upon group development and cohesion can detract from successful working and the overall purpose of the group. It may be more comfortable to remain with those who you feel you have more in common with, but it may also be simply remaining within your comfort zone and not testing your own ability to mix, accept and enjoy the company of those who you are not initially drawn to. As long as we are cognisant of the core conditions and sensitive to the guidelines supporting the group, our relationships should be safe and encouraging. The importance of this is that even activities such as socialising during breaks should still be regulated by the core boundaries of the group.

How might a group develop?

Despite groups being made up of selection of individuals with a shared goal, as groups evolve they tend to follow rather predictable routes. There have been many theorists who have studied stages of group development (Hough, 2006; Tuckman and Jensen, 1977; Yalom, 1985) and the majority are based on the elements of the initial creation, the management structure, members working successfully towards a goal and acknowledgement of some form of conclusion. These are laid out in Table 13.1.

This table illustrates that when you first join any group (consider for example your counselling class, which is a group) there is a shared sense of anxiety, politeness and orientation which can result in us being drawn to an individual to sit beside or talk to. Most, but not all, groups experience a second stage, which can involve disagreement, challenging and upset, and is a key period for members to either drop out or remain. The studies recognise at this point the ability of a group to find their feet, establish a successful routine and start working together. When a group has reached the end of its time (in this instance when

Table 13.1   Stages of group development

	Yalom (1985)	Tuckman (1965)	Hough (2006)
Initial stage	Orientation Hesitant participation Search for meaning Dependency	Forming	Anxiety
Second stage	Conflict Dominance Rebellion	Storming	Discord
Third stage	Development of cohesiveness	Norming	Trust
Fourth stage		Performing	Commitment
Fifth stage		(Mourning, adjourning)	Closure

members have completed the course) there can be a shared feeling of sadness as a core structure within the members' lives is coming to an end. Your lecturers will be aware of this ongoing process and will ensure that tasks and exercises are appropriate to the stage your group is at.

Methods of communication

Within your class group, there will be opportunities for different methods of communication. These might be formal, as in essays, presentations and counselling practice, or informal methods of contact, such as discussions and group work. Each can have a powerful impact upon the group as a whole, depending on whether they are framed in a positive or a negative manner. For example, if a member of your group is constantly complaining that they don't understand a current topic, the way that this is handled by other members of the group will result in either a supportive and trusting environment or a critical and judgemental one. This in turn will create pause for thought before others feel safe enough to share a personal concern. Clearly, we all have to take responsibility for our own learning, but how we choose to respond to others during this time does have an impact on them and us, and of course your tutor will be observing and noting how you communicate too.

Hints and tips for classroom communication

- Allow the person talking to complete what they are saying.
- Avoid jumping in with solutions.

- Focus on their feelings and experience, not your own.
- Avoid personalising everyone else's contribution (i.e. 'that happened to me too').
- Practise the core conditions.
- Become comfortable with silence.
- Concentrate on the person talking, including observing their body language.
- Use language appropriate to the environment.
- Self-edit (i.e. respond when you have considered your response).
- Consider links between theory and practice.

This applies to communicating with course lecturers and tutors too. Questions that clarify trains of thought or theoretical applications can often be useful if focused around contextualising a concept, such as through the use of examples. Always ensure you are comfortable with a new piece of information before moving on. Another suggestion would be to ask about theorists in this area so you are able to take notes which will help when it comes to writing assignments.

How you integrate with other students

During your course, your security and skills will develop over time and you will find that you begin to contribute, share and disclose in different ways. As far back as 1977, Gerard Egan identified different roles for group members that you might witness or adopt. These are usually temporary, with individuals tending to adopt different functions during different meetings of the group, so any individual's role will evolve and change over time. The 'detractor' is a member who disparages or devalues something or somebody, so has a negative input. An observer is a member who is more comfortable watching individuals and developments or interactions rather than taking an interactive role. A participant is a member who takes an active and involved role. Contributors are members who supply content and material to be discussed. The leader can be formal or informal and is a member who guides or directs others by showing them the way or telling them how to behave. Interestingly, Egan (1977) also felt that for a successful group, leadership and participation should be a shared experience.

ACTIVITY

Some of the issues below may arise during the development of your class group and it is helpful for you to consider how you may deal with each in a positive way:

collusion	own participation
dependence	reaction to conflict
disclosure	reaction to emotion
discomfort	relationship with facilitator
fear of rejection	relationship with group members
friendships	resistance
openness to feedback	scapegoating
openness to learn	taking responsibility

Purpose and practical use

Groups are used in an educational environment because the benefit of this upon a therapeutic environment can be considerable. This increased emphasis on experiential learning engages the student in a very personal and unique way, aiding the transition of theoretical knowledge to personal familiarity through regular practice. There are clear commonalities between how we are with co-students and how we communicate in general, and several studies have been conducted into the evaluation of personal development groups within counselling training (Small and Manthei, 1988; Izzard and Wheeler, 1994). The benefit to the student taking part in what is essentially a non-assessed experiential activity is outlined by O'Leary et al. (1994), who identified five significant components of growth resulting from involvement with personal development groups on counselling training courses. These components are self-awareness, congruence, spirituality, attention to positive and negative feelings, and the perception of growth as a dynamic process, which are valuable growth aspects in becoming a counsellor. As for the facilitator, Wheeler (1996: 81) observes that 'a well-trained group facilitator will be in an ideal position to comment on the way someone interacts with others, how open they are to feedback, how they manage feedback and how clear they are in communicating with others'. Therefore, the experience within a safe group setting allows students to experience many of the fears that clients face: concerns regarding trust, self-disclosure, self-editing and how sensitively they will be received by others. Learning takes place simultaneously in different ways in different parts of the brain, so the use of personal development groups can introduce theoretical influence, emotional responses, physical reactions, cultural differences and commonalities with professional practice. General student feedback has identified a resistance to this less formal method of delivery where considerably more responsibility lies with the student and there is a requirement for a deeper level of engagement.

The influence of orientation upon group development

'Group dynamics is best experienced and understood in groups rather than as a dry academic subject ... experiential learning' (Sanders, 2003: 14). How can you know what it is to be genuine and congruent if you have never really tried it with others? If your course does not include personal therapy or co-counselling, this integration should hopefully reduce any differences between the purely academic and subsequent exercises and thus embed theory within practice, reinforcing unconscious links in preparation for work with clients. However, not all training courses acknowledge unconscious links, as the theoretical orientation underpinning the course both influences and impacts upon the management of group work within the counselling training. For example, psychodynamic courses would ensure their groups are facilitated by an external facilitator/supervisor rather than a course tutor or lecturer to reduce the transference issues that can arise with an authority figure (Johns, 1996; Wheeler, 1996). A person-centred course would be more likely to avoid formal facilitation in preference to free-flowing encounter groups to encourage real connectedness between individuals and to allow for the experiential benefits of immersion within the dialogue of others.

Other orientations use differing methodologies, such as the use of an empty chair in Gestalt groups, although these are often used on integrative courses too to expand the options available.

THE CLIENT–COUNSELLOR RELATIONSHIP

The level with which we relate to our clients could be viewed as a scale or continuum as we are constantly sliding along the various levels of understanding (see Figure 13.2). Once experience of connectedness with fellow students has been gained within the classroom, it is then possible to gain a sense of the different levels achievable within a therapeutic alliance. Much has been written about the therapeutic bond that is central to successful counselling. It was Dave Mearns who, in 1996, first coined the term 'relational depth' as a way of working at the most engaged level. This isn't simply a condition for the counsellor, but rather refers to both client and counsellor being able to connect with each other on a deeper level. The amalgamation of Rogers' core conditions of empathy, congruence and unconditional positive regard is a necessary component, but successfully achieving such relational connectivity

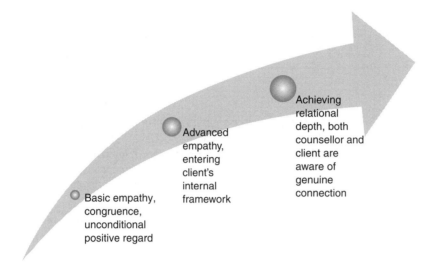

Figure 13.2 Developing client–counsellor relationship

requires more. Cooper (2008) describes this using the terms 'receptivity' and 'expressivity'; a reciprocal experience involving our willingness to be affected or moved by another with the capacity to share or give back. It is not possible to provide a prescriptive guide here as to how to achieve this additional depth, as it occurs when the counsellor and client are making a real connection without concentrating on the use of skills or proficiency; it is more to do with letting go and entering the realm of the client who in turn is aware of this intense understanding. Carkhuff (1969) developed a useful tool for measuring use of core conditions (see Chapter 10), but unfortunately it is not possible to design a similar tool for measuring such a unique connection within the relationship, which is essentially a shared encounter rather than an individual experience.

Theoretical orientation

Although the terminology and documentation of relational depth fall mainly within the humanistic model of counselling, and person centred in particular, be aware that this isn't exclusive. There are many methods of counselling that involve a shared understanding and alliance where this is equally as relevant. Even more directive or analytical orientations have practitioners who incorporate core conditions and as such place their practice on the continuum of deeper connectedness too.

ACTIVITY

Consider your personal experiences in counselling, either as a client or as a counsellor. Have there been any moments when you have felt that a strong connection was formed or that you were totally understood? Alternatively, have there been any moments where there was a clear lack of insight or comprehension? It may be helpful to document this process in your personal development journal if you keep one.

FURTHER READING

Merry, T. (2002) *Learning and Being in Person-centred Counselling*. Ross-on-Wye: PCCS Books.

14

Supervision and Support

The roles of monitoring, supervision and support are crucial to a counsellor both in training and in practice for many reasons, some of which we will examine in this chapter. Areas such as the debate surrounding the role of personal counselling, what supervision is, why it is necessary and how it can impact upon our practise are all covered.

PERSONAL COUNSELLING

There is little evidence to support personal therapy during counselling training (Aveline, 2007), although feedback from students supports it as a positive learning activity. Hough (2006) identified personal therapy as being useful for encouraging exploration of emotional life, forming a link between theory and practice, leading to a deeper understanding of the client experience, providing an opportunity to see and observe counselling, deepening awareness of the stages of counselling and helping identify personal problems and conflicts. By increasing self-awareness it is potentially reducing the risk of transference. These are some of the reasons that personal therapy has been a mandatory element of counselling training and accreditation for many years. However, this is no longer the case; it is now discretional, although still hugely beneficial to students. Often the additional cost can be off-putting for students but many colleges and universities provide counselling for their student population, which can be a compromise. A workable alternative is co-counselling, which can provide a safe environment in which to share personal issues. This is discussed in detail in Chapter 9.

Depending upon the theoretical approach, personal counselling might not even feature in class discussions (e.g. CBT and other directive therapies). However, if you are studying on a psychodynamic course, it might be a compulsory component. Norcross (2005) estimates that approximately three-quarters of all mental health professionals have engaged in personal therapy, with psychoanalytic practitioners attending more than average and behaviour therapists attending less than average.

Daw and Joseph investigated the role of personal therapy for practising counsellors and found that

> participants reported that personal therapy was a useful and valuable way to provide self-care. In every instance this was understood to be a positive experience. Second, participants discussed how personal therapy impacted on their professional practice. Through personal therapy therapists learnt experientially, and as a result they believed that they had deeper understanding of theories, models, and therapeutic processes. Similarly, experiencing the client role yielded deeper empathy and respect for clients. (2007: 231)

AIMS AND OBJECTIVES OF SUPERVISION

> Counselling supervision is a formal and mutually agreed arrangement for counsellors to discuss their work regularly with someone who is normally an experienced and competent counsellor and familiar with the process of counselling supervision. (BACP, 1996)[1]

The practice of counselling supervision involves many different processes but they all surround the monitoring of effectiveness for ethical reasons. Ensuring the safety of the supervisee and that of their clients is a core motive which incorporates self-care and development. It is rather like a car having a regular service; any potential concerns are identified and remedied before they cause further damage. In keeping with therapeutic alliances, the boundaries and structure of the professional relationship should be explicit, negotiated and agreed, which can be challenging if this is your first experience of counselling supervision.

Finding and employing a supervisor might be straightforward if you are referred to a specific individual by your tutor or provided with a list of

---

[1] © BACP (www.bacp.co.uk/admin/structure/files/pdf/566_ethical%20framework%20feb2010.pdf). This information is regularly updated and all up-to-date material can be found on the BACP website.

approved supervisors by the course. However, if you are to take responsibility for finding a supervisor yourself, it can be a more demanding process. For example, do you choose a supervisor from the same theoretical approach that you use or do you choose a different modality for alternative ways of viewing content? (It is usually recommended that to begin with you work with a supervisor who uses the same modality as your course so that it provides a wider understanding of the methodologies.) Will cost have an influence on who you choose, or reputation or location or style? By this I mean, have you considered what will take place? Within sessions, you may find that some supervisors are case centred where the focus is firmly placed on the content of sessions. Alternatively, some supervisors are more interested in the counsellor and their methods and choices. A more interactive and flexible model is usually considered more beneficial which encompasses a wide range of areas to provide a more holistic approach. It is basically a matching exercise once you are clear about what you are looking for and finding a supervisor that you feel you can work positively with. As with other counselling relationships, the relationship you establish with your supervisor influences the success and outcome of the sessions, which is why it is crucial that they are as impartial as possible. Having a line manager or colleague as supervisor would hinder honesty and openness for fear of inadequacies, flaws or weaknesses impacting upon the working relationship or even promotion opportunities. The benefits of supervision are that it:

- promotes therapeutic competence, knowledge and skills development
- enhances the quality of the therapeutic work
- safeguards the welfare of clients by monitoring ethical, professional and anti-discriminatory practice
- encourages the growth of insight and self-awareness through reflective practice
- provides the therapist with a protective mechanism against stress and burnout.

(Wosket, 2006)

The frequency of the sessions and the length of each meeting is usually dependent upon either the course requirements or those of the accrediting body whose ethical guidelines you adhere to; for example, the BACP require a minimum of 1½ hours per month, although if you have a heavy caseload or are under stress or experiencing difficulties, you may wish to increase this to meet your needs. In addition, group supervision may be of interest. This can be one-to-one supervision with a facilitator within a group setting, or a more free-flowing style with a supervisor responding to group members indiscriminately. Co-supervision is an option for more experienced counsellors, where the role is shared equally as it is with co-counselling. With these methods of shared supervision, the whole session cannot be used towards the time requirement but rather the percentage in which you were directly involved.

What actually takes place within the sessions?

Supervision does not normally include personal counselling, which should remain within your co-counselling or personal counselling sessions. Rather, it involves the appraisal and evaluation of your therapeutic work with clients. The supervisor does not sit in judgement but through discussion and exploration the supervisee is able to assess their own practice with the input of a more experienced therapist (see Figure 14.1). This is explained well by Hazel Johns:

> In a trainee's personal counselling, her feelings and issues will be in the forefront, though clients and what they trigger will be present too; in supervision, clients and their concerns and ethical needs must be in the forefront, but the trainee, her responses and needs are inevitably – and properly – present, if usually in the background. (1996: 88)

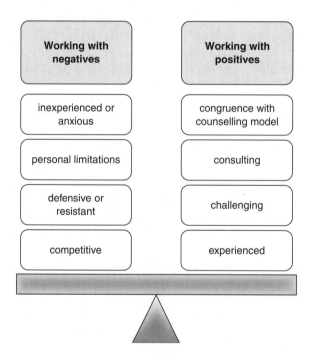

Figure 14.1   The supervisory dynamic

UNIVERSAL TASKS

Planning for a session

During supervision sessions, depending upon your counselling activities, there is quite often much to cover so it is useful to formulate a flexible plan beforehand of issues you would like to cover. This ensures that you are more likely to be focused and specific when you discuss your therapeutic work and use the time most constructively.

Experience self-disclosure and sharing

The use of self-disclosure is slightly different within supervision. For instance, a supervisor is more likely to self-disclose than a counsellor would as it is a tool that helps strengthen the supervisory bond. Page and Wosket (2001) provide evidence that the use of appropriate self-disclosure has two roles within supervision: that of improving the relationship but also helping to mend any problems should they arise. Their findings develop this further by claiming that supervisees can learn about relevant self-disclosure from its use by their supervisor which they can put into practice with their own clients; the more it is used correctly by the supervisor, the greater the alliance and success of the sessions, but too much self-disclosure has the opposite effect and damages the process. The sharing of struggles or difficulties by the supervisor corrects any imbalance of power and is welcomed by supervisees; in fact, the amount of its use within sessions can indicate the effectiveness of the relationship. This is a far more positive picture than that of the quandary that counsellors often battle with regarding the appropriate use of self-disclosure with clients.

Negotiating boundaries (including hours and remuneration)

The regularity and length of sessions tends to be dictated by your course or regulatory body but, if not, it comes down to your own personal requirements. There are guidelines you can follow to begin with until you establish your own needs. As already mentioned, the BACP recommend 1½ hours per month, although this can increase depending upon your client base, experience and any dilemmas. Cost of sessions tends to be similar to that of counselling in your area and is based on a rate per session. This can be a large financial responsibility if the cost is not covered by your course.

Initial supervisory contract

The negotiation of a contract during the first meeting is a crucial element of your supervisory relationship. Here you will agree on regularity, orientation, methodology, cost, location, content, etc. If you have considered this in advance, it makes the process smoother. Your supervisor will also be able to advise you about aspects that you are either unsure of or unclear about. It is important here to be honest and open about any wishes or concerns.

Learning and teaching

Supervision sessions are an opportunity for you to learn about yourself, your practice and counselling in general in a one-to-one environment which is often invaluable. Supervisors tend to be experienced counsellors so are able to view matters raised from a wider perspective. They are also able to provide alternative examples or scenarios, share their own experiences, alert you to potential difficulties and direct you to areas of further learning. This educational aspect is woven into the monitoring process.

Methodology and interactions

How the sessions are structured, and their content, is dependent upon your chosen supervisor, although you do have the opportunity for input here at your initial meeting or contracting session. The approach or model used by your supervisor dictates the methods and interactions used to some extent; for example, a psychoanalytical supervisor will be analysing your content, placing it in the context of your personal world and drawing your attention to any transference or counter-transference issues. A person-centred supervisor will be more focused on your relationship together, working in the 'here and now', and how you process the sessions with clients. Cognitive behavioural supervisors are not as prevalent, as supervision is not a requirement for most CBT practitioners. The only way to be sure that their techniques and practices will match your needs is to ask the supervisor at your first session.

Monitoring administration

Another important element of the supervisory relationship is to ensure that the supervisee is managing administrative duties to meet the requirements of the course or regulatory body. Case notes, personal development journals, evaluation documentation and training needs amongst others may all be discussed to ensure that professionalism and proficiency are not in question. Supervisors provide guidance here and some even offer pro-forma document-ation to show how this might be achieved.

Monitoring professional ethical issues

This links into the above section as monitoring the adherence to ethical guidelines is a fundamental task of supervision. Boundary issues such as confidentiality, referral issues, managing punctuality and non-attendance and any complaints can all be discussed and scrutinised to ensure safe and professional practice. It is clearly helpful if the supervisor and supervisee are working to the same ethical guidelines but, if not, the supervisor must be aware of the supervisee's regulations and work with them to avoid confusion.

Monitoring the therapeutic process, questioning and challenging

During sessions, a supervisor will ask you about *how* you are working with clients encouraging you to justify your chosen methods and purpose. You will be questioned about your feelings to your approach, but quite often you will be challenged. This may be through gentle enquiry or it might be more overt examination, depending upon the approach of your supervisor. However this is managed, challenge is a valuable tool to avoid stagnation, complacency or overconfidence. Having to justify your chosen methods of working therapeutically can renew and reinforce your choices or alternatively, can make you question yourself and question your motivations. This contemplative and introspective process is crucial to the safety of your client, as such reflection can expose the real drive and intention behind your working. It is an opportunity to consider alter-native ways of working if you are experiencing 'stuckness' or difficulties in your practice.

Qualifications

Usually counselling supervisors have completed further training specifi-cally in supervision although this is not always the case as it is not always

Table 14.1 Current supervision requirements

Organisation	Requirement when in practice	Source of information
BACP	You have an ongoing contract for counselling/ psychotherapy supervision for a minimum of 1½ hours per month for each month in which practice is undertaken.	BACP accreditation requirements 2008[1]
BPS	Trainees will seek high standards of professional conduct as counselling psychologists in the interests of all those with whom they come into contact and will: 7.1 understand the purpose and practice of receiving supervision.	TCCP Accreditation Criteria October 2008 (www.bps.org.uk)
CPCAB	'CPCAB is an awarding body and not a membership organisation. Our qualifications are mapped to BACP standards for individual counsellor accreditation, key standards, therefore once you are proficient in certain CPCAB qualifications, you will be able to apply for individual accreditation.'	www.cpcab.co.uk/learners/faqs. php 2006
COSCA	**Diploma students:** Practice supervision will be carried out to provide continual evaluation and monitoring of all client case work and the ratio of supervision hours to client contact hours will be 1:6. **Counsellors/psychotherapists** It is recommended that the proportion of time spent on counselling supervision to that spent on client work should be 1:12. **Experienced accredited counsellor/ psychotherapist member:** For counsellors who have been practising for more than 5 years post accreditation it is recommended that supervision is not less than 1 hour per month and is appropriate to the volume and nature of client work.	www.cosca.org.uk/new_ documents.php?headingno=5& heading=Supervision (COSCA: Counselling & Psychotherapy in Scotland)

[1] © BACP. This information is regularly updated and all up-to-date material can be found on the BACP website.

required. If supervision, is provided by your course, it may be that the external provision is supplied by experienced or recommended professionals who have a working knowledge of the ethos and aims of the course and can work positively within those boundaries (see also Table 14.1). It is also possible to access a list of supervisors directly from your accrediting or regulatory body.

Supporting the supervisee

Counsellors in private practice can experience a sense of aloneness if working without colleagues. Supervision is a crucial way to avoid professional isolation. There are several methods in which this can be achieved, one of which is inclusion of taped sessions (following the normal ethical procedures and with the client's permission) that can provide insight into the reciprocal narrative that takes place. This is an improvement on relying on memory for content as it also allows for the examination of content, dialogue, direction, pace, use of skills, silences and pauses, etc. that are not able to be present otherwise. This resource helps supervision focus directly on client work and opens up a new stratum for discovery. Supervisors should also able to direct supervisees towards new research, reading matter and CPD activities that might be of help with personal and professional development.

Interventions

As we know, supervision is different from a counselling relationship as it is not therapeutic but rather more focused on the process of counselling. As such, there are several different interventions that a supervisor might utilise. Heron (1975) developed a model of intervention that consists of six types of involvement:

- *Prescriptive* interventions involve the supervisor providing specific advice regarding how to proceed with a difficult situation. This might arise from their personal experience or knowledge.
- *Informative* intervention involves the supervisor passing on specifics that are appropriate or relevant to the current subject area.
- *Confronting* is different here to that in a counselling relationship, as in supervision it can be a prompt for drawing attention to or highlighting questionable areas of practice and as such may be more challenging.
- A *cathartic* approach when working with emotionally draining clients can allow you to 'get it off your chest', resulting in a re-energising or invigorating outcome.
- *Catalytic* 'light bulb' moments can occur during the process, in the same way that clients experience them in counselling when discussion sparks an idea or plan which might materialise, taking shape and develop.
- A *supportive* relationship should be the outcome, created through appropriate self-disclosure, a hugely supportive manner and a culture of sharing.

THEORETICAL SIMILARITIES AND DIFFERENCES

- *Person-centred supervision*: focuses on offering an environment which offers the supervisee an opportunity for growth and self-actualisation. The supervisory relationship is based on the core conditions so understanding, honesty and acceptance underpin the sessions, allowing the supervisee to view and assess themselves and their practice. Discussion may take place comparing the ideal and the actual self in the counselling room.
- *Gestalt supervision*: the here and now and creativity are major aspects of this model, so techniques and skills will be explored and the supervisor will develop improvisation to meet the supervisee's needs. There is also an evaluative process ongoing to ensure that the techniques themselves don't overshadow the therapeutic content of the sessions, within both the counselling and supervisory relationship. Gestalt supervisors will also be promoting the supervisee to be more self-accepting of themselves as a whole. Any ethical concerns surrounding levels of challenge and confrontation can also be opened up.
- *Psychodynamic supervision*: the supervisor will be highlighting unconscious motives and actions within the counsellor's work. Issues of transference and counter-transference will be examined and the counsellor's personal history and experiences may well be relevant. Within sessions, time might also be spent considering the supervisee's choice of methods and their effectiveness with clients.
- *Transactional analysis*: as with TA counselling sessions, the supervision agreement will begin with contracting to establish agreed goals, although it is common that this will be within a group setting rather than on an individual basis. Time may be spent on investigation into how the supervisees are maintaining equality within their counselling sessions where the balance between child, parent and adult is scrutinised. In the same way that there are dangers with the counsellor becoming 'parent' through transference, this is also true with the supervisor within supervision.
- *Cognitive behavioural supervision*: BACP do not currently insist that members have a supervisor, which is left to the discretion of the practitioner. CBT is a directive approach which, unlike the humanistic approaches, concentrates more on instruction and relaxation to change behaviours so the supervisor will be cautious to remain objective to avoid over-identifying with the supervisee. This distance allows for the application of logic to what might otherwise be an emotional situation. Homework might be set and the supervisee must take an active role in the process. Irrational or self-defeating thought patterns are challenged.

PROFESSIONAL ACCOUNTABILITY

Like counsellors, supervisors are also accountable, meaning that they too are in supervision to monitor their process with their clients and supervisees.

This is a continuous supportive cycle whereby all practitioners within the structure are receiving professional supervision for their various roles.

Interpersonal and intrapersonal use of self in sessions

> ## ACTIVITY
>
> - Identify the arguments for and against engaging in personal therapy during your course. What are your thoughts on this?
> - Consider the methodologies and reasons for counselling supervision.
> - Reflect upon the values, principles and personal moral qualities in relation to competent practice and counselling supervision.
> - Compare and contrast the different theoretical models of counselling supervision.
> - Think about the impact of different orientations on the supervisory relationship.

Any mention of support in relation to practical sessions should include a form of clear, specific assistance for you to follow, and as one of the most difficult points of counselling training is the ability to turn theory into practice, this seems a good choice. This is especially challenging when some courses believe firmly that this should not be a prescriptive process but one that evolves with the student interpreting the transition in their own way, making their practice their own. Most counselling practice at the start of a course prior to working with clients involves the use of triads, where three students adopt the roles of counsellor, client and observer for a set period of time before swapping roles. There is a list of general guidelines for practical sessions is provided in Chapter 10.

15

The Residential Experience

Many counselling courses include a formal or informal opportunity for a residential experience. Here we will examine the benefits and potential pitfalls of such an activity and consider the impact upon the individual and the group.

WHY DO WE HAVE TO GO AWAY?

Residential elements in counselling courses can be fascinating, fun and a positive learning experience. It may be that you have never before been immersed totally in your learning with like-minded people for such a condensed period of time. The learning that can take place can be considerable but not all courses include a residential element. Before we go any further, let's focus on the arguments for and against the inclusion of a residential component to help you understand why it may or may not be incorporated into your course and to help you identify the benefits and any potential pitfalls.

Simply, it may be that the tutors are hoping to observing students in a controlled environment so that they can watch for use of communication skills and interpersonal interactions. This can inform as to how you might bear up working in a stressful environment or as part of a team. Where the students have to take responsibility for the organisation of the trip, it allows staff to view you working collaboratively with others. This can be a very positive aspect as it can show how different students choose to solve disagreements and provide insight into negotiation processes.

However, there are numerous counter-arguments which disagree with a residential element being included in the course programme. Depending upon the theoretical orientation of the course, it could be argued that it is not directly relevant to counselling training as it is unlike most situations you might find yourself in with a client, so it can be hard to justify. A key issue is the cost of such an exercise. It can be a very expensive activity and not all students are able to afford the additional cost when things such as childcare are considered. Under-graduate certificate and diploma courses are less likely to include residen-tials for that reason, unless the cost is already included within the course fees. The organisation and preparation can be very time-consuming, whether it is staff or students who take on the task. There are also wider organisational restrictions such as health and safety issues, staffing and timetabling. It can be challenging to find appropriate accommodation that meets the requirements of the group and the activities but is also affordable. The staffing requirements can cause difficulties if there isn't a particular member of staff who is experienced in this area and is comfortable taking responsibility from the perspective of the training organisation. Finally, and very importantly, making structure of the time away beneficial is crucial: person-centred courses may prefer a more organic, flexible approach where no structure is enforced, whereas a psychodynamic residential experience might include prolonged group work.

WHAT CAN WE EXPECT TO HAPPEN?

This brings us onto the subject of what we can expect to happen when we take part. There are different general formats for the structure of residential experiences; however, most do share some specific activities, such as it being an ideal opportunity to spend time co-counselling if that is part of your course. Almost all residential events involve some sort of formal or informal group work where all students have an oppor-tunity to work on issues. With such a focus on interpersonal relation-ships, it can be a time when real friendships emerge or fragment. Such immersion into course material can be invigorating, especially if the trip is later in the curriculum when the initial excitement might have worn thin. At this point, it is the ideal time to catch up with any assign-ments or tasks that you might have let slip. The social aspect can be viewed as extremely testing if you are expected to be with each other for prolonged periods every day, but this depends up on the structure of the trip and the accommodation and facilities. Again, this comes back to cost.

An increased level of autonomy can be incorporated as some courses place total responsibility for the entire organisation firmly with the student group. This is a tactic used to measure interpersonal interaction and teamworking skills. Here, you might wish to revisit Chapter 13 to remind yourself how group theory such as Tuckman (1965) and Yalom (1985) informs the development and maturation of groups of individuals with a shared aim or aims. Again, the orientation of your course will impact upon how much information you are given beforehand, whether that be a timetable of planned activities or the freedom to evolve in the way that the group wishes. The unpredictability is a core learning experience as, even if the group has had a good relationship beforehand, you will see a different side of people or perhaps just get to know them on a deeper level. Being patient and understanding and not forgetting to use your skills will make an enormous difference.

Feeling empowered enough to voice your feelings and opinions both during the planning stage and whilst away is a fundamental key to feeling comfortable. Interestingly, whilst studying group work, the psychologist Bion identified that 'silence gives consent' (Lipgar, 2007), which may be worth bearing in mind during the organisation beforehand.

WHAT DO I HAVE TO DO?

This is not an easy question to answer as it is really up to you and how much you hope to become involved. This is a situation where the old adage 'you get out what you put in' really does apply. Your perception, enthusiasm and dedication to your learning all play a vital part in your mindset. If you are excited and interested, the chances are that you will have a valuable and worthwhile encounter where you discover much about yourself and others. However, if you are feeling resistant, dreading taking part or feel it to be a waste of time, try taking these feelings to supervision and spend time examining why you might be feeling this way. You may find that in raising your own awareness with relation to the activity itself, you actually learn more about yourself even before taking part.

If you consider that the emphasis will be on both inter- and intra-personal development, use the time to benefit yourself by spending it situating the course within the context of your life.

ACTIVITY

- Spend five minutes listing all the positive aspects that you hope to achieve whilst away.
- Now, list all the negative aspects that you can think of.
- Finally, for each list, consider how you might work with each issue, any preparation necessary and any strategies you might put in place to overcome possible negativity (e.g. taking calming music with you, or earplugs).

The purpose of the residential experience will help you prepare. Will it be purely therapeutic? Are activities (e.g. walks) planned? Will there be any demands made upon you and, if so, what?

HOW MIGHT RELATIONSHIPS CHANGE?

There can be enormous pressure of being together 24 hours a day, but this is often one of the reasons for going. Staff will be watching interactions to see how each person is coping in what is essentially an alien environment. Being together constantly is very different indeed from being in class on a regular basis, even if you have known each other for a considerable length of time. The sense of lack of escape can impact on different people in different ways.

Before leaving, it makes sense to speak to fellow students and staff that are also attending the residential and ask any questions you might have to help prepare you for your time together.

Here are some examples of questions that you could ask to clarify purpose, although you are bound to have more of your own:

- What is the purpose of the activity?
- What will take place whilst we are away?
- How might this help me develop?
- What sorts of activities have been planned?

- What will my role be?
- How can I use this time to the most benefit?
- How does this experience impact upon the course?

INFLUENCE OF THEORETICAL ORIENTATION

A worthwhile group activity prior to leaving is to spend time making links between the counselling approach you are learning and how this might impact upon the residential experience. It might help to consider the most basic ethos that underpins your practice and start to relate that to how you might learn and develop when away. By becoming comfortable with the purpose beforehand, this can help provide you with a personal plan or structure and reassurance that you will be engaging in a worthwhild learning activity.

16

Research

This chapter will look briefly at the role of research within counselling, how we might use the findings from published research but also how we might conduct our own research, because most courses involve using research in either or both of these ways.

WHAT IS RESEARCH?

Research is a detailed investigation that is achieved through the use of scientific and systematic methodology. We use it to learn more about counselling, to help us improve our practice, increase our knowledge or to test a theory we might have. There are many different methods that we can use, either alone or combined.

SO WHY DO I HAVE TO KNOW ABOUT RESEARCH?

Research is used by counsellors in two fundamental ways: first, to inform our practice, and second, to help us test theories and discover new information. This can be one of the primary activities on advanced courses and so, to be successful, you need to appreciate what research actually means and how you, personally, can use it to improve what you do. If you are on an introductory course, you may need to access published research to include in essays, and it will certainly help you understand why you are being taught the theories and skills that you are. Almost every counselling course will touch on research in one way or another.

IS RESEARCH REALLY ALL THAT IMPORTANT TO ME?

If you are to keep up to date, maintain your CPD and have informed discussions based on evidence with your colleagues, then research will probably become very important to you. Consider for a moment how much we know about which therapeutic techniques work and which don't. Research has provided evidence to show how successful different approaches can be. The methods and theories we learn about in courses are recognised and used as they have been studied for many years. It is because such research has been conducted that we can measure the impact on clients. Because of this, we are able to be confident that each method or theory has a history of success and continuing improvement. The difference between just gathering evidence in order to improve our understanding of a given subject or area and conducting academic research is importantly about the fact that research is a scientific process. What we mean by this is that there is a recognised, tested and generally accepted set of steps or procedures that must be followed in order to ensure that whatever is found or claimed as a result is based on sound practices and evidence. This is also part of the distinction we might draw between taking a 'common sense' approach to theory and practice and taking a 'scientific' approach. Common sense is actually very unreliable and is in effect based on no more that collections of culturally rooted preconceptions and values, when in fact we need to assess theory and practice through a more rigorous and controlled approach, that is to say, a scientific approach that is based strictly on the production of evidence through research. Often the results of research can be 'counter-intuitive'; in other words, the evidence generated through research can run counter to what seems clear and obvious. Human behaviour is complex and challenging and that alone means that our approach to understanding elements of behaviour must be up to meeting the challenge. In order to properly assess and understand the effectiveness, the strengths and the weaknesses of particular theoretical perspectives and the impact they might have on practice, we need to be able to evaluate the evidence of how they function. A vital part of that process of evaluation and central to the work of research is understanding the role and nature of sources.

WHAT IS A SOURCE?

We may call looking information up in a book or on an internet search engine 'research', but before we progress any further it is important to clarify the two specific sources, which are *primary* and *secondary* sources of data. Understanding the differences between primary and secondary sources of information helps us to make sense of what and where the information comes from. All research, whether conducted for academic or work purposes, is based on collecting evidence from sources. Sources can come in a variety of forms: medical reports, statistics, books, question-naires or even physical evidence.

WHAT ARE THE DIFFERENCES BETWEEN PRIMARY AND SECONDARY SOURCES?

Primary sources of information are discoveries that we make ourselves directly through our own investigations, such as a survey or case study, whereas secondary sources are studies that other people have conducted and which we might read about in books or professional journals. It isn't the case that one is better than the other; it's just that we need to appreciate that they are different; often secondary sources are very valuable forms of evidence. Research journal articles are often regarded as primary sources, since they give access to evidence gathered. This hopefully illustrates one of the most important reasons why journals and periodicals are so useful during your course and crucial when working in practice. They allow us to refer to examples of previous studies, gain insight into methods of presentation and draw upon conclusions that can be integrated into course assignments and also into your work with clients.

ACTIVITY

1 Visit your university or college library and locate one professional counselling publication and one counselling research journal.
2 List six differences between their presentation and content.
3 From the research journal, read one piece of research.
4 Identify why and how the research was carried out as well as the findings or conclusions.
5 In your personal journal, explain what you have learned from this research and how it might impact upon your previous knowledge.

HOW IS RESEARCH ACTUALLY CARRIED OUT?

Research can be carried out in many different ways. The researcher will decide upon an area of interest, will read published research and draw upon theoretical works in order to establish their interests and think about formulating a testable hypothesis. At the same time the researcher needs to think about how best to move forward to testing, what kinds of sources would need to be assessed, whether or not a qualitative or quantitative approach will be taken (which might well be determined by the theoretical area involved) and what resources would be needed in order to carry out the work.

This will lead to the creation of a set of 'research questions' which will enable the writing of the research proposal. Such proposals have to be put together in a way that takes account of ethical principles and often a regulating body will take a close look at any ethical implication of the research, including the important principle of informed consent. Any respondents or participants – those people who might be providing data as part of the research – need to be fully informed as to what the research is about and aware of how the data might be used.

The project might also begin by using a pilot study, that is to say, a small-scale version of the research could be carried out in order to test whether or not the appropriate methods and measures have been selected to test the hypothesis involved. If this goes well, any lessons learned from the pilot study will be incorporated into the design of the project and, assuming that all the resources needed are made available, the researcher will then move forward to gathering the data. Once the chosen research activity has been completed, the whole process must be accurately documented to show the exact methodology. This is so that the study can be replicated by other researchers to prove or disprove the findings or to apply the same method in slightly different conditions.

Here are examples of questions that I asked participants during qualitative interviews conducted with ex-students when researching the impact of the weekly community groups upon their learning experience:

1 Looking back, what are your feelings about the weekly community groups?
2 How safe did you feel in the group (e.g. boundary issues)?
3 What do you think were the benefits a) personally and b) to the group?
4 What do you think is necessary for a 'successful' community group?
5 What are your reflections regarding the development of the group throughout the year?
6 Please identify any differences you noticed between the agenda-less community group and the facilitated personal development groups.

Table 16.1 Responses to open-question survey

QUESTIONS	Looking back, what are your feelings about the weekly community groups?	How safe did you feel in the group?	What do you think were the benefits a) personally and b) to the group?	What do you think is necessary for a successful community group?	What are your reflections regarding the development of the group throughout the year?	Please identify any differences you noticed between the agenda-less community group and the facilitated personal development groups.
STUDENT A	Confusion regarding community group, wasted opportunity, too short	Trust, no fear, confident	None at start, great personal benefits, supportive and cathartic	Structure, instruction, loner groups	Flowering at end, progressed from shallow to deep	Instructed, in the moment as opposed to definite purpose
STUDENT J	Waste of time, no point or structure, free for all whingeing	Felt safe but had trust and confidentiality reservations	Great personal benefit, noticed benefits to others too	Longer groups	Divisions and cliques, discomfort, poor attendance affected development	Like night and day – PD groups had meaning and purpose
STUDENT E	Role of facilitator inappropriate	Not safe or comfortable	Witnessed acceptance and contributions of others	Facilitator to remain as educator, clear aims and goals	Members learning to listen to lecturer	Enormous benefit, reflection and self-questioning due to altered boundaries, lecturer and direction
STUDENT S	Dominated by some, unsure of role, good space for discussion	Size of group	Increased confidence and openness with decrease in being judgemental	Honesty, staff input, group size, transparency	Interesting journey, sense of achievement, creation of bond	Felt to be safer, enjoyed more, other members got more out of PD groups
STUDENT D	Confusion, conforming to norms	Fear of judgement, awareness of others paramount	Not in short term but in long run	Boundaries, loose guidelines, less domination	Subtle changes, increased challenge and support	Focus on activity, seen as task, good fun, all happy to take part, identified directive group v non-directed counselling
STUDENT W	At ease, uncomfortable with silence	Totally safe, role of confidentiality and boundaries	Minimal, less challenging	Structure, more time, direction	Lack of trust at start, quiet members challenged	Less domination in PD groups, confidence building, more contribute when instructed.

You can see that they are designed to allow the respondents to give as detailed and as personal account as they choose. The open design prevents any question being answered with a simple 'yes' or 'no' and so encourages detail but it is harder for the researcher to collate and formulate the answers into tables and graphs, so the answers are usually précied to show trends. This is the method I used in Table 16.1 to show the overall responses at a glance, but this is only possible with a small number of participants:

This qualitative (term explained later) example was conducted with a very small population but it is generally thought that the larger the group of people you include in your study, the more accurate or representative of the general population your findings will be. Who you choose to take part can influence your results, so *how* you choose participants is crucial for an accurate and unbiased result. This is known as 'sampling'.

There are numerous methods of sampling the population and they fall into two categories: probability sampling, where you as the researcher are able to control who is selected, and non-probability sampling, where you have little control over who is selected (see Figures 16.1 and 16.2).

The conducting of research is most common in undergraduate and post-graduate courses. Part and parcel of the course work is the business of conducting personal research – reading primary and secondary source material in order to keep well informed about developments in the field – and CPD will often involve working on source material and evidence.

Here are some examples to help your understanding of the context of qualitative and quantitative findings.

WHAT ARE QUANTITATIVE AND QUALITATIVE METHODS?

There are two broad categories that studies fall into: *qualitative* and *quantitative*. Qualitative methods are studies that are designed to discover detailed content and personal viewpoints; feelings, thoughts, values, aspects that are difficult or impossible to measure in some numeric way. Methodologies include interviews, open-question discussions, focus groups, participant observation, storytelling, case studies, etc. The advantages and disadvantages of qualitative methods of research are:

- *Advantages*: For counsellors, qualitative methods tend to sit more comfortably with our way of working and can be viewed as more person centred. The content of answers can provide detailed and specific information that relates directly to each participant's personal experience. It is fairly easy to identify areas of interest.

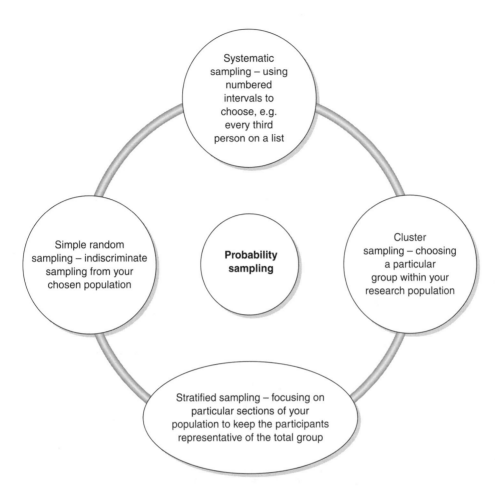

Figure 16.1   Probability sampling, where the researcher controls selection

- *Disadvantages*: Clearly by design, these studies are intended to focus on the individual experience, making scientific comparison and presentation very difficult indeed. Also the subjectivity of responses can make them hard to interpret accurately.

Quantitative methods (think 'quantity' or amount) are more objective, aimed at generalising results to a population, so designed to collate data and statistics that can be analysed, measured and compared in a more mathematical manner. Examples here include restrictive questionnaires, controlled randomised trials and rating scales. The advantages and disadvantages of quantitative methods of research are:

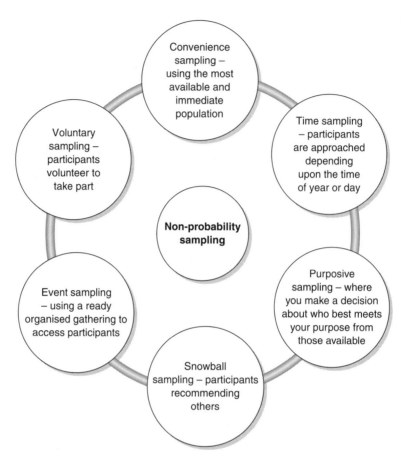

Figure 16.2   Non-probability sampling, where the researcher has little control over selection

- *Advantages*: The size and scale of the research findings can be more controllable and the analysis, presentation and interpretation of the results can be very clear.
- *Disadvantages*: These studies can be daunting initially due to the exacting structure of the methodology. Also, they don't sit comfortably with some theoretical orientations.

In Table 16.2 are some examples of possible qualitative and quantitative studies to highlight the relationship between the different methodologies and the potential findings.

Students on a counselling course were asked the question, 'Why did you decide to study counselling at this point in your life?' The responses were

Table 16.2 Possible qualitative and quantitative studies

Qualitative areas of interest	Quantitative areas of interest
How counsellors experience empathy	How many clients miss appointments
How supported clients feel	The success rate of CBT on addictive behaviours
The impact that PCT has on clients	What percentage of the population would consider attending counseling

collated into a bar chart (see Figure 16.3) to show how using numbers can clearly illustrate the overall responses.

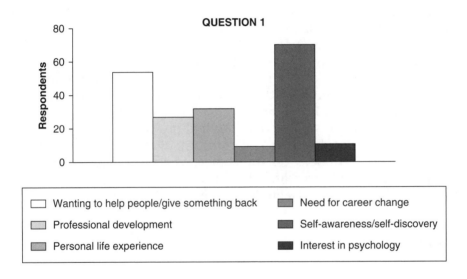

Figure 16.3   Example of how number of responses to questionnaire can be displayed visually

DOES RESEARCH MATTER TO PRACTITIONERS?

Your research question (or hypothesis), population that you choose to sample, the method you choose and your interpretation of the findings all tell the reader something of the assumptions, values and personal interests of the researcher. Once you have ensured that your approach is as unbiased as possible, your results will tell a story. This can then be used by counsellors working with clients in the settings that your findings apply to. A good example of this is the research showing that the strength of the relationship between client and counsellor is more important than the theoretical orientation or method that you are working with (Cooper, 2008). Until this research was conducted and published, there was less certainty as to what exactly influenced a successful (or unsuccessful) session.

HOW CAN A LIBRARY HELP ME DO RESEARCH?

Your university or college library will be of enormous help to you here as they are designed for locating and using relevant information. Most courses include some form of library induction, maybe including a guided tour, introduction to the Dewey system or instructions on how to use the indexing system. Many libraries have reciprocal agreements regarding inter-library loans, making it possible to order in resources from other establishments. The librarians themselves are highly qualified and able to guide you to access the information you are searching for. They may even be able to recommend sources that you had previously not considered.

The other, often neglected source of information is the bibliography or reference section in books on the subject you are interested in. These provide a ready guide to relevant data already collated, so you will be using secondary sources as a guide to primary sources.

RESEARCH METHODS

Be careful here as research *methods* are the processes or tools that you choose to use to gather your information, whereas research *methodology* refers more to your overall approach and theoretical predisposition. Here we consider some of the most common methods, but this list is in no way conclusive – there are many other methods which you might find more appropriate for your study.

- *Survey techniques*, such as interviews; questions where you select a sample of subjects and conduct interviews, not necessarily face to face.
- *Experimental studies* aren't used as often in counselling but variables are controlled to allow one change to become apparent which can be measured.
- *Semi-structured interviews* start with a basic or general set of questions to work with but allow for an exchange of information.

- *Observational techniques* such as cross-sectional studies and longitudinal studies where participants are watched and changes over time are recorded.
- *Case study* involves an in-depth study on an individual or group and a range of information can be gathered.
- *Participant enquiry* requires the researcher to be involved as the study is of a naturalistic group of which the researcher is already a member.
- *Action research* has the researcher and participant/s working together to try to alter a current situation, to try to establish how successful change might be made.
- *Participant observation* has the researcher joining a group to observe their practices from the inside to provide greater understanding. This can be overt (known) or covert (secret), although there are clearly ethical considerations here.
- *Grounded theory* works the opposite way round. Instead of trying to prove an already existing theory as the other methods do, grounded theory is trying to establish a theory as a result of the study. This means that the researcher conducts the research and then formulates a theory as a result of the findings.

ONLINE RESEARCH

We can waste a lot of time trying to find secondary data on the Internet because we are being too vague or not searching in the right place. If you are very specific in your search, you will not just save a lot of time and frustration but may well come across additional relevant information. Here are a few guidelines:

- Don't believe everything you find on the Internet. Unless it is an officially peer-reviewed site, the content might be completely made up.
- Always use names and dates in your search if you have them.
- Try to use the exact (and correct) title of the study.
- Remember to use dedicated search engines; e.g. Google Scholar will only search through academic studies, reports and journals, whereas if the study you are searching for was published as a book, only use search engines that are dedicated to finding books.
- Avoid reader contribution sites such as Wikipedia as there is no evidence to show that the content is accurate or true.
- If you are searching for secondary data to include in an academic submission, it is good practice to use more books and journals than websites.
- Be very careful with your referencing from websites; you still require an author and date as with any other reference, in addition to the site address and the date you accessed it.

The content of a research paper will typically include:

- Abstract
- Introduction
- Review of literature
- Methodology including ethical consideration
- Results
- Analysis of results
- Discussion
- Summary
- Conclusion
- References
- Bibliography

ETHICAL CONSIDERATIONS

Ethical considerations are crucial in the design and practicalities of counselling research when you might be including vulnerable clients as your subjects or population. Aspects such as confidentiality, safety, methodology, content, care and consideration must all be acceptable to the ethics committee (a board who judge whether your study is safe and ethically sound or not) when you submit your research proposal. Any changes to your plan can be made at this stage to ensure the participants are thoroughly protected. Ensuring that all participants grant informed consent is a key step.

WHAT DO I DO WITH RESEARCH?

Certificate-level courses tend to refer to research findings that are already published as a way of informing and updating the course content. As a student, you may choose to access research studies online or through journals made available through your place of study. The content of these can be referred to within assignments or class discussions. You may even wish to identify particular areas of study to help with how you process theory to use in your own practice.

Within graduate or degree courses, research takes on a more central role. Often units are included which require students to conduct their own research to validate or disprove a personal hypothesis. Before embarking on such a task, it is always a good idea to access a wide range of completed, published studies to read through to both help with ideas and to see the correct format which you can use for guidance in addition to the guidelines provided by your tutor. Post-graduate courses usually take this a stage further and research is often the core of the course. Here the expectation is to develop a more questioning way of approaching therapy; gathering evidence to prove or disprove a relevant point.

Research carried out by students on counselling courses is a valuable resource and studies that have been submitted can be accessed from depositories such as the BACP dissertation bank, Scottish Further Education Unit research bank or through associations or societies that gather research on different aspects according to relevance. There are many such banks accessible via the Internet.

THE ROLE OF RESEARCH IN PRACTICE

We have already looked briefly at how research can inform the counselling process to ensuring best practice. There are many research journals published in the field of counseling, although the BACP *Counselling and Psychotherapy* research journal would be a good publication to begin with as it incorporates such a wide range of subject areas.

> Ethical research is both time-consuming and complex. It involves constant negotiation and renegotiation and a reflexive approach to the process of enquiry, balancing the needs of all the stakeholders and maintaining professional standards. It should ensure that future researchers are welcomed, rather than regarded as plunderers. The key element is an approach which regards people not as objects to be researched, but as human beings possessing their own power, who can be regarded as equals and collaborators in the research process. (Abrahams, 2007)

STUDENT EXPERIENCE: KIM

When I started thinking about conducting research as part of my post-graduate course, I was really enthusiastic and came up with several areas of interest. I just wanted to make a start and find out the answers. It wasn't until my tutor started questioning my thoughts and made me justify everything that I was considering, did I realise that this wouldn't be as easy as I first thought. It took me ages to finally come up with a suitable hypothesis but I did find the literature review interesting; I discovered a lot of source material that I didn't know existed and it really helped me to shape my proposal. Finding participants to agree to take part wasn't as straightforward as I hoped and it meant that I had to reduce the scale of my study, but my tutor was pleased with this as he thought initially that I was being overly optimistic and setting my sights too high. Once this fell into place and I found the balance between a huge, unwieldy study and a tiny, insignificant one, I really enjoyed the process and passed my course with a good mark. Within a year I had started a second project.

FURTHER READING

Coombes, H. (2001) *Research Using IT*. Basingstoke: Palgrave.
Cooper, M. (2008) *Essential Research Findings*. London: Sage.
Dallos, R. and Vetere, A. (2005) *Researching Psychotherapy and Counselling*. Buckingham: Open University Press.
McLeod, J. (2003) *Doing Counselling Research*. London: Sage.
Wisker, G. (2001) *The Postgraduate Research Handbook*. Basingstoke: Palgrave.

17

Placement

More advanced counselling courses require students to gain experience within a relevant placement. At this stage, we will consider the importance of your placement, how difficult it can be to secure an appropriate arrangement and the range of choices available.

WHY DO I NEED A PLACEMENT?

Not all courses include a clinical or practical placement. It is usual that more basic courses place no pressure on you to engage in therapeutic work before learning about counselling skills and their underpinning theories. At this stage, practice is gained through triad work with fellow class members. On a more intermediate course, you may be asked to attend a placement as an observer or to practise counselling skills, but it is not until you are studying on a higher-level course that there is a requirement to be working therapeutically with clients in a counselling setting. There is enormous value in having placement experience on your CV, along with the fact that supervised practice hours are required for accreditation if that is what you are working towards. This experience can be daunting but there is real value in putting theory into practice. Basically, a supervised counselling placement helps you collate hours towards accreditation, whilst a placement in a helping environment that affords the opportunity to practise counselling skills will allow you to gain experience to progress within your training.

Professional or vocational courses require all students to engage in client work through a placement. Rules vary but if you are already working within a counselling environment, some courses allow you to use your current employment as a placement. More commonly, there is a requirement to find experience elsewhere. Although some courses provide placement opportunities for students, many request that you find your own. There may be several reasons for this; it depends upon the area you are studying in as to whether there are enough potential placements, if your course is supported by local agencies or whether the placement experience is assessed or not. If your placement is voluntary, the course requirement may be far less formal, for example, requesting that:

> All students are recommended to be either employed or volunteering on a regular basis within a helping agency or organisation that allows for the practice of counselling skills. A minimum of 1 day (or 6 hours a week) is expected. This will be documented in your reflective personal journal. (HNC Counselling placement requirements, Anniesland College)

The word 'recommended' here suggests that it is for the student's own benefit and not a prerequisite of the course. Clarify the exact requirements when you are interviewed prior to joining or with your tutor so that you are prepared in advance.

RELATIONSHIP BETWEEN COUNSELLING COURSES AND PLACEMENT

For you to feel supported and encouraged, it is hoped that there would be a close relationship between your course tutor, supervisor and placement mentor, although this is more likely on a course where the placement is compulsory. You may even be allocated a dedicated placement tutor to liaise with. A course handbook or written booklet with placement criteria clearly identified can be of great use, as can regular four-way meetings with your tutor, supervisor, placement mentor and you, the student, so that all parties involved are clear about the guidelines. Because of this, supportive relationships can develop over time between placements and courses which has advantages for the student.

When you first begin within your placement, even if it is your workplace, contracting should take place so that both you and your mentor are clear about the roles and responsibilities for the duration of your time there.

Time limits can put pressure on students, so additional periods might be required to complete practice hours. Don't let this put you off though, as the majority of counselling students find it challenging to gather sufficient hours. Between clients not turning up, appointments being fairly distributed between available counsellors, days attending your course, holidays and other unexpected reasons, it can take a surprisingly long time to accumulate the hours required.

HOW DO I FIND A PLACEMENT?

First, you need to decide how you are intending to approach this challenge. Are you hoping to start with advice from your course team, concentrate of specific areas of interest to you, focus on local agencies or scan adverts for vacancies? You may try writing or e-mailing, although telephoning or face-to-face visits tend to be more fruitful as you are able to speak directly to the individuals who make decisions. Before you make contact, make sure that you are prepared and able to answer any questions you might be asked, such as how many taught hours your course entails, any assessment requirements, level of support and contact from the course team, any mentoring obligations, length of commitment, weekly availability, relevant experience, etc. Of course, you can't know in advance all questions that might be asked but you can prepare yourself so that you can answer honestly and sound as though you know what you are talking about.

LENGTH OF COMMITMENT

How long you are to spend working within your placement depends upon the course requirements, the opportunities that the placement provider is able to offer, the level of support, any minimum requirements that the counselling service stipulates (e.g. some voluntary agencies don't charge for their training if you agree to volunteer with them for a minimum of two years). If you are based within a statutory service, your position might be restricted to one year as they will take on new students the following year.

APPROPRIATE PLACEMENTS

If you are new to counselling and have little or no experience of working with vulnerable people, it would be irresponsible to agree to a complex psychiatric placement, whereas if you already have counselling or helping experience, it is important that you stretch yourself and engage at a level where you are still learning. Managing to find that balance can be extremely difficult when placements can be hard to come across in the first place.

WIDE-RANGING PLACEMENTS AND THEIR VALUE

Deciding and applying for a placement can be a very time-consuming and drawn-out activity so it pays to consider your options in plenty of time, even as soon as you are offered a place on a course. First, consider the environment, client work and theoretical orientation of your training and make a list of possible counselling services your might contact. These might be in a local hospital, GP surgery or social work department. If you are enrolling on a more advanced course, an appropriate voluntary agency, such as one that works with mental health issues, addiction, homelessness, health issues, relationship issues, bereavement, etc., may also be an option. The list is extensive and you should begin by considering more than one choice – possibly half a dozen, as you may find that they don't take on students, already have filled available places or wouldn't be able to provide the client work that you require to meet the criteria for your course. Bear in mind that there can be enormous differences between working within a large statutory organisation that is used to accepting students and has a support network in place compared to working within a small agency where staffing, funding and client availability might be less predictable. Although it is advisable to gain experience in a wide range of environments with a wide range of clients, it is unrealistic to expect to gain this from a single counselling service. Honestly evaluate your own experience, level of training, confidence and support before taking on a placement that might cause you stress and not provide the clients with the service they were expecting. A placement should be an environment for learning; you shouldn't be expected to already have all the necessary skills, which is a difficult balance for your mentor to achieve.

Community-based work, including within a GP surgery, can often offer access to a wider range of clients and provide a more flexible placement where you might be offered a choice of days and hours in which to work. This might be more suitable if you have family responsibilities to consider.

WHAT IS MY ROLE IN A PLACEMENT?

When you first make contact with the counselling service, you need to establish exactly what experiences they are able to provide you with, how they can support you, how they can help you to meet the requirements of your course. Then ask yourself honestly if you are able to cope with this. If it is a new placement which hasn't taken students from your course before and you are expected by the course to conduct counselling sessions but your placement only offers you an observational role, there may have to be a period of negotiation where you can invite your course tutor to liaise with the placement.

First Option

Your role will vary according to the organisation you are working within. This can range from helping out in a supportive role, e.g. administrative tasks or observation to gain an understanding of how the agency works. This will not necessarily provide you with counselling experience, so tends be recommended for students who haven't worked within a counselling setting before and is a good first foot on the ladder of gaining relevant experience. It may be that this is an option for you before the course starts so that you are in a better position to secure a counselling placement once enrolled. However, it is important to be aware that any placement that does not involve structured, agreed counselling sessions in partnership with regular counselling supervision will *not* count as counselling hours and so *cannot* be counted towards accreditation.

Voluntary Setting

If you have secured a counselling placement within a voluntary agency or are working there as a volunteer, you may find that the agency insist that you participate in and successfully complete their in-house training course prior to engaging in therapeutic work with clients. These courses can range from a brief workshop right through to a formal, structured course with assignments, essays and recorded practical sessions. Although this may appear challenging to complete at the same time as your academic course, often you will find that there are strong parallels in your learning and the studying is not as challenging as you first feared. Also, your mindset will alter as you are offered new experiences, they trust you enough to invest in you and, at the end, it provides you with valuable practice that can be collated and logged towards your professional accreditation.

Recently, some voluntary agencies have started to charge volunteers to take part in their training courses. This is for several reasons:

- training can be expensive to provide
- these are charitable organisations so funding can be an issue
- many volunteers complete the training and then leave
- it establishes a level of commitment.

However, many feel this is inappropriate if you are giving up your own time to help out in an agency that relies on volunteer support. Ultimately, the decision is yours:

- Do you really want to work within this agency?
- Do you have alternative options?
- Is the cost reasonable (i.e. are they charging the exact cost of the training or is it an income-generation enterprise)?
- Will they be providing regular, appropriate supervision once you are working with clients?
- What is the reputation of the agency and their training course?
- Will this experience be invaluable to your personal development?
- Can you afford it in addition to your university/college course costs?

At the other end of the scale, you may find that your placement is provided by the course, in which case you need to ensure that the setting is in your particular area of interest. You may be offered the opportunity to start directly delivering formalised counselling sessions with clients, although this tends to be if you are enrolled on an advanced course and have previous experience of either counselling or working with people in a helping capacity. Many counselling students have already trained as professionals in a different field such as nursing or social work or may have personal experience of working through a therapeutic programme as a client. These relevant experiences often allow placements to fast-track students to begin counselling sessions sooner.

Statutory sector

Placements within hospitals, GP surgeries, prisons, schools, social work departments, etc. are slightly different. There is considerable competition for securing a placement in these establishments due to the formal structure of the setting. Placement requirements tend to be very specific, and often long-standing links are established with higher-level courses so that places are already 'reserved'. This can make life easier if you are enrolled on that course but will be frustrating and disheartening if you are not.

Using your current workplace

Although this might sound ideal in the first instance and certainly avoids some of the pitfalls of securing practical experience, the danger is that you continue with your regular routine and remain firmly within your comfort zone. To avoid this, it is vital that a new contract is drawn up to accommodate the criteria for the course and your line manager is made aware of the different role you might be undertaking. You also need to bear in mind that you will now be in a slightly different position and that therapeutic work with clients should be at a level that the course expects. There may also be concerns with boundary issues that may require addressing. All of these issues can be reflected upon within your personal journal, with your tutor, your line manager and with your counselling supervisor.

CAN I PASS WITHOUT A PLACEMENT?

Your course tutor knows the answer to this question and will be able to clarify the role of the placement at the very start of your course. As mentioned at the beginning of this chapter, it hinges on whether the placement is recommended (as in a lower-level course) or compulsory. Often the placement is separate from your course work and you are allowed time after the completion of the course to accrue placement hours prior to individual accreditation. This is so you are not under pressure for your clients to turn up for all their sessions, which is unrealistic. You may pass your course work and be issued with your certificate but still need to complete the required practice hours before you can apply for accreditation.

The questions in Table 17.1 may help to provide a framework for your thinking, either at the course interview or at the beginning of the course, in order to establish exactly what is required of you.

The information in the 'Placement Conditions' box below is taken from the BACP document 'Accreditation of Training Courses' 2009 and provides the framework for your placement if you are working towards accreditation.

Table 17.1   Questions that may help decide what is required of you as trainee counsellor

Question	Answer
What is the role of the placement on this course?	
Will my placement work be assessed?	
How many hours are required of me?	
What client group might I be working with?	
What if I am not happy there?	
What level of support will be available for me?	
Am I able to work in more than one placement?	
What am I required to do when I am there?	
Will supervision be provided or do I need to find my own supervisor?	
Am I covered by the placement's liability insurance?	
What are the responsibilities of my placement mentor, counselling supervisor, course tutor and myself?	

PLACEMENT CONDITIONS

B5.1 The course must require all students to complete a minimum of 150 hours of supervised practice (exclusive of missed sessions), in addition to the 50 hours in work-based learning or other duties related to service provision during the course, taking note of the following:

i. Before starting client work, students must be assessed individually for their readiness to take clients.
ii. It is not appropriate for students to take other students on the course as clients whether from their own or a different cohort.
iii. The client work undertaken by students should be congruent with the rationale and philosophy of the course.
iv. Inexperienced students in training should not gain their client work experience through private/independent practice.
v. The course has an obligation under the Ethical Framework to ensure that placement providers indicate student status to their clients.
vi. Details of the client work must be included in a professional log which the student maintains and presents at assessment as evidence of competence to practice. (Client confidentiality must be maintained in the log.)

B5.2 The course must have a procedure in place for students to extend the training period in order to complete the required practice hours:

i. the course must indicate clearly under what circumstances an extension is permitted and;
ii. over what time period this is allowed and;
iii. how students are being supported during that period.

Practice placement

B5.3 The course seeking accreditation will have clear, written and published procedures for practice placements.

B5.4 The course must demonstrate how it approves its placement providers as appropriate for the particular course.

B5.5 There must be an explicit written agreement/contract between students, the placement provider and the course, which is available to all. This must include:

i. A description of the course including its rationale and philosophy, procedures and resources and the requirements of students for client work and assessment (e.g. supervisor reports, electronic media recording).
ii. A confirmation from the placement provider that its aims, orientation and philosophy are congruent with that of the course.
iii. Details of where accountability lies for:

    a) the client work
    b) reporting relationships
    c) supervision arrangements

(Continued)

(Continued)

    d) limits of confidentiality
    e) complaints procedures
    f) health and safety issues.

iv. A contract between the course and placement provider that details the requirements for reports on students, reciprocal feedback, meetings etc.

v. Details of the placement providers' professional practice such as the initial assessment of clients, methods of referral to students, note taking/record keeping requirements.

vi. Details of the type and range of client work undertaken by the placement provider, the kinds of client work contracts offered and any limits upon these in relation to student experience or other factors.

vii. Details of how clients are assessed for suitability to work with students.

(BACP, 2009b)

© BACP (www.bacp.co.uk/accreditation/ACCREDITATION%20(FOR%20 TRAINING%20COURSES)/index.php). This information is regularly updated and all up-to-date material can be found on the BACP website.

FURTHER READING

Kahr, B. (2006) 'The clinical placement in mental health training', in R. Bor and M. Watts (eds), *The Trainee Handbook*, 2nd edn. London: Sage.

18

Certification, Registration and Accreditation

> The areas of certification, registration and accreditation don't remain constant for long so this chapter is not going to provide you with answers that become obsolete very quickly but rather, with how to access the most current information.

AWARDING BODIES

Awarding (or certifying) bodies are separate from accreditation. Examples might include universities, City & Guilds, Assessment and Qualifications Alliance (AQA), Scottish Qualifications Authority (SQA), Business and Technology Education Council (BTEC), Associated Examining Board (AEB) and Oxford, Cambridge and RSA (OCR), and they design, assess and certificate educational and vocational courses. They are not specific to counselling as they provide courses in many different subject areas. Each awarding body provides courses at a variety of academic levels, and these are taught in a range of settings including universities and further education colleges.

As this can all seem rather daunting, and purely as an example to illustrate comparison between courses, Table 18.1 is a basic chart to which I have added counselling courses available in Scotland. This is loosely based on the Scottish Credit Qualifications Framework design and allows at a glance to compare taught hours, placement requirements and awarding

Table 18.1 Comparison of various courses

LENGTH OF COURSE	BACP	OTHER	SQA	COSCA
480 hours	**PG Diploma** Length – 450 hours Placement – YES	**OU Foundation Degree** Length – 3–5 years Placement – YES **AQA Diploma in Counselling Practice** Length – 450 hours Placement – YES	**Counselling HND** Length – 480 hours Placement – YES **HNC Counselling** Length – 480 hours Placement – dependent upon centre	**Diploma in Counselling** Length – varies between courses Placement – YES
300 hours		**BTEC** Diploma in Developing Counselling Skills Length – 300 hours Placement – NO		
200 hours	**MSc** Length – 140/180 taught hours Placement – NO	**MSc** Length – 140/180 taught hours		**MSc** Length – 140/180 taught hours Placement – NO
120 hours		**CPCAB** Diploma in Psychotherapeutic Counselling Length – 120 hours Placement – YES	**PDA Addiction Counselling** Length – 120 hours Placement – NO	**Certificate in Counselling Skills** Length – 120 hours approx. Placement – NO
80 hours			**Counselling Skills** Length – variable Placement – NO	
40 hours		**CPCAB** Introduction to Counselling Skills Length – 30 hours Placement – NO	**Introduction to Counselling** Length – 40 hours Placement – NO	**Specialist courses** Length – 30/36 hours Placement – dependent on centre

body. It might be useful for you to consider developing an equivalent map for the courses available in your local area. This would show clearly progression routes, similarities and differences.

Similarities and differences

Your choice of course is dependent on several aspects, such as your experience in counselling, relevant qualifications (such as having studied a related subject, e.g. psychology or psychiatry) or if you are looking for a general counselling course or one that specialises by focusing on an aspect of counselling. Compare the choices available to you and carry out a matching exercise considering the level of the courses on offer in relation to your career plan.

Some points for consideration

Before enrolling on a course, consider the following in relation to your professional plans:

- Theoretical orientation
- Level of course, i.e. certificate, undergraduate, post-graduate
- Length of course, in taught hours
- Method of delivery, e.g. classroom based, distance learning
- Balance between theory, practice sessions, personal development and professional issues
- Part time or full time, weekends or evenings
- Content, e.g. general or specialised
- Method/s of assessment
- Cost of course
- Placement criteria and how this is managed
- Experience and qualifications of lecturers/trainers
- Reputation of centre
- Possible articulation routes and progression
- Potential for accreditation or registration.

It is important to point out here that there are a wealth of distance learning courses available online which may be ideal if you are looking for a leisure course; these are for your general curiosity or as a first step, but only face-to-face taught courses are recognised for accreditation purposes. This is simply due to counselling being so dependent upon interpersonal skills which can't be tested without meeting.

REGISTRATION

Up until now, anyone who has wanted to call themselves a counsellor has been able to do so whether or not they have completed professional training. This has raised issues of surrounding competence, professionalism and accountability. At the time of publication, registration for counsellors remains an issue for debate. It is intended that the Health Professions Council protect the title of 'Counsellor' and 'Psychotherapist' so that, in much the same way as nurses, doctors, art therapists and social workers, professionals who bear those titles will have completed courses and gained particular experiences which meet a national curriculum criteria. There are clear advantages of this, such as:

- clients will know that their therapist is trained to a national standard
- a professional levelling will be introduced that defines the differences between a counsellor and a psychotherapist
- vacancies for counselling posts will be required to demand specific qualifications
- it would be expected that with greater recognition would come increased professional approval
- at present, a counsellor who loses their accreditation through malpractice is still able to continue in practice as the accreditation process is voluntary.

This may not sound so complicated, but there are several counter-arguments which may have a massive impact of the availability of counselling services, such as:

- Many voluntary agencies rely on volunteers who may not have the time or inclination to engage in professional training.
- Waiting lists would grow if there were fewer counselling practitioners.
- There is a cost implication to additional training of all the practising counsellors who don't currently meet the new standards.
- Registration does not fit into the person-centred ethos. There is an innate hypocrisy in facilitating a course that purports the value of self-development, self-determination and autonomy but which you're unable to use professionally without meeting nationally set standards.

The Health Professions Council (HPC) is in consultation with the Psychotherapies and Counsellors Professional Liaison Group (PLG) to prepare recommendations for presentation to the Secretary of State for Health with the aim of protecting the titles 'Psychotherapist' and 'Counsellor' by formalising training requirements. Courses aimed at Master's level (level 7 on the National Qualifications Framework and level 11 on the Scottish Credit and Qualifications Framework) are appropriate for registration as a psychotherapist, and diploma-level courses (NQF 5 and SCQF 8/9) for registration as a counsellor. Any practising counsellor or psychotherapist who is already accredited should be eligible for registration when it is introduced. This is ultimately a political decision and will take time to instigate.

PROFESSIONAL ACCREDITING BODIES

As counselling and psychotherapy are currently unregulated within the UK, voluntary registers of professionally recognised psychotherapeutic practise have flourished. Practitioners of psychotherapeutic activities are encouraged to meet the training and experiential requirements which will allow them to request accreditation. This system is intended to provide clients with a safety network, a method of checking to see what standard of training their counsellor has attained and whether they adhere to particular ethical guidelines. Examples of such organisations include:

- British Association for Counselling and Psychotherapy (www.bacp.co.uk)
- United Kingdom Council for Psychotherapy (www. ukcp.org.uk)
- British Psychological Society (www.bps.org.uk)
- Counselling and Psychotherapy Central Awarding Body (www.cpcab.co.uk)
- Confederation of Scottish Counselling Agencies (www.cosca.org.uk)

Each organisation clearly lists their requirements for individual, organisational and training course accreditation. Most request that you first become a member before applying for accreditation, but membership alone is not the same as accreditation. If you meet the necessary standards, accreditation is designed to professionalise your practice. How this is done differs between organisations. The rest of this chapter covers the exact requirements for accreditation from the BACP, which have been placed into a checklist format for clarity.

You will notice that there are different routes to meet the requirements, which include via an accredited training course, via individual accreditation or through a more applied route based on counselling experience.

Route 4.1 is appropriate for you if you have successfully completed a BACP accredited training course. Table 18.2 is a checklist for the current criteria for application for BACP accreditation.

Route 4.2 is appropriate for you if you have successfully completed counselling courses that meet the criteria in section 4.2, i.e. included at least 450 hours of tutor contact hours, was carried out over at least two years (part-time) or one year (full-time), had a supervised placement as an

Table 18.2   Checklist for BACP accreditation following route 4.1

Criteria	Date evidence completed
1. A member of BACP	
2. Covered by professional indemnity insurance	
3. Practising counselling or psychotherapy	
Plus:	
4.1 **You have been awarded a qualification from a BACP accredited training course AND**	
Have been in practice at least three years when you apply for accreditation	
Have at least 450 hours of supervised practice accumulated within three to six years (they do not have to be consecutive years)	
Of the 450 hours, at least 150 of the hours of supervised practice must be after the successful completion of your BACP accredited course	
Have been supervised for at least 1½ hours per month throughout the period of practice submitted	
5 **You have an ongoing contract for counselling/psychotherapy supervision for a minimum of 1½ hours per month for each month** in which practice is undertaken	
6 **Continuing professional development (CPD)**	
6.1 Describe a CPD activity, relevant to your area of practice, that you have undertaken in the year before applying for accreditation	
6.2 Provide reason(s) for choosing the activity, with reference to your practice	
6.3 Show how the activity has influenced your practice	
7 **Self-awareness**	
7.1 *Describe an experience or an activity which has contributed to your own self-awareness*	
7.2 *Provide a reason(s) for choosing the experience or activity*	
7.3 Show how you use this self-awareness in your practice	
8 **Knowledge and understanding**	
8.1.1 Describe a rationale for your client work with reference to the theory/theories that inform your practice	
8.1.2 Describe the place of your self-awareness within your way of working	
8.1.3 Describe how issues of difference and equality impact upon the therapeutic relationship	
8.2 **Practice In your case material account for:**	
8.2.1 How your practice is consistent with your described way of working (in 8.1.1)	
8.2.2 How you use your self-awareness in the therapeutic relationship	
8.2.3 How your practice demonstrates your awareness of issues of difference and equality and the impact they have on your counselling/psychotherapy relationships	
8.2.4 Use of the BACP *Ethical Framework for Good Practice in Counselling and Psychotherapy*	

Table 18.2   (Continued)

Criteria	Date evidence completed
8.3 ***Supervision*** *In your case material demonstrate how supervision influences your practice by:*	
8.3.1 *Describing the awareness you have gained through reflection in and on supervision*	
8.3.2 *Showing how you apply that awareness in your practice*	
APPLICATION COMPLETED AND SUBMITTED	

© BACP (www.bacp.co.uk/accreditation/ACCREDITATION%20(FOR%20TRAINING%20 COURSES)/index.php). This information is regularly updated and all up-to-date material can be found on the BACP website.

integral part of the training and covered theory, skills, professional issues and personal development. See Table 18.3.

Route 4.3 is appropriate for you if you have successfully completed and are able to provide evidence of a combination of 10 units of training and practice, which contains at least two units of training and three units of practice. See Table 18.4.

Table 18.3   Checklist for BACP accreditation following route 4.2

Criteria	Date evidence completed
1. A member of BACP	
2. Covered by professional indemnity insurance	
3. Practising counselling or psychotherapy	
Plus:	
4.2 You have successfully completed and received an award for practitioner training that:	
4.2.1 Included at least 450 hours of tutor contact hours	
4.2.2 Was carried out over at least two years (part-time) or one year (full-time)	
4.2.3 Had a supervised placement as an integral part of the training	
4.2.4 Covered theory, skills, professional issues and personal development	
AND	
Have been in practice at least three years when you apply for accreditation	
Have at least 450 hours of supervised practice accumulated within three to six years (they do not have to be consecutive years)	
Have at least 150 hours of supervised practice after you have successfully completed your practitioner training	

(Continued)

Table 18.3   (Continued)

Criteria		Date evidence completed
	Have been supervised for at least 1½ hours per month throughout the period of practice submitted	
5	**You have an ongoing contract for counselling/psychotherapy supervision for a minimum of 1½ hours per month for each month** in which practice is undertaken	
6	**Continuing professional development (CPD)**	
6.1	Describe a CPD activity, relevant to your area of practice, that you have undertaken in the year before applying for accreditation	
6.2	Provide reason(s) for choosing the activity, with reference to your practice	
6.3	Show how the activity has influenced your practice	
7	**Self-awareness**	
7.1	*Describe an experience or an activity which has contributed to your own self-awareness*	
7.2	*Provide a reason(s) for choosing the experience or activity*	
7.3	Show how you use this self-awareness in your practice	
8	**Knowledge and understanding**	
8.1.1	Describe a rationale for your client work with reference to the theory/theories that inform your practice	
8.1.2	Describe the place of your self-awareness within your way of working	
8.1.3	Describe how issues of difference and equality impact upon the therapeutic relationship	
8.2	**Practice** In your case material account for:	
8.2.1	How your practice is consistent with your described way of working (in 8.1.1)	
8.2.2	How you use your self-awareness in the therapeutic relationship	
8.2.3	How your practice demonstrates your awareness of issues of difference and equality and the impact they have on your counselling/psychotherapy relationships	
8.2.4	Use of the BACP *Ethical Framework for Good Practice in Counselling and Psychotherapy*	
8.3	***Supervision*** *In your case material demonstrate how supervision influences your practice by:*	
8.3.1	*Describing the awareness you have gained through reflection in and on supervision*	
8.3.2	*Showing how you apply that awareness in your practice*	
	APPLICATION COMPLETED AND SUBMITTED	

© BACP (www.bacp.co.uk/accreditation/ACCREDITATION%20(FOR%20TRAINING%20 COURSES)/index.php). This information is regularly updated and all up-to-date material can be found on the BACP website.

Table 18.4 Checklist for BACP accreditation following route 4.3

	Criteria	Date evidence completed
1.	A member of BACP	
2.	Covered by professional indemnity insurance	
3.	Practising counselling or psychotherapy	
	Plus:	
4.3	***You must be able to provide evidence of a combination of 10 units of training and practice which contains at least two units of training and three units of practice.*** *One training unit is 75 hours of completed practitioner training, and one practice unit is one 12-month period in which supervised practice was undertaken.*	
	Of the practice units that you submit, at least three must have included a minimum of 150 hours of supervised practice and **at least one of these units must have taken place after you successfully completed the training in the units submitted.**	
	The three most recent of the practice units must have been supervised to the level of 1½ hours per month	
	Training should have covered theory, skills, professional issues and personal development (a S/NVQ Level III will count for four units of training)	
5	**You have an ongoing contract for counselling/psychotherapy supervision for a minimum of 1½ hours per month for each month** in which practice is undertaken	
6	**continuing professional development (CPD)**	
6.1	Describe a CPD activity, relevant to your area of practice, that you have undertaken in the year before applying for accreditation	
6.2	Provide reason(s) for choosing the activity, with reference to your practice	
6.3	Show how the activity has influenced your practice	
7	**Self-awareness**	
7.1	*Describe an experience or an activity which has contributed to your own self-awareness*	
7.2	*Provide a reason(s) for choosing the experience or activity*	
7.3	Show how you use this self-awareness in your practice	
8	**Knowledge and understanding**	
8.1.1	Describe a rationale for your client work with reference to the theory/theories that inform your practice	
8.1.2	Describe the place of your self-awareness within your way of working	
8.1.3	Describe how issues of difference and equality impact upon the therapeutic relationship	
8.2	**Practice** In your case material account for:	
8.2.1	How your practice is consistent with your described way of working (in 8.1.1)	
8.2.2	How you use your self-awareness in the therapeutic relationship	

(Continued)

Table 18.4   (Continued)

	Criteria	Date evidence completed
8.2.3	How your practice demonstrates your awareness of issues of difference and equality and the impact they have on your counselling/psychotherapy relationships	
8.2.4	Use of the BACP *Ethical Framework for Good Practice in Counselling and Psychotherapy*	
8.3	**Supervision** *In your case material demonstrate how supervision influences your practice by:*	
8.3.1	*Describing the awareness you have gained through reflection in and on supervision*	
8.3.2	*Showing how you apply that awareness in your practice*	
	APPLICATION COMPLETED AND SUBMITTED	

© BACP (www.bacp.co.uk/accreditation/ACCREDITATION%20(FOR%20TRAINING%20 COURSES)/index.php). This information is regularly updated and all up-to-date material can be found on the BACP website.

19

Professional Considerations

In some ways the easy part of becoming a counsellor is attending a course, learning theory and skills and putting these into practice in a placement, whereas
working as a professional counsellor comes with a considerably wider remit. To
remain up to date with current developments and to provide the best service for
clients, a counsellor has additional responsibilities to ensure they are proficient
and can remain accredited or registered.

THE ROLE OF THE COUNSELLOR

The everyday tasks and responsibilities of working with clients can be
unpredictable, exhausting, emotionally draining, surprising and gratify-
ing but, above all, unpredictable. Because of this, it can be daunting to
see yourself in the role of counsellor rather than that of trainee. Here we
will be considering some of the ongoing tasks required to be able to
work at your optimum. Before moving on to contemplate more practical
aspects of the role, it is crucial at this stage to be aware of the importance of self-care. Below, this student's feelings highlight how important
it is to value and care for yourself and how easy it would be to avoid
progression.

STUDENT EXPERIENCE: HELEN

Now that the course is coming to an end, I am terrified of having to take responsibility for my own actions and decisions in my practice in case I get it wrong. Being in placement is like being in a cocoon; I am busy in therapeutic work but feel as though I am hiding behind the title of student. No one expects me to be perfect yet and I am allowed to make mistakes. Maybe I'm just being too hard on myself but I just don't know if I am ready to be an independent counsellor. Does this mean I see counsellors as perfect and that they never make mistakes or am I just being overly hard on myself? Whichever it is, I am scared of the thought of work being work and not a placement.

We can see clearly here that Helen might have such an unrealistic view of what other counsellors are doing that she doesn't feel she is able to meet her own idealistically high expectations. Alternatively, she may genuinely not be ready. To be clear about our own abilities and how they can or cannot meet the needs of clients, we need to make sure that we establish methods of listening to ourselves right from the start as it is such a healthy habit to develop.

WHAT DO WE MEAN BY SELF-CARE?

How can we successfully care for others if we are unable to care for ourselves? If we are to become and remain a thriving practitioner, we have to be very alert to our own personal needs, to hear our own voice rather than silence it. This can be through physical signs such as tiredness or illness; emotional symptoms such as over-involvement or the inability to distance oneself from the client; cognitively, where we find our thinking and mental processing is sluggish; or even socially, through friendships changing or a drop in social interaction. If we are expected to apply the conditions of empathy, congruence and unconditional positive regard in our work, why shouldn't we be able to apply them to ourself so that we understand ourselves within the context of our lives?

This area of self-care is explained by Larcombe (2008), who identifies three specific aspects: first, to develop understanding and awareness of our own systems; second, to involve yourself in active management/self-regulation through the use of a positive structure; and third, to be mindful of maintaining a healthy balance. By bearing these aspects in mind, discussing them in supervision and using them as part of the framework that underpins our personal development journal, we are ensuring that we remain actively involved in our own care, which in turn impacts positively upon our care of our clients.

ACTIVITY

- What do you do at present to care for yourself?
- Do you have a healthy balance between your work time and your own time?
- How can you introduce a greater focus on yourself into your routine? How can you ensure this is beneficial?
- Where do you currently draw a line between your clients and yourself?

HOW DO I MAINTAIN MY SKILLS?

The maintenance and hopefully continuing development of skills will remain throughout your career as a counsellor (see Figure 19.1). Luckily for the client, there won't ever be a morning when you can wake up and declare that you now know everything there is to know about being a successful counsellor. CPD will become a way of life, although this doesn't have to be as onerous as it might sound due to the wide range of methods available to monitor ourselves and keep up to date. Consider how you might react if you visited your GP with a painful and ongoing condition only to be prescribed old-fashioned and outdated medication because they hadn't kept up with new developments. You may feel angry or disappointed and want to challenge your doctor for not doing their job properly. It's similar in counselling; not to the extent that you might change how you work every time a new theory is published, but you will need to be aware of new developments and be able to discuss academic progress and professional advancements with your colleagues, supervisor and possibly clients.

As a result of the growing demand and popularity of talking therapies, there are often articles in mainstream media which may feed clients' curiosity. To attend appropriate conferences can be massively helpful as you are not only updating your knowledge but also meeting fellow professionals, and it is often such networking opportunities that can be incredibly informative – learning about how others work in

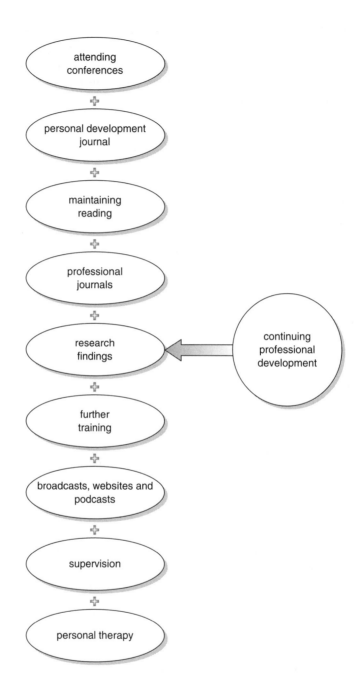

Figure 19.1   *Take charge of your own CPD*

different environments to ourselves. In addition, the upkeep of your personal development journal which you started on your counselling training will continue to act as a log or record of your personal learning, understanding and contextualising. This can be shared with your supervisor or even potential employers at any point within your career. This can't detract from the importance of reading to update knowledge and skills. To develop the habit of actively reading about counselling, whether that be through books, websites or journals, can easily provide a synthesis of knowledge gradually over time with little effort. It is remarkable how we process new, relevant information so that we forget that we ever didn't know it. Further training might also be useful, whether it be building upon your previous course/s, short workshop-based courses that concentrate upon a single element of learning or embarking upon studying a totally different orientation or approach that you are interested in. Further training might not be useful if you are enrolling on a new course to avoid facing up to using your previous course. If we learn more from the doing, then such avoidance might be counterproductive.

WILL I BE MONITORED?

The simple answer to this is yes, but not necessarily in ways that you might have considered. Rather than the Big Brother approach, at present counsellors expected to self-monitor. Here the focus is very much on personal insight, self-awareness and a core honesty combined with a wish to improve one's self. External monitoring comes through regular supervision, although this is not an external process as you, the counsellor, play such an active role in this (discussed in more depth in Chapter 14).

Depending upon the setting you are working in, funding methods may also play a role here. If you are working within the voluntary sector, funding bodies may request evidence to show whether the service is working or not (such as CORE-OM or CHRISTO). Some counselling services record DNAs ('did not arrives') per counsellor so that statistics can show which counsellors are least likely to have clients cancel, although it must be pointed out that this is about monitoring attendance rather than successful therapy.

Hopefully, this is starting to hint at the underlying importance of your relationships with your employer, your accrediting body, your clients, supervisor and yourself.

Table 19.1   Considerations for private practice (self-employed)

Freedom	Challenges
• Able to shape own routine and work pattern	• Develop all own policies and procedures
• Can choose environment in which to work	• Take responsibility for all financial aspects, e.g. marketing, tax
• Able to decide on own holiday entitlement	• Can feel isolated
• Autonomous	• Take full and ultimate responsibility
• Able to experiment and test alternative approaches	• Have to find own clients

Table 19.2   Considerations for employed situation (statutory/voluntary/private sector)

Freedom	Challenges
• Greater access to mentors	• Adhering to already established practice
• Part of a ready formed team	• Pay scale (usually) non-negotiable
• No overheads to pay	• No choice regarding colleagues
• Clients' appointments arranged for you	• Clients often have similar issues depending upon agency (e.g. addiction)
• Environment and facilities already in place	• Need to be comfortable with compromise if it is a large agency
• Can be a supportive atmosphere	• Difficult to secure full-time employment

EMPLOYED OR SELF-EMPLOYED?

This is often a difficult question when you first finish your course. Depending upon vacancies in your local area, your financial situation and your particular interests, it can be confusing to see where your next step might be. Some students are lucky enough to successfully apply for vacancies that may occur within their placement, but this is a rare occurrence as most placements remain as such from year to year. However, there are some important considerations. Tables 19.1 and 19.2 offer some ideas to help make the decision more straightforward.

ACTIVITY

It would be worth completing a blank table of your own similar to the two in this chapter, where you identify your own personal strengths and weaknesses regarding how you work best. Do you relish challenges or are you more comfortable simply concentrating on your client work? Have you experience in setting up a business? Do you work better alone or with others?

ARE THERE ANY JOBS OUT THERE?

It is a good idea to have read Chapter 5 on Counselling Contexts before moving on to this section as you will then be aware of the choices when it comes to practising as a counsellor. As a reminder, most counsellors are employed in a variety of environments which are either statutory, voluntary or private. Once you have decided upon the setting you would like to work in, you then need to be aware of where to find notice of vacancies; there are openings for counselling positions but competition is fierce.

One of the most obvious places to start would be adverts in relevant professional publications such as *Therapy Today*, the BACP journal, which contains a wide range of posts in each edition, local magazines and newspapers such as the *Big Issue* can sometimes contain information on local agencies and organisations which you not have been previously aware of. Particular websites for agencies you are interested in tend to have a vacancy section too, although it can be time-consuming searching through all your local services. This approach also assumes you know exactly where to look. By accessing vacancy search engines and entering your own requirements, you will only be forwarded appropriate vacancies according to your criteria. In Chapter 14, there is reference made to the value of attending conferences, but this is an excellent method of hearing about current and up-and-coming vacancies simply through word of mouth.

HOW ORIENTATION OF TRAINING CAN INFLUENCE EMPLOYABILITY

The theory and methods that underpin your training and practice can influence your chances of finding employment. For example, the statutory organisations such as the NHS and social work departments go through periods of favouring particular approaches. At the time of publication, they are currently actively recruiting practitioners of CBT as part of the IAPT government initiative (see below). If you are trained in person-centred therapy, you may find that many charitable organisations would welcome your skill base for your flexibility as your skills can be transferred to a wide range of clients. It really comes down to how you make connections between your knowledge, abilities and the vacant post, although there is often an element of fashion or trend here as well as the preference of the staff on the interview panel. The more confident you are in your application of your skills to the role, the more successful you are likely to be.

EMPLOYEE ASSISTANCE PROGRAMME (EAPS)

EAPs are external supportive services for employees, paid for by the employer and are currently on the increase. One of the core support services offered is counselling, mainly because employees are more comfortable receiving counselling outside the workplace. This is especially as most EAP confidentiality policies respect the employee's privacy and do not expect counsellor's feedback to be very detailed or to have overly personal information regarding the client/employee. Counsellors who are registered with an EAP agency for work are contacted if and when a client may be looking for counselling in the local area, so it is very much a freelance position with no guarantee of regular work. However, it does offer a spontaneous and unpredictable source of employment.

IMPROVING ACCESS TO PSYCHOLOGICAL THERAPIES (IAPT)

This government programme, which began in 2006, is designed to help Primary Care Trusts to meet the National Institute for Health and Clinical Excellence (NICE) guidelines so that adults living with anxiety orders and depression are more easily able to access psychological therapies such as counselling, in particular CBT. Pilot services in 2007 found that adults in this group were healthier and more able to remain in employment if they received therapy. As a result of this, government funding was pledged to increase the availability of psychological therapies in the hope that it will reduce the employment sickness levels that these conditions can cause. The focus is very much on evidence-based treatments that are clinically effective, which is why CBT fits in so well with this model.

Further information on IAPT, including government commitment to funding the programme and the current statistics regarding numbers of adults diagnosed with these conditions, is available from www.iapt.nhs.uk.

20

The End of the Course

It may be that you are reading this as you come to the end of your course or it may be that you are reading this in preparation for starting a counselling course. Here we will be considering three areas: the impact that a course ending can have on yourself, fellow students and those around you; progressing onto another course; or moving into employment.

HOW MIGHT I FEEL?

As we now know or will soon find out, being a student on a counselling course is not like studying on other courses. The skills, content and close relational contact that takes place means that you become far closer to other members of your group than you might when studying other subjects. The honesty, support and depth of feelings that are encouraged result in bonds and relationships that can last a lifetime.

Hence, when the end of the course is looming, there can be a tangible sense of loss and grief for some; the end of the regular structure and routines, friendships on a deeper level, a regular support network, can all provide a safety that some students are resistant to losing. The thought of being out there as a practitioner can induce a fear of such autonomy and of taking professional responsibility. Being honest with yourself and others and addressing any feelings of loss or fear may show you that you are not alone in this. So saying that, it is not everyone that feels this way. If you have been seconded onto the course from your workplace and are returning to your usual shifts, not attending the course can be a mixed blessing as it might be if you are stepping into a new job. The vocational aspect of counsellor training can lead to self-doubt and concerns about independent practice, which is one of the many reasons that having a successful relationship with your supervisor can help bridge the change; there is a supportive and expert relationship that will continue.

HOW MIGHT THOSE AROUND ME FEEL?

There are very clear commonalities or parallels between the ending of training and the subsequent dispersal of the group, with the client's experience at the end of the counselling relationship. Just as when the counselling relationship draws to an end, fears of dismissal or desertion may surface, indicative of a resistance to moving on. There are several reasons as to why this might occur; for example, this ending might resonate with negative experiences you have had with endings in the past leading to you doubting yourself and your abilities. The self-reliance and autonomy required at this point can be overwhelming, but this can be explored in supervision or during guidance with your tutor. Reminding yourself that endings are a natural part of life and that we all have to face them on a regular basis can reinforce the cyclic element of leaving the comfort and safety of a developed class group.

EXAMPLES OF FEEDBACK QUESTIONS

If you are now coming to the end of your course, you might find it useful to answer these questions which can help to consolidate your learning and development during your time at college or university. Your answers might also be useful in formulating a plan for the future as they will provide a wider picture of how your new counselling skills have been integrated into your life.

Remembering back to your initial choices on application

1 Why did you choose to apply for the course?
2 What generated your interest in counselling?
3 What were your reasons for choosing to study where you have?
4 When you first started, how did you hope to use the qualification?

Reflecting back on the course itself

5 What did you enjoy most about the course?
6 What did you enjoy least?
7 What has been the most challenging aspect for you?
8 Did you feel that the course progressed at the right pace for your learning, and why?
9 Did you feel that the tutors were approachable and supportive of your learning needs, and in what way?
10 Can you identify any changes in yourself that have taken place during the course?
11 What do you now consider to be your strengths and weaknesses?

Now, looking at you and your future

12 Have any of your goals or aims changed as you progressed through the course? If so, in what way?
13 How do you hope to use your new qualification?
14 Are you considering continuing your counselling education and if so, how and where? If not, why not?
15 In what ways do you feel ready (or not ready) to continue your work with clients?

By considering these questions, you are solidifying and contextualising your learning and making a place in your life for your new qualification. Not everyone who completes a counselling course continues on to become a counsellor. For some, the course is enough to convince them that this is definitely not a route they wish to go down. However, it may well be that your level of personal and professional development throughout the course has helped you to see who you are and how you are. Hopefully, it has also provided you with opportunities to change aspects of yourself that you didn't know you had or didn't like.

PROGRESSION OR PRACTICE?

How do you decide if you are ready to practice? There are several aspects to consider here, such as:

- Was my course set at a professional or vocational level that will allow me to practice?
- Do I now meet accreditation or registration requirements?

- Do my qualifications and experience meet the criteria requested in adverts for suitable posts?
- Has my placement experience provided me with the skills and confidence to work successfully and autonomously with clients?
- Am I in a supportive and successful relationship with my supervisor?
- Am I confident in my abilities or know where to seek support?
- Are my course tutors encouraging me to use my counselling skills professionally or recommending further study?

PROGRESSING ONTO EMPLOYMENT

Setting up in private practice can be a big leap when first qualified, so employment as a counsellor might be an easier option depending upon your experience, abilities and confidence. Making decisions regarding premises, internal design, funding and marketing can be a intimidating. Alternatively, you might be hoping to use your new skills and knowledge from the course in your workplace, in which case it would be wise to have a discussion with your line manager to update your job description and see if there are any opportunities for you to integrate some of your new skills and knowledge into your current role. It may be that your achievements on the course will allow you to diversify at work and begin to work in a more overtly therapeutic post. Whatever you choose, with such transferable proficiencies you are bound to find that colleagues and service users respond in a positive manner to your developed communication skills.

STUDENT EXPERIENCE: JANE

From my own personal view, I have gained a deeper, greater understanding of my own value and self-worth. No-one and nothing can alter that fact, so I now like me. I love being unique, being myself, my own person. I feel that I can approach life positively and have gained an inner drive and self-motivation. My counselling course was truly life changing. I don't want to work as a counsellor or progress with my counselling training, but my new skills have already helped me to become a better holistic therapist.

PROGRESSING ONTO ANOTHER COUNSELLING COURSE

Maybe you stumbled into your first course more by luck than good management, not really making an informed choice about the level, curriculum content or orientation, but if you are intending to continue studying, you are now more aware of the similarities than differences. You may well be more focused and goal orientated, with a more clearly defined plan. If this is not the case, there are several sources you can tap into to help you decide upon the most appropriate next step:

- Your tutor will be able to discuss progression routes available to you and advise you as to how they relate to your current course.
- Your supervisor knows you well enough by now to discuss your options.
- Local course providers will be able to provide information regarding the content of their courses and the entry requirements.
- Your placement mentor will be able to recommend courses and qualifications that are recognised and valued by employers.
- Yourself! From a person-centred perspective, you are aware of your abilities, interests and wishes for the future and know what you are able and not able to cope with. The time has to be right (funding, childcare, travel/access, accommodation and family responsibilities, etc.), a suitable course has to be available, and you have to be enthusiastic and driven.

Moving from a further education college to university can be a frightening step for many, particularly adult returners who have an image of students all being school leavers and leading a very different lifestyle to themselves!

STUDENT EXPERIENCE: HEATHER

Having felt a sense of disbelief that my course is nearing an end, I had a light-bulb moment and it dawned on me that perhaps I could go on to learn more. I am currently waiting to hear from the university which I have applied to for a post-graduate level counselling course. The HNC has laid the foundations for me to believe that so much is open to me than I ever thought possible. I have a while to go yet, but my desire to work as a counsellor has been strengthened now that my experience and confidence has grown. Each of the friendships I have made with other classmates has offered me a sense of believing in myself as their support and encouragement have been invaluable.

MOVING ON

Whatever you decide upon, your new way of being and the insight that accompanies it will stand you in good stead for further development in whichever area you choose.

Bibliography

Abrahams, H. (2007) 'Ethics in counselling research fieldwork', *Counselling and Psychotherapy Research*, 7(4): 240–244.

Aldridge, S. and Rigby, S. (eds) (2001) *Counselling Skills in Context*. London: Hodder & Stoughton.

Amis, K. (2007) *Providing a Community Service?: Are Community Groups Serving the Higher National Certificate Counselling Community?* Unpublished MEd research.

Amis, K. (2008) 'Working with client dependency', in W. Dryden and A. Reeves (eds), *Key Issues for Counselling in Action*, 2nd edn. London: Sage.

Andrews, J.D.W., Norcross, J.C. and Malgin, R.P. (1992) 'Training in psychotherapy integration', in J. Norcross (ed.), *Handbook of Psychotherapy Integration*. New York: Basic Books.

Atherton, J.S. (2005) *Learning and Teaching: Learning Curves*. Retrieved 26 May 2009 from www.learningandteaching.info/learning/learning_curve.htm

Aveline, M. (2007) 'The training and supervision of individual therapists', in W. Dryden (ed.), *Dryden's Handbook of Individual Therapy*. London: Sage.

BACP (1996) *Code of Ethics and Practice for Supervisors of Counsellors*. Lutterworth: BACP.

BACP (2007) *Towards Regulation: The Standards, Benchmarks and Training Requirements for Counselling and Psychotherapy*. Lutterworth: BACP.

BACP (2009a) *Ethical Framework for Good Practice in Counselling and Psychotherapy*. Lutterworth: BACP.

BACP (2009b) *Accreditation of Training Courses*, 5th edn. Lutterworth: BACP.

Bayne, R., Horton, I., Collard, P. and Jinks, G. (2008) *The Counsellor's Handbook*, 3rd edn. Cheltenham: Nelson Thornes.

Bion, W.R. (1961) *Experiences in Groups*. London: Tavistock.

Bolton, G., Howlett, S., Lago, C. and Wright, J.K. (eds) (2004) *Writing Cures: An Introductory Handbook of Writing in Counselling and Psychotherapy*. London: Routledge.

Bond, T. (2009) *Standards and Ethics for Counselling in Action*, 3rd edn. London: Sage.

Bond, T. and Mitchels, B. (2008) *Confidentiality and Record-keeping in Counselling and Psychotherapy*. London: Sage.

Bor, R. and Watts, M. (eds) (2006) *The Trainee Handbook*. London: Sage.

Bor, R., Gill, S., Miller, R. and Parrot, C. (2004) *Doing Therapy Briefly*. Basingstoke: Palgrave Macmillan.

Bor, R., Miller, R., Gill, S. and Evans, A. (2009) *Counselling in Health Care Settings: A Handbook for Practitioners*. Basingstoke: Palgrave Macmillan.

Buchanan, L. and Hughes, R. (2000) *Experiences of Person-centred Counselling Training*. Ross-on-Wye: PCCS Books.

Burnard, P. (2005) *Counselling Skills for Health Professional*. Cheltenham: Nelson Thornes.

Carkhuff, R.R. (1969) *Helping and Human Relations, Volume 2: Practice and Research*. New York: Holt, Rinehart and Winston.

Chu, J. (1988) 'Ten traps for therapists in the treatment of trauma survivors', *Dissociation*, 1(4): 24–32.

Claringbull, N. (2010) *What is Counselling and Psychotherapy?* Exeter: Learning Matters.

Clark, D. (2006) *The Disease Model of Addiction*. Retrieved 14 August 2007 from www.drinkanddrugs.net.

Connor, M. (1994) *Training the Counsellor: An Integratve Model*. London: Routledge.

Coombes, H. (2001) *Research Using IT*. Basingstoke: Palgrave.

Cooper, M. (2008) 'Working at relational depth', in W. Dryden and A. Reeves (eds), *Key Issues for Counselling in Action*. London: Sage.

Cooper, M. (2008) *Essential Research Findings in Counselling and Psychotherapy: The Facts are Friendly*. London: Sage.

Coren, A. (2010) *Short-term Psychotherapy: A Psychodynamic Approach*. Basingstoke: Palgrave Macmillan.

Cottrell, S. (2003) *The Study Skills Handbook*. Basingstoke: Palgrave Macmillan.

Cross, M. (2001) *Becoming a Therapist*. Hove: Brunner-Routledge.

Culley, S. and Bond, T. (2011) *Integrative Counselling Skills in Action*, 3rd edn. London: Sage.

Dallos, R. and Vetere, A. (2005) *Researching Psychotherapy and Counselling*. Buckingham: Open University Press.

Daw, B. and Joseph, S. (2007) 'Qualified therapists' experience of personal therapy', *Counselling and Psychotherapy Research*, 7(4): 227–232.

Dryden, W. and Reeves, A. (eds) (2008) *Key Issues for Counselling in Action*. London: Sage.

Egan, G. (1977) *You and Me: The Skills of Communicating and Relating to Others*. Pacific Grove, CA: Brooks Cole.

Egan, G. (1994) *The Skilled Helper*, 5th edn. Belmont, CA: Brooks Cole.

Egan, G. (2009) *The Skilled Helper*, 9th edn. Pacific Grove, CA: Brooks Cole.

Elliott, A. (2000) *Psychoanalytic Theory: An Introduction*. Durham, NC: Duke University Press.

Evison, R. and Horobin, R. (1983) *How to Change Yourself and Your World Co-Counselling*. Sheffield: Phoenix.

Evison, R. and Horobin, R. (1999) *Co-counselling as Therapy*. Retrieved 14 June 2009 from http://co-cornucopia.org.uk/coco/articles/cocother/.

Evison, R. and Horobin, R. (2006) 'Co-counselling', in C. Feltham and I. Horton (eds), *The Sage Handbook of Counselling and Psychotherapy*. London: Sage.

Feltham, C. and Horton, I. (eds) (2006) *The Sage Handbook for Counselling and Psychotherapy*. London: Sage.

Geldard, K. (2005) *Practical Counselling Skills: An Integrative Approach*. Basingstoke: Palgrave Macmillan.

Geldard, K. and Geldard, D. (2005) *Practical Counselling Skill: An Integrative Approach*. Basingstoke: Palgrave Macmillan.

Gibson, R.L. and Mitchell, M.H. (1999) *Introduction to Counselling and Guidance*. London: Prentice Hall.

Glasser, W. (1975) *Reality Therapy: A New Approach to Psychiatry*. New York: Harper & Row.

Graham, H. (1986) *The Human Face of Psychology*. Milton Keynes: Open University Press.

Guimón, J. (2007) 'Subgroups in training communities', *European Journal of Psychotherapy and Counselling*, 8(1): 47–60.

Heron, J. (1974) *Reciprocal Counselling Human Potential Research Project*. Guildford: University of Surrey.

Heron, J. (1976) 'A six-category intervention analysis', *British Journal of Guidance and Counselling*, 4(2): 143–155.

Heron, J. (1998) *Co-counselling Manual*. Retrieved 14 June 2009 from www.co-counselling.org.uk/resources/manual.html#theory.

Higdon, J. (2004) *From Counselling Skills to Counsellor: A Psychodynamic Approach*. Basingstoke: Palgrave Macmillan.

Horton, I. (1994) 'Counsellor training courses: external roles and procedures', *Counselling*, 5(3): 213–214.

Hough, M. (2006) *Counselling Skills and Theory*, 2nd edn. Abingdon: Hodder Arnold.

Houston, G. (1995) *The Now Red Book of Gestalt*. London: Rochester Foundation.

Howard, S. (2006) *Psychodynamic Counselling in a Nutshell*. London: Sage.

Ivey, A.E. (1971) *Microcounselling: Innovations in Interviewing Training*. Springfield, IL: Charles C. Thomas.

Izzard, S.A. and Wheeler, S. (1994) 'The development of self-awareness: an essential aspect of counsellor training? Does the provision of a personal awareness group as an integral part of counselling training enhance the development of self-awareness?' IRTAC Conference, Munich.

Jackins, H. (1994) *The Human Side of Human Being: The Theory of Re-evaluation Counselling*. Seattle, WA: Rational Island.

Jacobs, M. (2004) *Psychodynamic Counselling in Action*. London: Sage.

Johns, C. (2004) *Becoming a Reflective Practitioner*. Chichester: Wiley-Blackwell.

Johns, H. (1996) *Personal Development in Counsellor Training*. London: Sage.

Joyce, P. and Sills, C. (2001) *Skills in Gestalt Counselling and Psychotherapy*. London: Sage.

Kahr, B. (2006) 'The clinical placement in mental health training', in R. Bor and M. Watts (eds), *The Trainee Handbook: A Guide for Counselling and Psychotherapy Trainees*, 2nd edn. London: Sage.

Karter, J. (2002) *On Training to be a Therapist*. Buckingham: Open University Press.

Kauffman, K. and New, C. (2004) *Co-Counselling: The Theory and Practice of Re-evaluation Counselling*. London: Routledge.

Klein, M. (2006) *The Psychodynamic Counselling Primer*. Ross-on-Wye: PCCS Books.

Lapworth, P., Sills, C. and Fish, S. (2001) Integration In Counselling and Psychotherapy: Developing a Personal Approach. London: Sage.

Larcombe, A. (2008) 'Self-care in counselling' in W. Dryden and A. Reeves (eds), *Key Issues for Counselling in Action*. London: Sage.

Lazarus, A. (n.d.) Retrieved 17 May 2007 from http://rebt-cbt.net/My_Homepage_Files/Page16.html.

Legg, C. and Donati, M. (2006) 'Getting the most out of personal therapy', in R. Bor and M. Watts (eds), *The Trainee Handbook*. London: Sage. pp. 217–231.

Lindon, J. and Lindon, L. (2008) *Mastering Counselling Skills*. Basingstoke: Palgrave Macmillan.

Lipgar, M.R. (2007) 'Learning from Bion's legacy to groups', *European Journal of Psychotherapy and Counselling*, 8(1): 79–91.

Lister-Ford, C. (2002) *Skills In Transactional Analysis Counselling and Psychotherapy*. London: Sage.

Loewenthal, D. and Snell, R. (2006) 'The learning community, the trainee and the leader', *European Journal of Psychotherapy and Counselling*, 8(1): 61–77.

Macdonald, A. (2007) *Solution-focused Therapy: Theory, Research and Practice*. London: Sage.

Mander, G. (2000) *A Psychodynamic Approach to Brief Therapy*. London: Sage.

Maslow, A. (1954) *Motivation and Personality*. New York: Harper.

Masson, J. (1992) *Against Therapy*. London: Fontana.

McLeod, J. (2003) *Doing Counselling Research*. London: Sage.

McLeod, J. (2007) *Counselling Skill*. Maidenhead: Open University Press.

McMillan, M. (2004) *The Person Centred Approach to Therapeutic Change*. London: Sage.

Mearns, D. (1996) 'Working at relational depth with clients in person centred counselling', *Counselling*, 7(4): 306–311.

Mearns, D. and Cooper, M. (2005) *Working at Relational Depth*. London: Sage.

Merry, T. (2002) *Learning and Being In Person-centred Counselling*. Ross-on-Wye: PCCA Books.

Merry, T. (2002) Learning and Being in Person-centred Counselling. Ross-on-Wye: PCCS Books.

Messina, J.J. (2005) *Integrative Perspective in Therapy*. Retrieved August 2007 from www.coping.org/write/C6436counselther/lectures/C6436-12th-Integrative.ppt.

Milner, J. and O'Byrne, P. (2002) *Brief Counselling: Narrative and Solutions*. Basingstoke: Palgrave Macmillan.

Moon, J. (2006) *Learning Journals*. London: Routledge.

Nelson-Jones, R. (2009) *Introduction to Counselling Skills: Text and Activities*. London: Sage.

Norcross, J. (2005) 'The psychotherpist's own psychotherapy: educating and developing psychologists', *American Psychologist*, 60: 840–850.

O'Connell, B. and Palmer, S. (eds) (2003) *Handbook of Solution-focused Therapy*. London: Sage.

O'Leary, E., Crowley, M. and Keane, N. (1994) 'A personal growth training group with trainee counsellors: outcome evaluation', *Counselling Psychology Quarterly*, 7(2): 133–141.

Page, S. and Wosket, V. (2001) *Supervising the Counsellor*, 2nd edn. London: Brunner-Routledge.

Palmer, F. and Murdin, L. (eds) (2001) *Values and Ethics in the Practice of Psychotherapy and Counselling*. London: Open University Press.

Palmer, S. and Woolfe, R. (eds) (1999) *Integrative and Eclectic Counselling and Psychotherapy*. London: Sage.

Perls, F., Hefferline, R.F. and Goodman, P. (1951) *Gestalt Therapy*. New York: Julian.

Plato (360 BC) *Phaedrus*. Translated by Benjamin Jowett. Available online at http://classics.mit.edu/Plato/phaedrus.html.

Reynolds, B.C. (1985) *Learning and Teaching in the Practice of Social Work*. Washington, DC: National Association of Social Workers.

Rogers, C. (1951) *Client-centered Therapy*. Boston, MA: Houghton Mifflin.

Rogers, C. (1980) *A Way of Being*. New York: Houghton Mifflin.

Rogers, C. (2004) *On Becoming a Person*. London: Constable & Robinson.

Rose, J. (2007) *The Mature Student's Guide to Writing*. Basingstoke: Palgrave Macmillan.

Rowson, R. (2001) 'Ethical principles', in F. Palmer Barnes and L. Murdin (eds), *Values and Ethics in the Practice of Psychotherapy and Counselling*. Buckingham: Open University Press.

Sanders, D. and Wills, F. (2005) *Cognitive Therapy: An Introduction*, 2nd edn. London: Sage.

Sanders, P. (2003) *Step in to Counselling: A Students' Guide to Learning Counselling and Tackling Course Assignments*. Ross-on-Wye: PCCS Books.

Schon, D.A. (1991) *The Reflective Practitioner: How Professionals Think in Action*. Aldershot: Ashgate.

Shostrom, E.L. (Producer and Director) (1965) *Three Approaches to Psychotherapy*. Motion picture. Corona del Mar, CA: Psychological and Educational Films.

Sills, C. (Ed.) (2006) *Contracts in Counselling and Psychotherapy*. London: Sage.

Smail, D. (1987) 'Psychotherapy and "change": some ethical considerations', in S. and G. Fairbairn (eds), *Psychology, Ethics and Change*. London: Routledge & Kegan Paul.

Small, J.J. and Mathei, R.J. (1988) 'Group work in counsellor training: research and development in one programme', *British Journal of Guidance and Counselling*, 16(1): 33–49.

Smith, M.L., Glass, G.V. and Miller, T.I. (1980) *The Benefits of Psychotherapy*. Baltimore, MD: Johns Hopkins University Press.

SQA (Scottish Qualifications Authority) (2007) *Higher National Unit Spefication*, F1EM 34. Glasgow: SQA.

Thorne, B. (2003) *Carl Rogers*. London: Sage.

Tuckman, B. (1965) 'Developmental sequences in small groups', *Psychological Bulletin*, 63: 384–399.

Tuckman, B.W. and Jensen, M.A.C. (1977) 'Stages of small group development revisited', *Group and Organizational Studies*, 2: 419–427.

Tudor, K. (ed.) (2008) *Brief Person-centred Therapies*. London: Sage.

Tudor, L.E., Kemar, K., Tudor, K., Valentine, J. and Worrall, M. (2004) *The Person-centred Approach: A Contemporary Introduction*. Basingstoke: Palgrave Macmillan.

van Deurzen, E. and Arnold-Baker, C. (2005) *Existential Perspectives on Human Issues: A Handbook for Therapeutic Practice*. Basingstoke: Palgrave Macmillan.

Westbrook, D., Kennerle H. and Kirk, J. (2007) *An Introduction to Cognitive Behaviour Therapy: Skills and Applications*. London: Sage.

Wheeler, S. (1996) *Training Counsellors: The Assessment of Competence*. London: Cassell.

Wisker, G. (2001) *The Postgraduate Research Handbook*. Basingstoke: Palgrave.

Wosket, V. (2006) 'Clinical supervision', in C. Feltham and I. Horton (eds), *The Sage Handbook of Counselling and Psychotherapy*, 2nd edn. London: Sage.

Yalom, I.D. (1985) *The Theory and Practice of Group Psychotherapy*, 3rd edn. New York: Basic Books.

Young, R. (2002) *How Are We to Work with Conflict of Moral Standpoints in the Therapeutic Relationship?* Retrieved 14 May 2007 from www.psycho analysis-and-therapy.com/human_nature/free-associations/young.html.

Index

Page references in italics refer to figures and tables

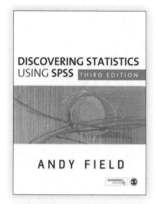
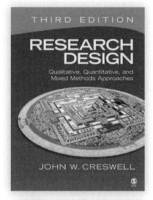

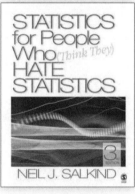

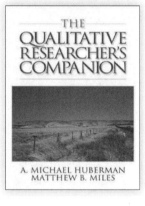
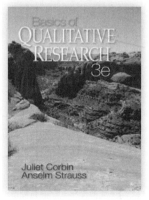

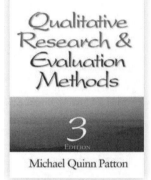
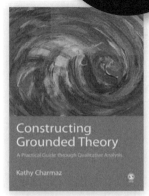

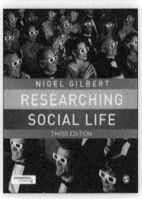
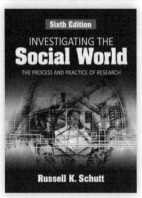